D0065211

Colección Támesis

SERIE A: MONOGRAFÍAS, 179

# A COMPANION TO
# SPANISH-AMERICAN LITERATURE

STEPHEN M. HART

# A COMPANION TO
# SPANISH-AMERICAN LITERATURE

TAMESIS

First published 1999 by Tamesis, London


ISBN  1 85566 065 2

Tamesis is an imprint of Boydell & Brewer Ltd
PO Box 9, Woodbridge, Suffolk IP12 3DF, UK
and of Boydell & Brewer Inc.
PO Box 41026, Rochester, NY 14604–4126, USA
website: http://www.boydell.co.uk

A catalogue record for this book is available
from the British Library

Library of Congress Cataloging-in-Publication Data
applied for


This publication is printed on acid-free paper

Printed in Great Britain by
St Edmundsbury Press Ltd, Bury St Edmunds, Suffolk

# CONTENTS

For Jordan

# FOREWORD

This book is designed for the moderately specialised reader who reads Spanish and wants an introduction to the main works of the Spanish-American literary canon. It takes its point of departure from an historical coincidence, namely that the discovery and colonisation of the area of the earth now called Latin America largely coincided with the birth of a new technology of the transmission of knowledge, that is, printing. The world has never been quite the same since Johann Gensfleisch zum Gutenberg printed his 42-line Bible in Mainz, Germany, in 1452–1456 (Steinberg 21). Gutenberg's discovery of movable type spread like wild fire in the Europe of his day; as Steinberg suggests, '[w]ithin fifteen years after Gutenberg's death in 1468 printing presses had been set up in every country of western Christendom from Sweden to Sicily and from Spain to Poland and Hungary' (Steinberg 27). Twenty-five years after Gutenberg's death, the American continent was discovered and it is no exaggeration to state that the discovery, conquest and colonisation of that land took on a unique quality in the imagination of the West precisely because of the recent discovery of print. The newly-created presses of Europe printed copies of Christopher Columbus's letters to the Catholic Monarchs, they circulated printed versions of Hernán Cortés's letters, as well as Theodor de Bry's images of the New World, which were eagerly bought by the new mercantile classes then emerging in Europe. An earlier age had to be content with the Bayeux tapestry. As this work hopes to show, the printed word was a crucial component in the cultural configuration that Spanish America would gradually create over the next five centuries.

I take this opportunity to thank the librarians at the libraries I visited while conducting the research on which this book is based, at the Fondo Reservado, in the Biblioteca Nacional, Mexico City, the Biblioteca Nacional in Bogotá, Colombia, the Bodleian, Oxford, the University Library, Cambridge, the British Library, London, and particularly Dr Barry Taylor, a former colleague at Westfield College, London, and now librarian in the Spanish Department in the British Library, and to whom I owe a special debt both personal and academic.

I should also like to take this opportunity to thank Dr David Watt, former Vice Chancellor of Research and Graduate Studies at the University of Kentucky, whose generosity allowed me to research in the special collections in the National Libraries in Mexico City in 1994 and Bogotá in 1995, Dr Fitzgerald Bramwell, Vice President for Research and Graduate Studies, who supported a research trip to the Biblioteca Nacional, Lima, in 1996, and Dr Richard Edwards, former Dean of the College of Arts and Sciences, whose support in the form of a Research Assistantship made the task of compilation much easier. I am pleased to record here my gratitude to the Latin American Studies Program at the University of Florida which provided me with a research grant during the summer of 1995, thereby allowing me to conduct research in the Stetson Collection in Gainesville. Special thanks to my former colleagues in the Department of Spanish and Italian, University of Kentucky, especially to Drs Susan de Carvalho, Brian Dendle, Jay Allen, Lourdes Torres, and Daniel Reedy, whose willingness to discuss some of the concepts in this book helped me to make less errors than would otherwise have been the case. I express my gratitude to Fernando Botero and the Museum of Modern Art in New York (and particularly Ms Mikki Carpenter who person-ally helped me secure the copyright) for permission to reproduce *The Presidential Family* on the cover. Thanks too are in order for the generous assistance of the editorial team at Boydell & Brewer, and especially Pam Cope who prepared the book for publication. Lastly, I thank the anonymous reviewers of the manuscript whose wisdom saved me from many an error; the others, of course, are mine.

S.M.H.

# INTRODUCTION: UNPACKING THE CANON

The present study is different from previous studies in three main ways. The typical survey of Spanish-American literature published in the last twenty-five years fails to address two issues which recent research in adjacent disciplines has discovered to be central to the notion of canon formation which underpins, consciously or not, any literary survey. The first issue concerns the treatment given to pre-1900 literature and, in particular, the indigenous cultural tradition in a study of the Spanish-American literary canon. For example, in her important study, *An Introduction to Spanish-American Literature* (1969), Jean Franco devotes her introduction to literature of Spanish America written between the conquest and c.1750 (Franco 1–27), and, within that, gives barely 4 out of 390 pages to the treatment of indigenous literature (Franco 5–8). Most critics agree that, in its ability to combine general sweep with detailed discussion, Franco's study is unmatched. Since the publication of *Spanish-American Literature*, however, our notion of the Spanish-American literary canon has drastically altered and the importance of colonial and indigenous literature has increased accordingly. The present study reflects that trend and gives more space to literature written before the nineteenth century and, in particular, before the conquest. It also attempts to integrate a discussion of a period of literature (the post-Boom novel, poetry and theatre in the 1970s and 1980s) which was not treated in Franco's book simply because of its time of publication, as well as giving more space to significant women writers, especially in the modern period.

The second point of difference between the present study and previous works concerns the issue of evaluation. In this study I have not been exhaustive in selecting works for inclusion. Enrique Anderson-Imbert, in the introduction to his major study, *Historia de la literatura hispanoamericana* (1954, 1966, and 1982), has identified two of the main dangers which an historian of literature risks, namely, of writing on the one hand 'a history of literature containing very little history' or, on the other, 'a history of literature containing very little literature' (Anderson-Imbert, II, 441). Especially in the modern period, Anderson-Imbert, in his desire to be all-inclusive, includes writers whose work is of minimal literary value; he mentions, after all, in his introduction that he has included a 'farrago' of secondary writers. I have decided not to follow that path in the present study, preferring to limit the number of writers included in order to give them the space they deserve. For the benefit of the general reader, I have also included a very brief plot summary of the novels discussed in order to clarify the subsequent analysis. The list of canonical authors studied here is based on a survey conducted in 1995 of the main literary works taught in departments of Spanish in United States research institutions.

The third point of difference between my analysis and previous studies concerns the importance given here to the social value of the literary work, the way in which it functioned within the society which gave it life, and the role that the writer played in that society. The present study needs to be read alongside two crucial recent studies, the *Cambridge History of Latin American Literature*, in three volumes, edited by Enrique Pupo-Walker and Roberto González Echeverría, and published in 1995, and the *Encyclopedia of Latin American Literature*, edited by Verity Smith and published in 1997. The first offers more detailed information about some of the writers covered in the present volume, while the second provides an up-to-date view of the Spanish-American canon. What the present study attempts to do is provide a continuous, brief narrative about the main writers and works of the Spanish-American canon, and frames that historical narrative in the context of literary print culture. Footnotes and reference to the criticism have been kept to a minimum, while some indication of the main bibliographical trends has been made in the Suggestions for Further Reading. It is hoped that this overview of Spanish-American literature will be useful as a refresher course for the student preparing for Masters and Doctoral exams, as well as the general reader.

Some words here about how the term 'literature' is used in this study are necessary. A number of manuals do tremendous injustice to the proper under-standing of the term 'literature' when they define it in universal, anti-historical terms. The entry on literature in the *Enciclopedia Universal Ilus-trada Europea-Americana*, for example, begins by stating that literature is a work of art written for aesthetic effect only ('Género de producciones del entendimiento humano, que tienen por fin próximo o remoto expresar lo bello por medio de la palabra'; 1076), but then contradicts itself by giving space in the same article to ecclesiastical literature, judicial literature, and even military literature (1076–87). Through its reliance on universalisms (for example, literature is a 'medio universal de expresión de todas las ideas'; 1077), the article in effect remains blind to the premise on which its argument is built. A more historicised approach to the meaning attached to the term lit-erature clearly becomes necessary. In effect, the idea of literature changed during the Romantic period in Europe as much as in South America and, as a result, the term itself came more and more to signify a literary work written for aesthetic effect, a meaning which has remained with us until the present day. As Terry Eagleton has pointed out, literature, before the nineteenth century, meant 'the whole body of valued writing in society: philosophy, history, essays and letters as well as poems' (Eagleton 17). However, 'by the time of the Romantic period, literature was becoming virtually synonymous with the "imaginative"; to write about what did not exist was somehow more soul-stirring and valuable than to pen an account of Birmingham or the circulation of the blood' (Eagleton 18). The first recorded example of literature used in this sense in English was in 1812, although the term itself was in existence by at least the fourteenth century.[1] A similar situation exists for Spanish. Though 'literatura' is recorded as in use by 1490, it was in the nineteenth century that its more narrow, specialised sense of 'literary work written for aesthetic effect' came to replace the earlier more inclusive meaning of 'something written'.[2]

The three main differences mentioned above – reference to pre-Columbian literature, emphasis upon representativeness at the expense of all-inclusiveness, and the use of literary print culture as a paradigm to contextualise individual works – should not detract from the fact that the present book is offered as a complement to other studies on that complex protean creature, Spanish-American literature. If it inspires future scholars to take up and critically test some of the ideas expounded here, in the classroom or elsewhere, its purpose will have been well served.

---

[1]   The *Oxford English Dictionary* defines literature as 'writing which has claim for consideration on the ground of beauty of form or emotional affect', noting that this sense is 'of very recent emergence both in English and French' (VIII, 1029). The older original meaning of literature as 'acquaintance with letters or books' is recorded as early as c.1375 (VIII, 1029).

[2]   'Literatura' appears in Alonso Fernández de Palencia's *Universal Vocabulario en latín y en romance* (1490); see Corominas & Pascual, III, 636. 'Letras' to mean 'carta misiva' is recorded in Spanish as early as 1250, and 'letrado' is already found in medieval texts by Berceo (1220–1250) (Corominas & Pascual, III, 636). This more narrow notion of literature emerged during the nineteenth century as a direct consequence of the specialisation of other fields of knowledge; the social sciences, for example, were born in the nineteenth century and, as a result of their mapping out their territory, literature was forced to retreat into a smaller, more cramped, domain. The term most frequently used in Spain and Spanish America during the pre-Romantic period ('letras') meant anything printed and included what we now understand by the term literature (i.e. writing normally published and written for aesthetic effect), as well as other disciplines such as law, history, religion and science.

## Chapter 1

# THE AMERINDIAN LEGACY AND THE LITERATURE
# OF CONQUEST AND DISCOVERY

The Amerindian cultures did not possess an alphabetic script but they did have cultural artifacts that resembled the European book in some respects. The codices of the Mayas and the Aztecs were sacred books which dealt with the ritual calendar, divination and the actions of the gods; their notation was a combination of pictography, ideograms and phonetic symbols. They were kept in temples and used by the priestly caste in their divine ceremonies. Some indication of the hermetic nature of the knowledge they encapsulated is suggested by the following passage in the *Cantares mexicanos*:

> Yo canto las pinturas del libro
> lo voy desplegando
> cual florido papagayo,
> hago hablar a los códices.
>
> (qtd. in Oviedo, *Historia*, vol. 1, 35)

Because of their religious content only a small number of the codices escaped destruction by the Spanish. In 1562, for example, Bishop Diego de Landa held a triumphalist *auto-da-fé* in Maní, Yucatan, in which he burned all the Maya books with hieroglyphic writing that he was able to capture. As Landa recalled in chapter LXI of his *Relación de las cosas de Yucatán* (1864): 'Hallámosles gran número de libros de estas sus letras [hieroglyphs], y porque no tenían cosa en que no hubiese superstición y falsedades del demonio, se los quemamos todos, lo cual sintieron a maravilla y les dio mucha pena' (Diego de Landa 117–18). There are only three Maya codices and a handful of pre-Columbian Aztec codices now in existence (for more information see 'The Codices' below). As a result of the brutal rupture brought about by the conquest, many of these repositories of cultural knowledge -- ranging from the *quipus* (Incan accounting tools made of rope) to Maya texts – remain undeciphered to this day.

Much of what we now know about Amerindian culture comes down to us filtered through a vast enterprise of transliteration by the Spanish invaders. This process can be compared to that of the last will and testament taken from a dying man whose language is imperfectly understood by the scribe: the testimony is meant to summarise the whole of the individual's previous life and, given the circumstances, it is inevitably characterised by gaps. Add to this the role of the scribe who transliterates the testimony and who – unconsciously or not – moulds the narrative to fit his own view of the world, and we can see how difficult it becomes to separate out the various strands within this process of transculturation. When considering the texts below, we must bear in mind that all were created in the process of transliteration which occurred after the conquest and produced what might be described as a 'negative transparency' of Amerindian culture. Even the sacred verbal texts, such as the *Popol Vuh*, were transliterated *after* the conquest, even if their textualization was based on an oral account which had been passed down through the generations.

The best example of this transliteration process is the work of Bernadino de Sahagún (1499–1590) who was one of the first Franciscans to arrive in New Spain. Soon after his arrival there in 1529 he quickly learned Nahuatl, the language of the Aztecs, and, with the help of twelve chieftains from the town of Tepulco, and four interpreters, he began to write the *Historia de las cosas de Nueva España* (1569). The chieftains provided him with a verbal as well as a pictographic account of the history of their people; Sahagún incorporated the images into his text, transliterated the Nahuatl account and provided a translation into Spanish in an adjacent column. A vast encyclopedia about the history and customs of the Aztecs, the *Historia de las cosas de Nueva España* is particularly valuable since, in the final chapter, it describes the conquest of Tenochtitlan from the Aztec point of view, and it has been used by León-Portilla to good effect in his compilation *Visión de los vencidos* (see 'The Amerindian View of the Conquest' below). Given its hybrid nature – it is a chronicle since it has an historical narrative, and a codex since it has illustrations (thus it is also known as the *Codex Florentino*) – the *Historia de las cosas de Nueva España* offers an unparalleled glimpse into the transculturation process which occurred in Spanish America after the conquest.

## The *Popol Vuh*

The most important of the Amerindian sacred verbal texts is the *Popol Vuh*, literally 'Book of the Community', but customarily known as the Sacred Book of the Quiché Maya. The original Quiché manuscript of the *Popol Vuh* had been transliterated probably by one Diego Reynoso, a member of the Maya priestly caste, possibly between 1554 and 1558, and was discovered by Father Francisco Ximénez in the late seventeenth century while he was serving as parish priest of the village of Santo Tomás Chichicastenango in the highlands of Guatemala. He copied it and then produced his own dual-language version (Quiché original with Spanish translation) of the original manuscript. From that point Ximénez's manuscript lay dormant in the library of the university of San Carlos in the city of Guatemala until discovered by

Carl Scherzer, a Viennese doctor, who published the Spanish text in Vienna in 1857. This book was followed four years later by the publication in Paris of the original Quiché text together with a French version, introduction and notes by Abbé Brasseur de Bourbourg entitled *Popol Vuh, Le Livre Sacré et les mythes de l'antiquité américaine, avec les livres héroïques et historiques des Quichués* (1861).[1] Any hope that the *Popol Vuh* might be a completely pre-Columbian text is dispelled in the introduction in which the (unknown) author refers to writing 'under the Law of God and Christianity' (*Popol Vuh* 79–80). The text has, since Abbé Brasseur de Bourbourg's suggestion, been divided up into four parts and, although there is nothing in the text to indicate that this is necessary, it clarifies its structure. Part I begins like the Old Testament book of Genesis with the creation of the human race, although in the *Popol Vuh* this is only successful on the third attempt; the first two attempts, with mud and wood respectively, do not produce the desired result, and it is only when ears of corn are used that the creation is to the satisfaction of the gods (I, i–iii, 81–93; III, i–ii, 165–69). As with the Genesis, the *Popol Vuh* stresses the continuity between the first examples of mankind, in this case the four men Balam-Quitzé, Balam-Acab, Macutah, Iqui-Balam, and the Quiché people of which the author is a member, mainly through the genealogy lists given in Chapter III, Part iii (170–73), and Chapter IV, Part xii (228–35). These creation stories are mixed freely with stories from individuals of the principal houses of the Quiché peoples such that the empirical and the supernatural, history and religion, are merged to form one narrative. The world of the Quiché is presented as coming to an end with the invasion of the Spaniards. The arrival of Pedro de Alvarado, called Donadiú, the sun, by the Quiché since he burned their kings (IV, xii, 230), coincided with the twelfth generation and, as the narrative concludes: 'And this was the life of the Quiché, because no longer can be seen [the book of the *Popol Vuh*] which the kings had in olden times, for it has disappeared. In this manner, then, all the people of the Quiché, which is called Santa Cruz, came to an end' (IV, xii, 234–35). As the penultimate sentence makes quite clear, the *Popol Vuh* is not to be understood simply as a symbolic transcription of the laws of the Quiché people but rather as an outward sign of the inter-generational continuity of a living community. Though we have the book (*Vuh*), the community (*Popol*) to which it testifies is no more.

---

[1] The original copy of the manuscript – i.e. probably transcribed by Diego Reynoso – has been lost but Father Ximénez's original handwritten text is now held in the Edward E. Ayer collection in the Newberry Library of Chicago.

*The Codices*

The codices are a unique Latin-American art-form; they were often made of deer-skin, covered with a chalk-like varnish to preserve them, and, typically, folded like a screen (*leporello*). Some were drawn on *amatl*, a native paper made from the inner bark of trees belonging to the genus *Ficus*, and they are normally read from right to left, backwards and forwards in a zig-zag like motion (Caso 10). The codices which, as mentioned above, are partly ideographic, partly phonetic, are normally divided into three distinct types: those which focus on the annals of a people and/or their gods and divine rituals; the Techialoyan books, that is, petitionary documents used to defend lands and communities against changes in the law; and the Testerian manuscripts whose main purpose was Christian instruction (Brotherston, *Mexican Painted Books* 3). What follows will concentrate in the main on the first category of codex (both the Maya and the Mexican), although some mention will be made of the second type. It would, of course, be a mistake to see the codices as offering unmediated access to the truth about Amerindian culture since, ironically enough, many owe their very existence to the Spanish invasion and, for that reason, demonstrate a hybridic character.

There are only three known Maya codices in existence, the *Codex Dresden*, the *Codex Pérez* and the *Codex Madrid*, two of which are named after the city in which they are now held. The *Codex Pérez* is exemplary; it was named after the Yucatecan Don Juan Pío Pérez (1798–1859) who collected, collated and copied a number of Maya manuscripts which he came across in Ticul (Craine & Reindorp xv–vi). It is a compilation of various 'books' authored by different Jaguar priests, but it does have a unified focus; the Maya notion of time (with its combination of the 365-day 'vague' year and the 260-day ritual almanac), around which all else orbited in the thought-universe of the Mayas. It also contains a version of the important sacred text *The Book of Chilam Balam of Maní* (literally, 'The Book of the Jaguar Priest of Maní'), and a charming short narrative entitled 'The Maiden Teodora', which recounts how a young beautiful girl entices the court of the King Almanzor with her unrivalled intelligence and good looks (*Codez Pérez* 59–62). A close reading of the *Codex Pérez* suggests that the narrative which predicted the return of the Maya culture-hero, Kukulcán, was tampered with to produce a text which predicted 'the coming of the Spaniards and Christianity, both of which should be welcomed with enthusiasm' (*Codex Pérez* 69, footnote 21).

The Aztec codices, many more of which survived, reveal similar evidence of transculturation. One of the most famous of these, the *Codez Mendoza*, which derives its name from the first Viceroy of Spain, Antonio de Mendoza, who commissioned it, is divided into three parts: the first concerns the Mexican annals from the founding of Mexico (1324) until Moctezuma II's death (1520) (fols. 1–18r); the second describes the tributes paid to the

Mexican lords (fols. 18v–71v), and the third part concentrates on the social and political life of Mexico (fols. 56v–71v) (Madan & Craster, entry 3134). It was compiled some twenty years after the conquest by native scribes under the supervision of missionary priests; while it appears that the document as a whole was prepared for the Spanish crown, there is little doubt that Parts 1 and 2 were copied from earlier pictorials dating from pre-contact times (*Codex Mendoza*, ed. Berdan & Anawalt vol. 1, xiii). Some of the codices were clearly revisionist, post-conquest documents. The *Codex Aubin* (or *Codex 1576*), for example, portrays the Mexican gods as devils ('salieron llevando al diablo a quien adoraban como un dios'; *Códice de 1576* 5); it is significant that the only Castilian word to appear consistently in the Nahuatl portion of the text is 'diablo'.

There are also a number of codices which were composed some time after the conquest and which document the harshness of colonial rule. The *Codex Kingsborough*, for example, drawn in the middle of the sixteenth century in water colours and accompanied by a narrative in Spanish, was first published by Lord Kingsborough (1795–1837) in a volume entitled *Various Papers* (1831); the original of the *Codex Kingsborough*, now separated into two separate codices, is held in the British Museum.[2] In this codex the Spaniards are depicted as malevolent, almost out of place in the mental universe of the Tepetlaoztoc Indians with its abundance of natural symbols (fish, frogs, etc.). The scene on page 250 is typical, showing two Spaniards standing on top of two reclining figures wrapped in funeral robes, and a severed head on top; the symbolism could not be more brutal. One of the most intriguing of these later more politicised codices is the *Codex Osuna* which documents the early municipal life of the indigenous population of Mexico City. Originally published in 1878 from the library of the Duque de Osuna as a forty-page document, it is now known to be part of a longer document of over four hundred folios which is, in essence, a law suit dated 2 March 1564, brought by the Indian governor, mayors and chieftains against the Viceroy and *Oidores* of New Spain on the occasion of Don Gerónimo de Valderrama's visit to New Spain as official *Visitador* of the crown (1563–1566). The document accuses the Viceroy and others of legal malpractice, greed, cheating, and immorality (frolicking naked with naked women in the steam baths in full sight and knowledge of all and sundry). The first folio, for example, accuses the Viceroy Luis de Velasco, with drawings as evidence, of having received 215 'cargas' of lime to repair his residence but without returning just recompense

---

2 Its original reference was MS Add. 13964. The *Codex Kingsborough* has subsequently been disbound, since it was seen to contain two different texts, the Tepetlaoztoc Codex and a Cochineal Treatise (*Relación de lo que toca a la Grana Cochinilla*), which, in the exhibition Mexican Painted Books before and after the Spanish Conquest, held in the British Museum from the 4 June to 6 September 1992, were listed separately; see Brotherston, *Mexican Painted Books* 29.

(Chávez Orozco 264); it also records how the *Oidor* Doctor Vasco Puga was given lime for which he did not pay, as did the *Oidor* Villalobos (*Códice Osuna* fols. 465–3v; fol. 466–4r). It was usual for legal documents of this kind to contain drawings since Indians during trial proceedings often needed interpreters and relied on pictography to present their case. The *Codex Osuna* therefore offers invaluable insight into the conflict between Spanish and Amerindian culture, as well as the interplay between written text and pictography during this period.

## Quechua Runasimi

Any expression of Amerindian culture was expressly prohibited during the colonial era by viceregal decree. Thus a council in Lima in 1583 ordered that all *quipus* be destroyed, and, in 1613, Father Arriaga rejoiced at the destruction of Incan musical instruments and religious icons; the following year festivals and indigenous dances were prohibited, especially those in which Quechua was spoken or sung. After the 1780 rebellion of Tupac Amaru, Quechua was outlawed in the viceroyalty of Peru; a good example of the excessiveness of this prohibition is that even Garcilaso de la Vega's *Comentarios Reales*, which in the final analysis supported Catholicism, was banned (Aybar xxvii–xxviii). It comes as no surprise, therefore, to learn that Quechua literature was not 'discovered' until the nineteenth century and even then by foreign scholars such as Markham, Tschudi, Middendorf, and Trimborn (Aybar xxviii).

Referring to a body of knowledge passed on from generation to generation by oral means – as happened with Quechua, its language and its culture – in terms of 'literature' is, of course, problematic. Literature was understood as 'runasimi' by the Incas, that is, verbal art, rather than 'literature' in the Western sense of the term (written, normally printed, designed to have an aesthetic effect). 'Runasimi' was used by the Incas in their religious ceremonies of communication with the Sun God, Inti, in a ceremony called Inti Raymi. Edmundo Bendezú Aybar mentions a number of ways in which the 'runasimi' could be expressed: the *hayllis* (a joyful war song), the *hauri* (a mournful, nostalgic song), a theatrical performance in a public space called a *mellquis*, and the recitation of short songs or stories of a fabulous nature and usually told to children (Aybar xxiii). During the colonial period, Quechua literature went into a state of what Aybar calls 'ukupacha' (the underground world), although some works emerged later on, such as *Yauri Titu Inca*, *Usca Páucar*, and, most famous of all, *Ollantay* (see pp. 47–48). Some of these texts expressed a terrible vision of the collapse of Incan civilisation, such as *La Tragedia del Fin de Atahuallpa*, discovered in Bolivia by Jesús Lara. The two genres which survived during the colonial era and, indeed, surfaced, were poetry and short narrative.

Some of the most interesting material is the poetry. It is difficult to tell of those poems which have survived from the Incan period whether they are truly untouched by the influence of the Spanish. Certainly those poems which express non-Christian sentiments ('Beberemos en el cráneo del enemigo/ haremos un collar de sus dientes/ haremos flauta de sus huesos/ de su piel haremos tambores/ y así cantaremos'; Aybar 18) may be safely seen as pre-Columbian. Those which emphasise the Christian notion of sin and penance ('Tú, el que previene y manda/ ¿lejos estás o cerca/ del pecador?/ Sálvame de esta cárcel,/ tú, gobierno del hombre, dios'; Aybar 21) appear to be post-Columbian. Although it would be foolish to discount the role of acculturation (some of the poems we know of come, after all, from Garcilaso de la Vega), the poems collected by Aybar constitute a good collection, and offer a fair indication of the main themes of Quechuan verse. The first thing that needs to be underlined is that the typical Incan poem is performative, not only in the sense that it exists in performance in a social context with an audience in attendance, but also in the sense of being an enactment of the community's desire, rather than the description of a personal emotion. Many of the poems, after all, ask Viracocha for his guidance (normally in the form of advice), and for his protection from want and from war. A good example is the poem 'Viracocha', perhaps the oldest of the Incan hymns, which opens as follows:

> Es Viracocha
> señor del origen,
> 'sea esto hombre',
> 'sea esto mujer'.
> De la fuente sacra
> supremo juez,
> de todo cuanto hay
> enorme creador.
> ¿Dónde estás?
> ¿No te veré acaso?    (Aybar 5)

One other characteristic of these poems, evident in this hymn, is their emphasis on the separation of the sexes. Viracocha created man and woman deliberately, and this sense of separation is very distinctly carried over in the communal songs in which the men and women of the community recite their lines antiphonally and sequentially. In '¡Ea, el triunfo!' for example, the men speak of their work in the fields ('¡He aquí el arado y el surco! ¡He aquí el sudor y la mano!') while the women spur them on in recalling their prowess. The penultimate 'estribillo' ('¡He aquí la infanta, la hermosa!') brings to mind the notion of the commerce of love after the work has been done. Other poems which emphasise courtship and love ('Morena mía . . .' 20–21, 'Canción amorosa' 28, and 'Canción' 31), likewise underline that these poems were written for specific social ends such as building a sense of community, and expressing the religious urge to petition Viracocha's protection. The language of love and courtship here becomes pragmatic and performative.[3]

## *Aztec Poetry*

The corpus of extant Aztec poetry is based on four main sources, which are: (i) the twenty sacred hymns collected by Bernardino de Sahagún, (ii) the songs scattered in various testimonies of the 'ancient word' or 'huehuehtlahtolli', (iii) the *Cantares mexicanos* held in the National Library in Mexico, and (iv) the *Romances de los señores de Nueva España* housed in the Nettie Lee Benson Latin American collection, University of Texas Library at Austin (León-Portilla, *Fifteen* 18).[4] The major bulk of these songs were transcribed alphabetically in Nahuatl soon after the conquest based on oral performances given by indigenous singers, or poets, which were inspired by pictoglyphic books. The poets see themselves as unique interpreters of that knowledge: 'I am a precious bird/ for I make the books speak,/ there in the house of the painted books' (qtd. in León-Portilla, *Fifteen* 5). These poems fall into a number of genres which are as follows: 'xopancuicatl' (songs of springtime), 'xochicuicatl' (flowery songs), 'totocuicatl' (songs of birds), 'michcuicatl' (songs of fish), 'icnocuicatl' (songs of orphanhood), 'cozcacuicatl' (necklace songs), 'teuccuicatl' (songs of the lords), 'tlaocolcuicatl' (songs of suffering), 'cuauhcuicatl' (songs of eagles), 'yaocuicatl' (songs of war), 'atequilizcuicatl' (songs of puring water), 'cihuacuicatl' (songs of women), 'cococuicatl' (songs of doves), 'cuecuechcuicatl' (provocative songs), and 'huehuehcuicatl' (songs of old people) (*Fifteen* 28). León-Portilla has identified and named fifteen Aztec poets, reconstructing their biography and works painstakingly, based on the scant evidence available. While their work clearly demonstrates individual features, the similarity of the themes treated in their poetry is overwhelming. Perhaps most noticeable is the obsessive preoccupation with the brevity of life. A good example is the 'Song of the Flight' by Nezahualcoyotl of Tezcoco (1402–1472) which begins as follows: 'In vain was I born, in vain have I come forth/ to earth from the house of the Lord' (*Fifteen* 90). The gloominess of the poetic emotion expressed is reinforced by the parallelism. 'Sad Song of Cuacuauhtzin' by Cuacuauhtzin of Tepechpan (mid fifteenth century) offers a similar lesson in fatalism: 'Where would we go/ that we never have to die?' (*Fifteen* 109). A striking feature of these

---

   [3]  For a brief discussion of literature written in Guaraní, see Oviedo, *Historia*, vol. 1, 69–70.
   [4]  I have focussed in this section on Aztec poetry since it is the genre of Aztec literature about which most is known; for a discussion of pre-Columbian drama, see the Theatre section of this chapter.

poems is their sense of metaphysical uncertainty. In the 'Song of Axayacatl, Lord of Mexico', for example, by Axayacatl (1449–1481): 'Will there perhaps be an end to pain?/ Perhaps they will come again?/ Who can teach me about this?' (*Fifteen* 169). At times this metaphysical certainty is borne out of distressing historical events such as the loss of material power. In one poem, for example, the loss of leaders is expressed in terms of orphanhood, as in the 'Song of Axayacatl' quoted above (*Fifteen* 168). Yet, at other times, this uncertainty is transformed into an eerie sense of loss of identity: 'Am I perchance a shield of turquoise,/ will I as a mosaic be embedded once more in existence? Will I come again to the earth?' (*Fifteen* 145), and also of life being no more than a dream: 'We only rise from sleep,/ we come only to dream,/ it is not true, it is not true,/ that we come on earth to live' (*Fifteen* 153).

In terms of style, the overriding feature of Aztec verse is its consistent use of an interlocking mesh of images, as when one image is related to another, painted books to song, song to music, music to birds, birds to flowers, flowers to intoxication, intoxication to spring, spring to earth, and earth to (fleeting) life. Typically these images are constructed paratactically (which is to be expected, perhaps, given the grammar of Nahuatl which works 'by the process of compounding and derivation' [Campbell & Kartunnen I 10]), and are treated as a woven artifact to be offered as a sacrificial offering to God the Giver of Life. A good example of this is the 'Song of Springtime' by Nezahualcoyotl of Tezcoco which progresses through a series of images (painting-singing-music-flowers-birds-intoxication), and yet does so by weaving backwards and forwards in a gentle see-saw motion in which 'singing' becomes the axial image. One other striking feature of Aztec poetry is its ludic, sexual side, the best example of which is 'The Song of the Women of Chalco' by Aquiauhtzin of Ayapanco (c.1430–c.1500). This poem teases its addressee, Axayacotl, challenging him to make love to its female author, sometimes bluntly ('Do it in my warm vessel, much/ light on fire./ Come, put it in, put it in'; *Fifteen* 274) and sometimes poetically ('Look on my flowering painting: my breasts./ Will it fall in vain,/ your heart,/ little man, Axayacatl?/ Here are your small hands,/ now take me with your hands. Let us take pleasure'; *Fifteen* 279).[5] The sexual explicitness of this female Aztec writer is extraordinary if one takes into account the time in which this poem was written (sometime in the sixteenth century).

---

5   There are some similarities between Aztec verse and Maya verse, particularly in the choice of imagery; see Oviedo's discussion of *Libro de los Cantares de Dzitbalché* (Oviedo, *Historia*, vol. 1, 59–60).

## The Legacy

As is clear from the analysis above, the legacy of Amerindian culture, though rich, comes down to us in chequered form. Linguistic-oral culture such as the *Popol Vuh*, the 'Song of Springtime' by Nezahualcoyotl of Tezcoco, and the Inca poem dedicated to Viracocha, show us a world in which oral culture and religious ritual are mutually porous. The codices, for their part, offer a fascinating glimpse into the Amerindian world. They range from the ritualistic (namely, a pictorial, non-linguistic representation of the activities of the gods of the Maya and Aztec panthenon), to part-illustration, part-verbal description of the history of a particular people, to an account – from the Indian's point of view – of the excesses of Spanish colonial admin-istration; they are immeasurably valuable in providing insight into the vitality of Amerindian culture. While it is only right to discuss them before analysing the literature of conquest and discovery, it is important to remember that these texts were not historically evident to the Spaniards who arrived in the New World from 1492 onwards. They were, indeed, deliberately ignored or, in the case of Bishop Diego de Landa, wilfully destroyed. (It is naive to assume any other type of reaction from a colonizing culture, perhaps.) It was only in the era of independence, and particularly the middle of the nineteenth century, that a receptivity to these texts emerged. As already noted, Juan Pío Pérez began collecting Maya manuscripts in about 1835, the *Popul Vuh* was re-discovered in the 1850s, and many of the Mexican codices were discov-ered and published for the first time in the nineteenth century, often by French and British scholars. The ideology of the discoverer as much as of the conquistador, was one which required the New World to be a blank page on which they would write their exploits and their destiny.

## Conquest and Discovery

The conquest of the Americas by the Spanish was first and foremost a military event, but it was accompanied by a massive intellectual conquest through the written word. Literacy and military conquest, indeed, went hand in hand during this period since, as C. M. Cipolla has pointed out, 'after the fifteenth century, technological progress in warfare required, and at the same time was based on, an adequate supply of literate soldiers . . . Societies which produced an increasing number of literate soldiers had a decisive advantage over those that failed to do so' (qtd. in Cruickshank 812). We have already noted that New World culture was seen by the European invaders as a blank page on which they would write their own deeds, and the book played an important role in this process given the authority and power invested in print during the fifteenth and sixteenth centuries. Printing came to Spain in the early 1470s (Cruickshank 800) and, as we shall see, the printed word was used by the conquistadors and their accomplices as a means of asserting ownership of land in the New World.[6] The literature examined in this section consists in the main of chronicles, treatises and letters which focus on the conquest and discovery of the New World; some of these texts were published in Spain soon after composition, but many only achieved published form many years later. No work, religious or otherwise, was published in the New World before 1535, and the book, or intellectual, industry, was heavily dependent on Spain for many years after that date. Intellectual traffic was, like trade, minimal between the viceroyalties and was normally one-way from Spain; the average edition of this period, the fifteenth century and the first half of the sixteenth century, involved a print-run of about two hundred copies (Steinberg 140).

Some of the texts examined in this section could arguably be seen as examples of Spanish rather than Latin-American literature but, given precedent and the undeniable logic of analysing these texts, they are here presented as an integral part of the roots of Spanish-American literature. These works specifically mark themselves as part of the print-language of Spanish, in contradistinction to the oral-vernacular diversity of the Indian languages, which Nebrija refers to in his *Gramática castellana* as 'peregrinas lenguas' as opposed to the 'language of empire' of Spanish ('siempre la lengua fue compañera del imperio', he notes in his opening words of justification to the Catholic Monarchs; Nebrija 11, 5). Much of the writing of the early chronicles is based on the Spanish medieval tradition of recording historic events for the benefit of the national collective memory. The mood of many of the authors of these early texts has been well described by Greenblatt:

> The Europeans who ventured to the New World in the first decades after Columbus's discovery shared a complex, well-developed, and, above all, mobile technology of power: writing, navigational instruments, ships, war-horses, attack dogs, effective armor, and highly lethal weapons, including gunpowder. Their culture was characterised by immense confidence in its own centrality, by a political organisation based on practices of command and submission, [and] by a willingness to use coercive violence on both strangers and fellow countrymen . . . Such was the confidence of this culture that it expected perfect strangers – the Arawaks of the Caribbean, for example – to abandon their own beliefs, preferably immediately, and

---

6   In the sixteenth and seventeenth centuries in Spain, the printed word was held to possess great authority. This is suggested by an exchange in Lope de Vega's play, *La octava maravilla*, written in about 1609, in which a master and servant are discussing printed ephemera. As Cruickshank elucidates: 'The servant has come across a pamphlet which states that in Granada a man has given birth. The master is scornful. The servant, surprised, asks: '¿Está de molde, y te burlas?' (roughly translated as 'It's in print, and you still mock the idea') (Cruickshank 808). Though treated ironically in Lope's play, this incident suggests the power of print in the early seventeenth century (and presumably before) in Spain and, one must assume, in the Spanish colonies in the New World.

embrace those of Europe as luminously and self-evidently true. A failure to
do provoked impatience, contempt, and even murderous rage.

(*Marvelous* 9)

It is ironic that the first published text in Spanish focussing on the reality
of the New World should have been written by an individual who was a non-
Spaniard with a defective knowledge of Castilian and who was unaware of
what he had witnessed, namely, Cristóval Colón (as his name is printed in his
*Diario*). What we know about the discovery of the New World by
Christopher Columbus (1451–1506) is contained within the log-book journal
he kept of his four voyages to the New World (1492–1493; 1493–1496;
1498–1500; 1502–1504), as well as the famous letter dated 15 February 1493
which he sent to Luis de Santangel, the Catholic Monarchs' scribe, in which
he announced the discovery of a New World. Columbus also wrote other
letters to the sovereigns based on his subsequent voyages, namely, a memorial in April 1493 proposing that trading posts be established in Hispaniola, a
letter to the same on 18 October 1498 and a letter to Doña Juana Torres, Isa-
bella's confidante, in 1500 giving details of his third voyage, and the *Lettera
Rarissima* to Philip II on 7 July 1503 (Murray 38–54). The *Carta a Luis de
Santangel* (1493) is in effect, if not in intention, a proclamation of the discovery of a New World. While still labouring under the misapprehension that he
was visiting islands off the coasts of China, Columbus described the Caribbean islands he had visited in such terms that would lead to further investment by the Catholic Monarchs, enticing them with the hope of possession of
foreign lands. The mountains are so enormous they reach the sky, the trees
never lose their leaves, there is evidence of abundant spices and the rivers
flow with gold ('traen oro'). The rest of the letter takes care in pointing out
that the people encountered there are docile and would be easy to Christian-
ise; they have neither iron nor arms, and are 'temerosos a maravilla'. Columbus's concluding paragraph gives to understand that the islands he has visited
are an abundant source of commodity, mineral and human capital: 'pueden
ver sus Altezas que yo les daré oro cuanto hubieran menester con muy
poquita ayuda que Sus Altezas me darán ahora' (Chang Rodríguez & Malva
E. Filer 13–14). It was a letter which would fire the imagination of the West
for many years to come but it simultaneously spelt death for the inhabitants
of the Caribbean whose lands and domestic environment would soon be sav-
agely destroyed by the arrival of Spaniards hungry for gold.

The connection between ownership and writing is also played out in the
the letters of the greatest of the conquistadors, Hernán Cortés (1485–1547),
conqueror of Mexico, Governor and Captain-General of New Spain and later
Marquis of the Valley of Oaxaca. His letters, like Columbus's before him,
were written to the Catholic Monarchs during the years of conquest
(1519–1526) to inform them of current developments but also to persuade
them that this venture was worth further monetary investment. Their impor-

tance is based on two things: they provided Spanish and other Europeans 'with their first great paradigm for European encounters with an organised native state' and, 'through their swift publication in several European languages', reached a wide audience in the Old World (Clendinnen 87).[7] Cortés's letters, however, also had the purely pragmatic aim of ensuring that his own land privileges were retained; thus he is at great pains to record the various acts of treachery carried out by others (such as Diego Velázquez and Pánfilo de Narváez, fellow conquistadors whom Cortés casts as villains of the piece in the first and second letters). The value of the letters nowadays is more to be found in what they show us about the process of transculturation. Cortés tells an unconsciously amusing anecdote: when the first conquistadors arrived on the Mexican mainland they understood the indigenous population to say that the land they had arrived in was called Yucatán, although the words pronounced actually meant 'we do not understand your words' (Cortés 3). The scene epitomises the drama of the conquest: on the one hand we have a native population which finds the words and actions of the European incomprehensible, while, on the other, we have the European coloniser mapping out a new world based on a misreading.

## The Chroniclers

There were a great number of chronicles published in Spain and Latin America soon after the conquest, and still more have emerged into print in more recent years, such that it would be impossible to give an account of all or even some of them in an introductory study of this kind. What I propose to do therefore is to take a few chronicles as representative texts and discuss their information value and techniques of persuasion. It is important to recall that the works of this period were not necessarily written for the benefit of posterity. As the letters by Columbus and Cortés already show us, texts written during the early years of the postmath of conquest were more concerned to persuade their audience of the justice of their claim to wealth, position or land. A good example of this is the manuscript 'Nueva obra y breve en metro y prosa sobre la muerte del adelantado Don Diego de Almagro, hecha por un testigo de vista – por los años de 1550', held in the Biblioteca Nacional in Lima (Sala de Investigaciones A124, 5ff.). This work, which was notarised by Fray Félix Ponce de León (fol. 5v), seeks to restore the reputation of Diego de Almagro who, as this manuscript suggests, as a

---

[7] The publication of these letters and their wide circulation was an indication of a paradigm-shift which occurred in the sixteenth century as a result of the creation of print. As Cruickshank has pointed out, while manuscript transmission involved a slow process, '[t]he press could make an author famous overnight' (Cruickshank 800), and this is essentially what happened in the case of Cortés's letters.

result of the foul deeds of 'Don Francisco y sus hermanos', was deprived of 'honra, vida y hazienda' (fol. 1v). This work crosses between the realms of literature (in the sense of a work written for aesthetic effect), history (understood as a chronicle), and legal document (in the sense of claiming the right to property, etc.). Typical of its era, 'Nueva obra y breve . . .' conflates various discourses for the purely pragmatic end of persuading the addressee of its truth-value.

Among the body of 'crónicas', two divergent trends can be identified. On the one hand were the official accounts of the conquest, such as *Historia general y natural de las Indias* (1526) authored by Gonzalo Fernández de Oviedo y Valdés (1478–1557), which were either commissioned by the Catholic Monarchs or received the royal seal at some stage during their composition. The official nature of Oviedo's text, for instance, is underlined by his claim that members of the Council of the Indies saw and corrected the manuscript; it is dedicated to Cardinal Fray García Jofre de Loaysa, President of the Royal Council of the Indies. Oviedo's work won fame in Europe, and justly so, for being the first ever description of the Sub-Continent's flora and fauna (Brading 43). In contrast to official chronicles of this kind were those accounts which reported the first-hand experience of an individual's life (normally of a traumatic kind), such as *Naufragios* (1542) by Alvar Núñez Cabeza de Vaca (1490?–1559?). Núñez accompanied Pánfilo de Narváez on his expedition to colonise the provinces of Florida, occupying the position of treasurer and *alguacil mayor*. The expedition set out from Spain on 27 June 1527. Núñez's *Naufragios* covers the voyage with Narváez, the fate of the expedition and specifically his adventures with a contingent of Spanish sailors, while sea-wrecked along the coast of North America and wandering through the mainland of the Northern Continent, gaining the friendship of the Indian tribes through their apparent ability to heal sick people, living on nuts, berries and tuna fish, until they met up with some Spaniards from the settlement of San Miguel, and were finally transported to Mexico City, where they arrived in July 1536. To this day, Núñez's route is disputed, and there are at least eight different hypotheses concerning which route he took (Hellenbeck 243–306). With a matter-of-factness which at times seems unsuited to the events described, Núñez recounts the various misadventures which befell him over a period of nine years. Particularly gripping is his description of the plight on the island which the Spaniards named Malhado, given their experience there. Again its identity is a matter of dispute, although Hellenbeck advances Galverston Island as the most likely candidate (Hellenbeck 119–27). Having beached on this island on or around 6 November 1528, after being separated from the other boats and lost at sea with no knowledge of where they were for nine days, Núñez and his companions had a spell of good luck, since they were fed by the Indians they encountered there, although this was probably as much due to Cabeza de Vaca's 'skill as a cultural negotiator' (Ahern 225). But when they had sufficiently recovered they put to sea once more on the barge which promptly capsized because of an enormous wave, and three of the crew were drowned. Núñez Cabeza de Vaca's account of the perils of sea voyages is the matrix text of a rich auto-biograpical tradition in Spanish America; Carlos de Sigüenza y Góngora's *Infortunios de Alonso Ramírez*, for example, provides an important stepping-stone between these narratives and the first fully-fledged novel in Spanish America, *Periquillo Sarniento*.

Most of the accounts of military action in the New World, following in the vein of Cortés's letters, took the bias of the invading forces. Such was certainly the case with the *Historia general de las Indias* (1552) by Francisco López de Gómara (1511–1564), and this is not surprising since he was for four years Cortés's chaplain (1541–1545) and subsequently resided in the conquistador's house. Gómara's account of the Amerindian population is harsh to say the least: of the inhabitants of the Caribbean he charged that their god is the devil (XXVII, 45), the women are lascivious and the men are sodomisers, lazy, deceitful, ungrateful, capricious and uncultured (XXVIII, 47). Unlike Gómara's account, which was penned by someone who had never set foot in the New World, Díaz del Castillo's *Verdadera historia de la conquista de la Nueva España* (1632) is concerned with the daily grind of the conquest. His is an eyewitness account; he was a 'testigo de vista' (Bernal Díaz, I, 65). It is for his emphasis on ocular evidence and his lack of interest in annotation that Bernal Díaz is favoured by the modern historian.

In the *Chronica del Peru* (1554) by Pedro Cieza de León (1518?–1560), the author depicts himself, and in this he establishes a precedent which later writers such as Ercilla would emulate, as a soldier-writer; his two professions are 'escreuir, y seguir a mi vandera y Capitan' (fol. 3r). Cieza de León's approach to the Incas is that of a Christian seigneurial colonist; like other chroniclers he has no hesitation in calling the Incas' god the 'devil' (the solemn feast of Hatum Raimi is described as 'witchcraft'; Book II, chap. xxx), but unlike some hardliners such as José de Acosta, he is willing to cede that the Spanish have some blame to bear for their treatment of the Indians. At the end of Book II, chap. xxv, for example, Cieza de León implores God to give the Spanish the grace necessary to re-pay the Incas the enormous human debt they owe them as a result of the conquest. Without a doubt the most skilled of all the chroniclers was El Inca Garcilaso de la Vega (1539–1616), according to one critic, 'the first New World native and the first person of Amerindian descent to be published and read widely throughout Europe' (Zamora 3), the son of a leading conquistador, and descendant of a highly literate family which included among its ancestors the Marqués de Santillana, Jorge Manrique and Garcilaso de la Vega, and of the Inca princess, Isabel Chimpu Occlo, a grand-daughter of the Emperor Tupac Inca Yupanqui. Like earlier chronicles such as Cieza de León's *Chronica del Peru*, Garcilaso's *Comentarios Reales* (1609) shows a keen awareness of transculturation; as Garcilaso points out in the first chapter of his chronicle, it was as a result of the clash between the print-based culture of the Spaniards and the oral-based culture of the Incas that he decided to write down the history of the Incas. His knowledge had been culled from the conversations he had with his family while a young man and offers a remarkable insight into the Inca way of life which, in effect, makes the commentaries not only historiographical but also autobiographical.

Apart from the military chroniclers there was also a group of religious who wrote accounts of their experiences in the New World. An important early chronicler was Fray Toribio de Paredes o Benavente (1490?–1568), also known as Motolinía, a name based on the Yucatec word for poverty which he adopted for himself; his major work was *Historia de los indios de la Nueva España* (1541). Motilinía saw the New World as the work of the devil; thus he translated the Yucatec word for temple, 'teocalli', as 'templo del demonio' (chap. III: 24). A similar desire to depict Amerindian culture in satanic terms underlies *Historia Natural y Moral de las Indias* (1590) by José de Acosta (1540–1600), who described the New World as a gigantic parody of the Christian world created by the devil (V, xxx; Acosta 181). His view of Aztec hieroglyphics was also uncompromising: 'la pintura es libro para los idiotas que no saben leer' (VI, iv; Acosta 185). Similar in tone and intention to Acosta's *Historia Natural* is the *Relación de las cosas de Yucatán* (1864) by Fray Diego de Landa. Diego de Landa's chronicle, though, throws light on the ambiguous space inhabited by the religious in the middle of the six- teenth century in the New World. On the one hand they were enemies of the conquistadors and the *encomenderos* (see chapter XVII, 36–37); on the other hand, they were hostile to the Amerindian culture and especially its religious precepts as embodied by the Jaguar priests. Thus, he calls the Yucatecans' priests 'idolatrous' and describes their social function as 'dar al pueblo las respuestas de los demonios' (XXVII, 55).

Though written by a man of the cloth like Motilinía, José de Acosta and Diego de Landa, the version of the conquest found in the chronicles of Bar- tolomé de las Casas (1484–1566) could not be more different. His most cele- brated pamphlet is the *Brevísima historia de la destrucción de las Indias* (1552), which, in one fell swoop, established the so-called Black Legend which would plague the Hispanic world for centuries to come. Las Casas's text was eagerly taken up by Spain's imperial rivals – the Dutch, French and the English – in order to discredit the methods whereby the Spanish estab- lished their overseas empire. It describes the recently colonised empire region by region, beginning with Hispaniola and ending with Río de la Plata, and describes the initial peaceful overtures made by the Indians, followed by the treachery of the Spaniards (torture, forced slavery, rape, murder, etc.). Las Casas's main point in this essay is to underline the irony of the Spanish purporting to be ambassadors of Jesus Christ while acting like devils. There were also some chronicles which, like the *Codex Osuna*, highlighted the evils of conquest from the Indian perspective. Such is the case of *Nueva corónica y buen gobierno* by Felipe Guaman Poma de Ayala (c.1535–c.1615), a sixteenth-century Quechua-speaking *ladino* Indian from the Ayacucho region. His text did not have a sympathetic hearing in the era in which it was written and languished in manuscript form for nearly three hundred years before it was finally discovered in the National Library in Copenhagen in 1908 by Richard Pietschmann and published in facsimile form in 1936. Guaman Poma de Ayala's basic point – the West imposed on the inhabitants of newly discovered lands a creed they did not live up to themselves – has had a sympathetic hearing in our anti-colonialist times.

## The Amerindian View of the Conquest

Though fragmented by a colonial power not overkeen on hearing the story of the conquest as seen through Amerindian eyes, the 'other' version of the conquest has gradually emerged. By Miguel León-Portilla's computation, there are twelve surviving documents, in written or pictographic form, which describe the conquest from the Amerindian point of view (*The Broken Spears* 129). One very important source is Fray Bernadino. de Sahagún's history of New Spain based on oral accounts of the conquest given to him by Indian informants as described above, the *Historia general de las cosas de Nueva España*, also known as the *Codex Florentino*. Other important extant Amerindian accounts of the conquest are: *Anonymous Manuscript of Tlaletolco* (1528), *Codex Aubin* (or *Codex 1576*), *Códice Ramírez* (probably compiled from the data assembled before 1580 by Fray Diego de Durán, and published in 1944), Fernando de Alva Ixtilxochitl, *XIII relación* and *Historia chichimeca* (written in Spanish and based on Nahuatl sources no longer extant), *Lienzo de Tlaxcala* (dating from the middle of the sixteenth century and published in 1892), Diego Muñoz Camargo, *Historia de Tlaxcala* (written in Spanish during the second half of the sixteenth century and published in 1892), Fernando Alvarado Tezozomac, *Cronica mexicana* (1944), and *Cronica mexicayotl* (1975) by the same author, and the *VII relación* by the historian of Chalco, Domingo Francisco de San Anton Munon Chimalpain Cuauhtlehuanitzin. Though centreing on different geographical areas, these texts were culled by authors concerned to keep this history alive, and were based on information given by oral informants in Nahuatl which was then transcribed phonetically and recorded in written form; many of these original manuscripts are now scattered in libraries around the world but have now been published. A highly influential collection of these texts was published by León-Portilla, translated into Spanish as *Visión de los vencidos* (1959).

The passages of the *Codex Florentino* relating to the conquest are the most dramatic. They present a picture of the Aztecs whom Cortés faced as riven by internal political tensions, caught in an uneasy truce with the various Mesoamerican peoples surrounding them, and as led by a leader, Moctezuma, paralysed by indecision and submitting to the invasion with a fatalistic resignation. All of these factors Cortés was able to exploit cleverly to his own advantage. The *Codex Florentino* provides an internally and chronologically coherent version of the events leading up to the destruction of Tenochtitlan, beginning with the eight bad omens (the most incredible of which was the appearance of 'tlacantzolli', or men with two heads, symbolizing, perhaps, the *mestizo* race soon to emerge),[8] the first sightings of the Spanish galleons, the alliance of the peoples hostile to the Aztecs, and leading to the description of the Spaniards' relentless march on Tenochtitlan, the capture of Moctezuma, the massacre of the Aztec warriors during the Feast of Toxcatl on the orders of Diego de Alvarado (seen by the Aztecs as an example of the most perverse treachery), the subsequent expulsion of the Spanish army, and concluding with their return to Tenochtitlan which they revengefully razed to the ground (1519–1522). One of the most striking features of the *Codex Florentino* are the illustrations which accompany the narrative. Examples are the description of Cortés firing a gun at which the Indians faint (fol. 9r), La Malinche speaking from a rooftop on behalf of Cortés to an Indian (fol. 29r), and the carnage during the Feast of Toxcatl (fol. 33r–v, fol. 34r), as well as the Spaniards escaping from Tenochtitlan (fol. 43r). Certain symbols are used to tell the story over and above the words. While the war has not been lost by the Aztecs, the figures show a triumphant eagle (fol. 54r, fig. 2, and fig. 3 in which a cactus takes the place of the eagle, and later on fol. 50r, figs. 2 and 3). But when the war is nearing its conclusion, the eagle is depicted as cowering in fear, its wings unspread and held close to its body (fol. 50v, fig. 3). The eagle is absent from the last twenty-two illustrations as if to indicate that the Aztec empire has now fallen (fols. 63r–69v). It is surely not insignificant that the last pages of the text (fols. 70r–87r) bear no drawings, as if to suggest the reality was too painful to illustrate in visual terms.

Other Nahuatl documents can in the main be used to support this basic narrative; Tezozomac's *Cronica mexicana*, for example, contains the first detailed eyewitness account by a poor *macehual* (common man) of the Spanish in their ships, described as 'two towers or small mountains floating on the waves of the sea' (*The Broken Spears* 16), and expanded in the following account:

> Our lord and king, it is true that strange people have come to the shores of the great sea. They were fishing from a small boat, some with rods and others with a net. They fished until late and then they went back to their two great towers and climbed up into them. There were about fifteen of these people, some with blue jackets, others with red, others with black or

---

[8] The most miraculous of the signs is the captured bird with a mirror on its head ('tenya esta ave, en medio de la cabeça, un espejo redondo, donde se parecia el cielo') in which Moctezuma saw a 'muchedumbre de gente iunta que venyan todos, armados encima de cavallos'; fol. 3r.

green, and still others with jackets of a soiled colour, very ugly, like our *ictilmatli*. There were also a few without jackets. On their heads they wore red kerchiefs, or bonnets of a fine scarlet color, and some wore large round hats like small *comales*, which must have been sunshades. They have very light skin, much lighter than ours. They all have long beards, and their hair comes only to their ears. (*The Broken Spears* 17)

The beauty of this passage is that it reveals the unfamiliarity of the sight of the Europeans for the Amerindian mind (the ships' masts become 'mountains' or 'towers'), in reverse to the account of the Spanish chroniclers who see the Amerindian world as strange and barbaric. A similar defamiliarisation technique is evident in the description provided by the *Codex Florentino* of the Spanish in their military garb. With regard to the cannons, we hear 'de los truenos que quyebran las orejas, y del hedor de la polvora, que parece cosa infernal, y del huego que echan por la boca, y del golpe de la pelota, que desmenuza un arbol de golpe' (chap. 7; fol. 11r). As for the Spaniards, their swords are iron; their bows are iron; their shields are iron; their spears are iron, and 'tenyan las caras blancas, y los ojos garços, y los cabellos rojos, y las barbas largas' (chap. 7; fol. 11v). Their horses are called 'deer' which 'carry them on their backs wherever they wish to go' and are 'as tall as the roof of a house', and they have dogs which have 'burning yellow' eyes which 'flash fire and shoot off sparks' (*The Broken Spears* 30–31). To judge by descriptions such as these it is no wonder the Aztecs were terrified by the arrival of the Spanish.

It would be naive, however, on the basis of the above to assume that all the extant Amerindian versions of the conquest are univocal. There are, indeed, differences in emphasis between the texts and, at times, disagreements about the course of events due to political considerations (as is the case with the Spanish chronicles, a good example being the contestatory versions of Cortés's achievement as found in Gómara and Díaz Bernal del Castillo, respectively). There is a notable gap between the version of the massacre of Cholula as it appears in the *Codex Florentino* and in Camargo's *Historia de Tlaxcala*. In Sahagún's version the Tlaxcaltecans, a neighbouring tribe of the people of Cholula, used the presence of the new invaders to settle old scores whereas, according to Muñoz Camargo, the Cholultecans provoked their own demise by callously flaying an envoy sent by the Tlaxcaltecans advising them to surrender to the Spanish (*The Broken Spears* 37–49).

An important feature of these Amerindian texts is that they testify not to a culture which was suppressed in the early fifteenth century, but rather to a living though repressed community. Not only the texts mentioned above but later Nahuatl texts such as *An Eighteenth-Century Nahua Testimony* and *The Manifestoes of Emiliano Zapata of April 1918* (the latter written in Nahuatl to mobilise the Mexican peasantry; *The Broken Spears* 158–68) testify to the strength and continuity of the Amerindian cultural tradition, as indeed do more recent texts such as Miguel Angel Asturias's novel, *Hombres de maíz* (1949), and Menchú's testimonial text *Me llamo Rigoberta Menchú* (1982) (see below, Chapters 5 and 7).

## *Theatre*

The branch of Amerindian drama about which most is known is Aztec drama. As Miguel León Portilla has pointed out, Nahuatl drama can be divided into four basic forms, which are: (i) hymns in the form of a dialogue, (ii) comic acting and entertainment, (iii) representations of significant myths, and (iv) themes related to family and society (*Teatro*). The important point here is the pre-eminence of ritual, because of this drama's continued connection to its origins in religion and magic; the 'presentation of cosmic balance remains one of the chief functions of drama' at this time (Weiss 28). Particularly for the Aztecs, in whose culture human sacrifice was most prevalent, the prisoner or volunteer was coached in the dialogue and the ritual acts that he would perform as he was taken up to the place of sacrifice. It is perhaps best to see pre-Columbian drama, if it can be so called, as an offshoot of religious ritual. Certainly the many descriptions of human sacrifice which appear in Book II of Sahagún's *Historia de las cosas de Nueva España* follow a similar pattern. The captives, whether they be children, slaves, or war prisoners from another tribe, are adorned with feathers and flowers, and then the people sing and dance in front of them, after which they are led away for sacrifice; sometimes, as in the festival of Tlacaipeoaliztli, the prisoners were flayed and various ceremonies performed by soldiers wearing their skins (Sahagún, *History* 52). The songs could involve ritual dances and the wearing of masks, and dramatic dialogues could be performed, normally emphasizing the continuity of family lineage. These details give a sense of what should be meant by the term drama used here. Three elements common to these practices should be mentioned as related to the symbolic language of drama; all have to do with identification through performance. The first is that the sacrificee 'becomes' the god as a result of the ritual; in the festival of Toxcatl, for example, a youth was treated regally for one year and, in the ritual twenty-day month immediately before the sacrifice, he becomes Tezcatlipoca and is revered as such (Sahagún, *History* 54–55). The second element involving identification concerns the flaying of the sacrificee, based on the notion of becoming the sacrificee in his or her newly gained divine identity. Thirdly, the flesh of the sacrificee was often consumed, and this action again emblematised identification through the ritual of drama: the sacrificee becomes the god, the actor becomes the person.[9] It is as a result of this

---

[9] In special ceremonies the identification through drama reached the audience as well; in the feast of Atmalqualilitzi, for example, the people dressed in costumes,

element of identification that we can describe the practices described above as drama.

The only extant pre-Columbian play is the Maya drama, *Rabinal Achí*, an anonymous work which dates from fifteenth-century Guatemala. It was first heard by the Maya specialist Abbé Brasseur de Bourbourg, from the lips of a Guatemalan Indian, one Bartolo Ziz; Brasseur de Bourbourg subsequently published the original Maya text, accompanied by a French translation, in Paris in 1862. *Rabinal Achí* is a ritualistic text which focusses on the dialogue between the chief of one tribe – the Rabinal – who 'captures' the chief from another tribe – the Quiché (the capture is enacted in the first scene). The bulk of the drama is taken up with an elaborately rhetorical exchange between captor and prisoner in which the former attempts to establish the virility, or lack thereof, of the latter, with the natural world acting at once as backdrop and jury of this process, which reaches its climactic finale with the sacrificial death of the Varón de Quiché. It has been suggested that the sacrificial element of these Amerindian practices 'was taken up in the sacramental auto which, with its sacrificial substitution of Jesus Christ, was imported and adapted by Catholic missionaries from Mexico to Brazil' (Weiss 33). While this may be true with hindsight, it is important to recognise that, apart from the obvious difference that a human being is not literally sacrificed during the *auto sacramental*, there is also the difference that the Amerindian drama is not marked off as a symbolic space separate from everyday life, as was the case with theatre in contemporary Europe, in the sense of being entertainment for which an entrance fee is paid. Just as the Mexican codex had no legend to explain its symbolic meaning (unlike the European map which bears a legend which explains the code of the represented territory), so Amerindian drama did not require a symbolic space marked off from the discourse of everyday life; it was, indeed, part of everyday life.

The first examples of theatre brought by the Spanish were related to Franciscan missionary activity, of which the earliest were the *auto* (the Iberian version of the miracle play), the *Pastores* (Shepherds' Play), and the *Moros y Cristianos* (legendary-ritual play). Four more genres were added over time: the *paso*, the *entremés*, the *loa* and the *coloquio*. There were some examples of secular drama (by the late 1500s, the *comedias* of the Spanish Golden Age were gaining popularity in the colonies and conquistador Pizarro had ordered some *comedias* to be performed for the entertainment of his troops) but, by and large, the lion's share of drama was linked to proselytisation. Missionary drama notably took the form of the presentation of the fundamentals of the Christian gospel in the church-sponsored Corpus Christi celebrations. The

---

impersonated birds, butterflies and beatles, and even carried on their backs a sleeping man whom they called sleep (Sahagún, *History* 146).

earliest reference to any form of dramatic performance involves the Corpus Christi festivities held in Mexico City cathedral in 1525. Noticing that dance and song were integral parts of the Aztec ceremonies of worship, Pedro de Gante composed songs for worship at the nativity scene. When the chiefs of Texcoco, Tlatelolco, Clalco and Huejotzinjo heard native Americans singing in their own language, they were greatly impressed, agreed to be baptised and to let their children attend the school the Franciscans had built (Weiss 47). Amerindian-language plays followed; in Tlalolco in 1533 a Spanish *auto* translated into Nahuatl by Father Andrés de Olmos was performed and, in Tlaxcala in 1538, a native-language Corpus Christi ceremony was arranged by Fray Toribio de Benavente. In Tlaxcala the following year, in 1539, an impressive Nahuatl version of 'The Fall of Adam and Eve' was presented on Easter Wednesday; Fray Jerónimo de Mendieta said of the latter ceremony that it was 'la cosa más agradable a la vista que en mi vida he visto' (II, 50).

A good example of early missionary drama is the anonymous *Coloquio de Nueua conberción Y bautismo delos quatro Vltimos Reyes de Tlaxcala en la Nueua España*; written and performed at the end of the sixteenth or beginning of the seventeenth century (some give the date of performance as 1619), the manuscript of this play was discovered in the 1920s in a collection in the University of Texas Library. It was subsequently published by the man who discovered it, Carlos E. Castañeda, in the *Revista Mexicana de Estudios Históricos* in 1928, and attributed to Gutiérrez de Luna; this attribution has been questioned by José Rojas Garcidueñas (*Tres piezas* 151–81). The play focusses on the conquest of Tlaxcala by Hernán Cortés in 1519, an event which played a crucial role in the subsequent subjugation of the Aztec kingdom. Contemporary indigenous texts, such as those included in *The Broken Spears* (see above), suggested that the reason why the Tlaxcaltecans sided with Cortés was in order to settle old scores with the Cholultecans. The *Coloquio*, however, could not be more different. The four kings of Tlaxcala are presented in the opening scene as wrestling with the dilemma posed by the arrival of the Spanish. They are first visited by their god, called Hongol and later revealed to be none other than the devil, then by an angel of the Lord, who manages to persuade them to convert instantly to Christianity. Cortés and La Malinche subsequently pay them a visit, the kings are baptised and the play concludes with the partaking of mass; though called a *coloquio*, thus, the play is essentially an *auto sacramental*. That this is an early colonising text is suggested by the naivety involved in the naming of the Indians' god. As Angel María Garibay points out, Nahuatl does not have the 'g' sound (*Tres piezas* 163); the name of the Tlaxtaltecan god is probably a version of the name of one of the prominent leaders of the Araucanian Indians who appears in Ercilla's *La Araucana*, namely Ongol (*Tres piezas* 168). Whatever its source – it may even have come from Lope de Vega's *El nuevo mundo descubierto por Cristóbal Colón* – the use of the word Ongol betrays an historically inaccurate but convenient shorthand notation for denoting cultural otherness.

The important point to be retained from the above is that the early missionary activity as expressed through drama was profoundly assimilationist and synchretistic. Mendieta, for example, had commented on the great ability with which the Mexicas learned to write Spanish and Latin, to sing in choirs, to play instruments, and learn grammar (II, 38–40). They were so successful, indeed, that their compositions were indistinguishable from Spanish compositions: 'Y, lo que más es, que pocos años después que aprendieron el canto, comenzaron ellos a componer de su ingenio villancicos en canto de órgano a cuatro voces y algunas misas y otras obras, que mostrados a diestros cantores españoles, decían ser escogidos juicios, y no creían que pudiesen ser de indios' (Mendieta, II, 40). The Mexicas were also able to enclose Christian ceremony within their own culture-specific religious ceremonies: 'Acabados los maitines a las dos o a las tres de la mañana, ya están aparejados en el patio de la iglesia los que han de comenzar el baile a su modo antiguo, con cánticos aplicados a la nueva fiesta' (Mendieta, II, 50). The vogue of religious dramas flourished until the 1550s in Mexico and Central America, and until the 1560s in South America (Weiss 42). The Dominicans and the Jesuits, who were later on the scene, copied the Franciscans in the use of drama for proselytisation. But this was not without its problems; in 1586, in Etla, near Oaxaca, during a performance arranged by the Dominican friar Andrés de Moguer, the balcony of the convent collapsed, killing many people, including a friar (Weiss 55).

The most significant drama of the early colonial era was the *Tragedia intitvlada trivmpho de los sanctos en qve se representa la persecucion de Diocleciano, y la prosperidad que se siguio con el Imperio de Constantino* (1579), probably written by two Jesuits, Vincencio Lanuchi and Juan Sánchez Baquero, and published by Antonio Ricardo in Mexico City. The play is medieval in design in that it contains characters who are emblems of abstract concepts, such as Iglesia, Fe, Idolatría, Crueldad, etc., and Senecan in pedigree in that the enunciation of long-winded, morality-based speeches by the characters is the norm. The theme, as suggested by the title, is a comparison of the vice of Diocletian (245–316) who, while emperor of the Roman empire (284–305), was responsible for the persecution of Christians, and the virtue of Constantine I (280?–337), the first Roman emperor attested to have become a Christian. Just as interesting as the play itself is the social ritual which accompanied its performance, for it was part of a week-long celebration in Mexico City in November 1578 in which some holy relics donated by Pope Gregorius XIII were officially transmitted to the Jesuits. On All Saints' Day, a procession of great pomp and ceremony attended by every significant state and ecclesiastical dignitary took place in which the relics were transported from the cathedral where they had been deposited to the Colegio Máximo de San Pedro y San Pablo. On the following day, 2 November 1578, the *Tragedia* was staged in the Jesuit College; the performance was four hours long and was attended by the Viceroy, the members of the *Real Audiencia*, the Inquisition, as well as other state and ecclesiastic officials (*Tres piezas* 3–10). At the conclusion of the play, the character Iglesia addresses the 'amado pueblo mío MEXICANO' exhorting it to follow Constantine's example and embrace Christianity (line 666; *Tres piezas* 146). The play, intriguingly enough, also has a post-Tridentine political edge in that the character Fe subsequently exhorts the Mexican people to accept the sacred treasure of the relics 'a pesar del engaño luterano' (line 681; *Tres piezas* 146). Some critics have criticised this play for its turgid style, with Seneca mentioned as the culprit (notably H. L. Johnson; qtd. in *Tres piezas* 22–26), but it is surely more important to observe that the intended audience for the *Tragedia* – essentially the executive elite of society, both secular and ecclesiastic – may well have enjoyed, and even expected, a type of drama in which characters on a stage before them pronounced decrees ratifying executive decisions intended to guide the future direction of Christendom; they would have felt 'at home', so to speak.

Chapter 2

## COLONIAL AND VICEREGAL LITERATURE

The literature of the colonial period in Spanish America was more closely linked to political power than tended to be the case with post-independence literature. It was not unusual, for example, for a candidate to a government position in the New World to provide reference to a literary work as evidence of ability to serve office. The second generation of settlers in the New World used print where their predecessors had used military exploits; as one commentator points out, the 'sword was yielding to the quill as an instrument of material advancement, and a familiarity with letters and learning was becoming a surer guarantee of social preferance than military skill' (Leonard, *Books* 198). From its inception printing in Spanish America was associated with royal privilege. Throughout the colonial era permission in the form of a licence from the Spanish sovereign was necessary before a printing press could be set up. Thus the printed word in Latin America – namely, Spanish as the language-of-state – was linked indirectly to the crown and directly to the viceroyalty in the New World, since the inception of printing in the New World coincides almost exactly with the establishment of the first viceroyalty. Don Antonio de Mendoza's viceroyalty began in 1535 and a printing press may have been operational in Mexico City in that year (if we subscribe to José Toribio Medina's notion that one Esteban Martín was at work in the capital of New Spain from 1535 to 1538), or at least by 1539 when a native of Brescia, Giovanni Paoli, or Juan Pablos as he came to be known, worked as a printer in Mexico City on behalf of the leading Seville printer, Juan Cromberger, in the service of Archbishop Zumárraga under a contract negotiated with Antonio de Mendoza (Thompson 12–13). In a contract drawn up between Cromberger and Pablos on 12 June 1539 Pablos agreed to go to Mexico with his wife and stay there for at least ten years; he was to be manager-cum-compositor and, demand permitting, given power to contract labour and print 3,000 sheets a day (Griffin 85). It was not long before Mexico became the pre-eminent book publishing centre in the Spanish colonies; during the seventeenth century, New Spain was able to contribute to other parts of the empire not only textiles, clothes, jewelry and leather goods, but also books (Adrien 35).

Printing early on in the colonial era, in New Spain as much as in Peru, was in the main restricted to the publication of works for missionary purposes (catechisms and the like).[1] From its beginnings in New Spain, the art of printing gradually spread to the rest of the Spanish empire, reaching La Ciudad de los Reyes, or Lima, by 1584, Old Paraguay by 1700, Cuba by 1723, New Granada (specifically Bogotá) by 1738, the Río de la Plata region by 1766, and Chile by 1776 (Thompson 34, 47, 94, 76, 87). A quick survey of some of the books published early on in the colonial era gives some insight into the culture of the period, based as it was on a view of print as performative rather than descriptive, law-enforcing rather than politically mediational. The first work published in the New World of which reliable information exists is Bishop Zumárraga's *Breve y mas compendiosa doctrina christiana*, published in 1539 on Juan Pablos's press, and of which no copy is now extant (Menéndez Pidal viii–ix). During the second half of the sixteenth century print culture diversified to include theology (notably Fray Alonso de la Vera Cruz's *Recognitio Summularum* published by Juan Pablos in 1554), medicine (the first medicinal text was Francisco Bravo's *Opera medicinalia* published by Pedro Ocharte in 1570), philology (the first dictionary of an Indian language was Alonso de Molina's *Vocabulario en la lengua Castellana y Mexicana* [1555]), and nautology (such as Diego García de Palacio's *Instrvcion nauthica para el bven Vso y regimiento de las Naos* [1587]). Unlike the missionary publications, these works were dedicated to and funded by prominent individuals, typically the Viceroy; the catechisms were simply dedicated to God and funded by the Church. The bulk of the early literary works were published in Latin, such as Francisco Cervantes de Salazar's six dialogues in Latin (1554), and the Jesuits' edition of Ovid and some *Emblemata* by Alciato (1577). But some original literary works were published in Spanish, such as Bartolomé de las Casas's *Cancionero Espiritual* (1546), and Cervantes de Salazar's *Túmulo Imperial* (1560) inspired by the funeral honours for Charles V in Mexico City. But we have to wait until the seventeenth century until a major original literary work is published in the New World: Balbuena's *Grandeza Mexicana* (1604), closely followed by Mateo Alemán's *Ortografía* (1609).[2]

Before passing to a discussion of the three main genres of literature of this period, it is important to emphasise that its sources were European. During the pre-independence period the intellectual in the Spanish colonies saw Europe as the source of ideas, statecraft, money and power, and America as an inferior replica of the European model. This is clear from three book orders which survive from the early colonial period, two from Mexico City

---

[1] This is largely to be expected of the time since, as Steinberg has pointed out, the 'great publishing successes of the sixteenth century were achieved in the realm of theology' (Steinberg 142).

[2] It is important to recall in this context that, as far as printed books were concerned, Spain was one of only two countries (the other being England) in which 'vernacular books outnumbered Latin ones from the beginning' (Steinberg 118).

(21 July 1576, and 22 December 1576), and one from Lima (22 February 1583). The promissory note of 21 July 1576 orders 341 volumes from Spain, of which half are theological; the creative literature ordered is mostly by Latin authors (Lucan, Martial, Seneca, Terence, Horace, Suetonius, and Ovid) (Leonard, *Books* 200–204). In the promissory note of 22 December 1576, which orders 1,190 books, a preference for Latin authors in the literature section is also evident (Vergil, Ovid, Cicero), although original works by Castilian authors such as Marqués de Santillana, Jorge Manrique, and the *Celestina* are also requested; the most popular work, of which 26 copies were ordered, was Nebrija's *Arte de la lengua* (Leonard, *Books* 205–206). The book order made by the *limeño* bookseller, Juan Jiménez del Río, on 22 February 1583, with one Francisco de la Hoz, lists a little under 2,000 books, of which 44 per cent are ecclesiastical, 32 per cent non-fiction, and 24 per cent for belles-lettres (Leonard, *Books* 220). All three of the book orders show a Eurocentric bias; as Leonard suggests, '[t]his apparent indifference to local themes and preoccupation with Spanish and European literature characterise the entire colonial period and illustrate the complete spiritual and literary as well as political and economic subordination of the colonies to the mother country' (*Books* 224). This helps to explain why the first texts studied here – namely, Ercilla's and Balbuena's – were published in Spain rather than the Spanish colonies.

## Poetry

The social experience of poetry in this period was more likely to be in the form of a public reading than what we normally understand by reading poetry privately nowadays, given, *inter alia*, the exorbitant material cost of printed volumes during this period. Very common during the colonial period, especially in the large viceregal capitals of Mexico and Peru, were the poetic contests in which aspiring poets of the day read their verses before an audience. The 'certamen poético' would typically take as its theme an important historical event – the arrival of a new viceroy or archbishop, the celebration of a martial victory, the reiteration of an article of faith – and would be underwritten by a generous patron, normally a member of the aristocracy. Often the requirements of the tournament were quite specific; one organised by the University of Mexico in 1683 required that the subject be the Immaculate Conception and stated that the metrical model to be imitated would be verses 71 to 98 of the third book of Vergil's *Aeneid*. The rules circulated for the occasion also mentioned that authors should avoid 'a false playing on words of double meaning' and that 'words shall be kept in all their proper meanings' (Leonard, *Baroque* 136–38). To win one of these contests was a sure way of achieving literary visibility. Bernardo de Balbuena, for example, whose work is discussed below, won a poetic contest held in Mexico City in

1685, against three hundred other contestants (Leonard, *Baroque* 132), and later proved to be one of the most significant poets of his day in New Spain.

*La Araucana*, three volumes of which were published successively in 1569, 1578, and 1589 by Alonso de Ercilla y Zúñiga (1533–1594), is the most significant epic poem treating the theme of the conquest. The high respect which it gained in its day is suggested by an incident described in Cervantes's *El Ingenioso Hidalgo Don Quijote de la Mancha*; it is one of the few books in Don Quijote's library which is not consigned to the flames by the barber and the priest.[3] The documents which precede the text of the epic proper, most of which are not reproduced in modern editions, and which include the letter by the scribe, Pedro del Marmol, and the *imprimatur* by Antonio de Eraso on the King's behalf, the author's prologue and declaration, and two sonnets which praise Ercilla's martial valour, all bespeak the patronage system of publication customary throughout the colonial era (*La Araucana*, facsimile copy: 1967). For the last two volumes at least, Ercilla drew on first-hand experience of warfare in Chile from 1577 to 1579; his work provides a surprisingly favourable depiction of the enemy of the Spanish army, the Araucanian Indians. Apart from empiric experience, it is generally acknowledged that the single most important literary source for his work was *Orlando Furioso* (1510–1532), which was one of the best-sellers of the period (Steinberg 144–45). Ercilla echoes Ariosto's playful control of his subject matter, and specifically borrowed the Italian's technique of interjecting his poetic persona into the story at certain crucial junctures, leaving the warriors in the middle of the battle to create suspense, for example (Bautista Avalle-Arce). But there are some significant differences between Ercilla and Ariosto. For example, while the Italian was celebrating events set in a mythic past, Ercilla's subject matter is drawn from contemporary events (the wars with the Araucanian Indians were raging during the years when Ercilla's volumes were published).

*La Araucana* is typical of the heroic verse poems published in the pre-Tassesque period in which we encounter 'Aeneas-like heroes who stand for national tradition and endeavour' (Pierce xii) before the Counter-Reformation required more catholic subject matter (an example being Diego de Hojeda's post-Tridentine *La Christiada* [1611]). Given the leisurely pace of its publication (cantos i–xv, 1569; cantos xvi–xxix, 1578; cantos xxx–xxxvii, 1589), it is not surprising that the poem becomes gradually more sprawling and more disorganised in form as it proceeds, such that the third

---

[3]   In Part I, chap. 6 of the *Quijote* the priest comes across *La Araucana,* as well as Juan Rufo's *La Austríada* and Cristóbal de Virus's *El Montserrate,* and makes the following comment: '– Todos esos tres libros – dijo el cura – son los mejores que, en verso heroico, en lengua castellana están escritos; y pueden competir con los más famosos de Italia: guárdense como las más ricas prendas de poesía que tiene España –' (Cervantes, II, 126–27).

volume contains much material which is extraneous to Ercilla's specific purpose, namely, describing the war between the Spanish and the Araucanians; in cantos xxxii–xxiii, for example, we hear about Dido's life, and in canto xxxvii we are treated to a fulsome defence of Phillip II's right to the kingdom of Portugal. In this he is typical of his age; Ercilla could not resist various digressions into areas not obviously germane to his subject, such as the Spanish triumph at San Quentin, or the naval battle of Lepanto, or, still less relevant, the discussion towards the end of the poem of the monarch's rightful claim to foreign kingdoms. The poem is written in the Octava Real, or Octava Rima verse form, in stanzas of eight hendecasyllables with alternating rhyme (ABABABCC), a form originally introduced in the Spanish lyric from the Italian tradition by Boscán (Navarro Tomás 206). The most common stress pattern used throughout the poem, not surprisingly given its subject-matter, is the heroic endecasyllable, that is with stress on the second and sixth syllables (Navarro Tomás 263). Each stanza constitutes a separate sense-unit (there is very rarely any semantic run-on between stanzas), and, very often, the stanzas themselves are split into two sense-units of four lines each. This leads to an impression of severe regularity that at times makes the poem monotonous, especially in some of the long, turgid speeches made by the Araucanian Indians and the Spaniards.

Arauco domado (1596) by Pedro de Oña (1570–1643) consciously imitated Ercilla's masterpiece in theme but not in political bias. Like Ercilla before him, Oña had first-hand experience of military warfare, having participated in an expedition to quell an uprising in Quito, Ecuador. His description of these events in cantos XIV–XVI of Arauco domado was thought so offensive by members of the Audiencia of Quito that their protests caused the first edition to be withdrawn. It was only with the publication of the second edition in 1605 that Oña achieved fame for his poem. Oña's aim in writing, following established practice of the day, was to secure a high government post. In this he was successful since, soon after its publication, the by-then Viceroy of Peru, García Hurtado de Mendoza, whom he had extolled in his poem, rewarded him with the post of Corregidor of Jaén de Bracamoros in Peru. Arauco domado could not be called a well-constructed poem; it spends too much time on elaborate digressions, such as the description of the Quito rebellion which Oña had helped to suppress and his description of the defeat of the English pirate, Richard Hawkins, none of which is related to the body of the narrative. To make matters worse, Oña fails to find time to describe the subsequent capture of the Araucanian chieftain, Caupolicán, surely the main historical event encapsulating the meaning of the title of Oña's poem. Despite his first-hand experience of warfare, Oña's description of clashes between Spaniards and the Araucanian Indians is awkward, and has none of the verve of Ercilla's narrative.

Grandeza Mexicana (1604) by Bernardo de Balbuena (1568–1627) is arguably one of the finest poems written in the colonial period. Given his occupation – Balbuena was a priest for most of his life – and the sedentary way in which he fulfilled his duties, Balbuena's work does not have the cut-and-thrust adventure characteristic of the epic poem. *Grandeza Mexicana* describes a colonial city set in the heart of the Spanish empire, confident of its position in the world, not involved in costly wars subjugating foreign tribes, and not split by internal dissension. Some years before publishing *Grandeza Mexicana*, Balbuena had written *Siglo de oro en las selvas de Erfile* (though it was only published in 1608), which sharpened his skills in composing eclogues. Like the earlier work, *Grandeza Mexicana* is essentially a bucolic poem but it focusses not on the countryside, as do the eclogues of the most famous contemporary practioner of the genre, the Spaniard Garcilaso de la Vega (1503–1536), but rather on the urban environment of Mexico City, except possibly in chapter VI of the poem, which devotes some time to the countryside. *Grandeza Mexicana* consists of an eight-line *argumento* followed by eight chapters, the titles and themes of which are taken successively from the eight lines of the *argumento*. The poem thus functions as a three-tiered structure with the empirical world of Mexico City encapsulated within the eight chapters of the poem, which in turn are encapsulated within the *argumento*. Balbuena's poem is therefore not simply a (medievalising) gloss but involves a playful exploration of the notion of perspective and, in particular, miniaturism. The poem is introduced as a missive to an illustrious Mexican lady, Doña Isabel de Tovar y Guzmán, which emphasises the aristocratic social framework of patronage into which the poem inserts its discourse. The whole of the *Grandeza Mexicana*, apart from the *argumento*, is written in endecasyllabic tercets, which are interconnected in the sense that the second line of each stanza rhymes with the first and third lines of the subsequent stanza, and so on throughout the entire length of the poem. The tercet was traditionally used, at least in the sonnet with which it is normally associated, as the point of semantic summation of the poem. The form of *Grandeza Mexicana*, thus, gives it an almost breathless feel as if Mexico's wonders could only be described in hyperbolic terms.

   *La Christiada* (1611) by Diego de Hojeda (1571?–1615) is an epic poem which tells, in twelve cantos, the story of Christ's Passion from the Last Supper to the Resurrection. Like many of the works published at this time, its author was well-connected in religious and political circles; Hojeda had founded a Dominican convent in Lima in 1606 and had been made a Master of Theology in appreciation, and his poem was dedicated to the then Viceroy of Peru, the Marqués de Montesclaros (almost *de rigueur* as a custom in the early colonial period, as we have seen). The verse form is identical to that used in Ercilla's *La Araucana*, namely, the Italianate Octava Real which had stanzas of eight hendecasyllables with alternating rhyme (ABABABCC). One of the problems faced by the poem (one that has led to its being less popular with modern audiences) is the disjunction between its poetic form, which suggests the epic with all its contemporary associations with nation-building, hero worship, warfare and a swift-moving narrative, and its subject matter. The historical events which took place from a Thursday night (the Last Supper) to a Friday afternoon (the crucifixion) and, indeed, their written account in the synoptic gospels, do not lend themselves as obviously to epic treatment as do Ercilla's. *La Christiada* is a devotional poem which consciously diverts attention away from action understood in a canonic epic sense to digressionary material which leads to contemplation and which includes the psychological (in the form of the agonised thoughts running through Christ's mind), the doctrinal (mainly in allusions to the mystery of Christ's incarnation as man and God), and what for lack of a better term might be called the 'Baroque imaginary'. All three of these types of digressionary material tend to slow up the poem's forward propulsion, yet it is in the third type that Hojeda's skill is most apparent. A good example of the latter occurs in Canto I when the New Testament account of Christ carrying the sins of mankind in the Garden of Gethsemane is transformed into a fifty-stanza Baroque exposé detailing the sins of mankind as etched on Christ's clothes (Pierce 99–110).

The authors mentioned thus far were well-connected. In order to publish it was important either to know personally the Viceroy or a member of his court or somebody influential in the church hierarchy. If a writer openly criticised a figure of authority, his chances of being published and of achieving a position in the state hierarchy were, for obvious reasons, small. Such was the fate of two writers who were writing at the end of the sixteenth century, Fernán González de Eslava (1533?–1601?) and Francisco de Terrazas (1525?–1600?). González de Eslava wrote some satirical *entremeses* criticizing the recently imposed 'alcabala' (sales tax) which appeared within a play of his (*Coloquios III*) staged in Mexico City in 1574 during Archbishop Pedro Moya de Contreras's inauguration: some satiric *pasquines* which attacked the King appeared on the wall of the cathedral ten days later, and González de Eslava, suspected of being the author, was imprisoned (along with Francisco de Terrazas) for seventeen days on the orders of the Viceroy of New Spain, Martín Enríquez de Almaza. Those works which have survived show a finely-honed exploitation of irony and a trained eye for the vicissitudes of everyday life. González de Eslava's 'Entremés del ahorcado' for example, is a funny skit about a ruffian who pretends he has been hanged when he sees one of his enemies approaching, and has to restrain himself when hearing the insults poured on his head; the 'Entremés de Diego Moreno y Teresa' depicts a hilarious argument between a wife who complains to her husband about their poverty and suggests they go to China, and the husband who is unwilling to go (Luzuriaga & Reeve 54–59).

As the seventeenth century progressed, however, and publishing activity began gradually to extricate itself from royal influence, satire emerged much more clearly as a vibrant social energy. As Julie Greer Johnson has shown in her important study, *Satire in Colonial Spanish America: Turning the New*

*World Upside Down*, there were a number of writers who turned to satire to express their vision of New World society, but two names stand out and these are Mateo Rosas de Oquendo (1559?–1612?) and Juan del Valle y Caviedes (1651?–1697?). *Sátira hecha por Mateo Rosas de Oquendo a las cosas que pasan en el Pirú, año de 1598*, to give the text its full name, by Rosas de Oquendo, though written in 1598, was not published until it was discovered in the Biblioteca Nacional in Madrid at the beginning of this century; it first emerged in excerpts prepared and published by Antonio Paz y Melia in the *Bulletin Hispanique* in 1906. As Pedro Lasarte has pointed out, however, the manuscript clearly made an impact in the seventeenth century, being cited in at least two contemporary documents: Baltasar Dorantes de Carranza's *Sumaria relación de las cosas de la Nueva España*, of 1604, and a satirical ballad known to have been circulating in Lima in 1621 (Rosas de Oquendo, xv, n. 1). The *Sátira*, which consists of 2,120 octosyllabic lines, provides a fascinating insight into viceregal society at the turn of the seventeenth century and, though vindictive (Rosas de Oquendo's outlook was soured by his inabilty to make much headway socially during his stay in Peru, as suggested by the unsuccessful period he spent in the service of the Viceroy of Peru, Don García Hurtado de Mendoza), may contain much that was true. The *Sátira* is a well-structured work; it begins with an exhortation to all and sundry, from white men to black women, to come and listen to his tale since it deals with a theme which is relevant to everyone, 'propio onor', or social reputation (line 47; Rosas de Oquendo 2). It then provides some background information about the author himself (lines 59–110), which is followed by the introduction proper which argues that Peru is a topsy-turvy world in which the rich are poor, and the poor rich, the guilty walk the streets, and the innocent are in prison (lines 111–289). After this introduction the poem proper begins, and roughly the first half is concerned with describing the multifarious venal sins of the population of Lima, and particularly the female residents. In this section, in which no woman seems to be spared satire (included are married women whose husbands are away, married women looking to bring extra money into the houshold, old lascivious toothless women, young women not yet married but who know how to feign virginity later on, and so on), Rosas de Oquendo shows his poetic ingenuity through elaborate metaphors of sexual commerce; the technical language of sewing, that of journeys (particularly sea journeys), the action of entering and leaving an abode, the language of war, of tutoring, even the language of the rites of Christian penitence, all are grist to Rosas de Oquendo's mill in his search for elaborate means of describing by innuendo the sexual act. Perhaps most striking about the poem is its ability to expose the lies beneath the official version of events. Thus, in his account of the military conquest of the southern region of the viceroyalty of Peru, in which he had participated, Rosas de Oquendo contrasts the written report sent to the Viceroy, which described how they had founded a city after fighting three days with two hundred enemy Indians, with what actually happened (they built four yards, and were welcomed by the Indians who, to boot, offered them food; Rosas de Oquendo 42–43). Though clearly suffering from its own type of bias – that of a *peninsular* expecting to succeed in the colonies and being sorely disappointed when this does not happen – Rosas de Oquendo's *Sátira* offers an entertainingly sardonic picture of the carryings-on of viceregal society, only surpassed in its wit by Caviedes.

Juan del Valle y Caviedes is, with the exception of Sor Juana, the most significant writer of this period. Although he also wrote religious and didactic poetry his fame largely rests on his *Diente del Parnaso* (c.1689), in which Caviedes, in a style reminiscent of the Spanish poet, Francisco de Quevedo (1580–1645), directs mordant satire at, *inter alia*, the doctors of his day. At least twelve of the doctors mentioned have been identified as real-life individuals practising medicine in Lima in the second half of the seventeenth century (Reedy 66). Only three of his poems were published in his own lifetime, in 1687, 1689 and 1694; for this reason his work mainly circulated in manuscript form (Caviedes x).[4] The butt of his mordant satire can vary, ranging from a hunchback (whom he advises to cure himself by piercing his hump with a sharp instrument, 'Receta que el poeta le dio a Liseras que sanase de la giba'; Caviedes 72–74), to a mulatto who believes he is marrying a white girl but is mistaken ('Al casamiento de Pedro de Utrilla' 141–42), to a contemporary poet whose work Caviedes compares to excrement ('pues son tus letras tan sucias/ que me parecen letrinas', 'Un poeta que de hacer versos le dieron cursos'; Caviedes 200–201 [p. 201]). Singled out for particularly ribald treatment are those whose lives are ruined by the misfortunes engendered by lust. Thus, he recounts in meticulous and sordid detail the agonies suffered by a prostitute named as Anarda who is attempting to recuperate from syphilis in a hospital. This situation provides Caviedes with the opportunity to make a *conceptista* pun based on sweat. The laxatives she has been prescribed make her sweat now as much as she used to make others sweat in the past: 'Vivirá de su sudor/ si viviere de hoy ve más/ la que de ajenos sudores/ vivía antes de enfermar' (Caviedes 159). A pimp from Cuzco, likewise, is satirised for selling her daughters 'in pieces' as a result of her business: 'Una mestiza consejos/ estaba dando a sus hijas,/ que hay de mestizas consejos/ como hay el Consejo de Indias./ Al diablo se estaban dando/ todas en cosas distintas: la vieja se da por tercios,/ por cuartos se dan las niñas' (Caviedes 252).

Caviedes's wittiest and most sardonic poems, though, are reserved for doctors. 'Fe de erratas', for example, uses the analogy of editorial amend-

---

4   At the present time there are ten manuscripts of Caviedes's poetry whose whereabouts is known, according to María Leticia Cáceres Sánchez ('Don Juan del Valle y Caviedes, foco de interés en el quehacer de la crítica hispanoamericana', paper given on 4 September 1996 at the I Encuentro de Peruanistas held at the Universidad de Lima).

ment to emphasise the connection between doctors and death: 'En cuantas partes dijere/ *doctor*, el libro está atento;/ por allí has de leer *verdugo*,/ aunque éste es un poco menos' (Caviedes 6–7). As a general rule, Caviedes's poetry tends to function in terms of the repetition of the underlying motif rather than by amplification of a given theme. 'Coloquio que tuvo con la muerte un médico estando enfermo de riesgo', one of Caviedes's most famous poems, with great humour presents a doctor trying to persuade Death to let him live since that will bring a greater yield of fatalities in time. One of his most witty poems, 'A un doctor que curaba las cataratas y los cegaba peor de los que estaba', draws out an analogy between the literal blindness that the doctor visits upon his patients ('Cupido de medicina,/ pues ciegas a los que curas', Caviedes 136) and the metaphorical, spiritual blindness engendered by delusion ('Mucho más que la primera/ es la ceguedad segunda,/ porque se viene a los ojos/ que hace ciencia de la astucia', Caviedes 138). For his mordant satire, and his inventive word-play, rather than his versatility, Caviedes will be remembered as one of the most significant poets of the colonial era.[5]

## Prose

During this period, as a result of a number of royal decrees (the first of which was promulgated in 1531), the publication, circulation and reading of novels in the New World was prohibited because, it was believed, their fantastic contents could induce immorality, especially among the young, women and Indians. This prohibition, nevertheless, was consistently violated during the colonial period in the sense that novels found their way to the colonies from Spain (see Oviedo, *Historia*, vol. 1, 210–12), but it did have its effect on the works produced in the Spanish-American viceroyalties in that the prose works of this period were often hybrid and, as we shall see, had recourse to the ploy of mixing the genres of history, autobiography and fiction in order to escape the dull hand of censorship.

One of the most significant prose writers of the colonial period was Juan Rodríguez Freile (1566–1640), son of a first-generation immigrant who made his wealth in farming. He is remembered above all for his *El Carnero*, which he began writing at the age of seventy, namely in 1636, and finished in 1638, and which was first published in 1859; two manuscript copies of the work are held in the Sección de Raros y Curiosos in the National Library in Bogotá, Colombia (Rodríguez Torres 6). *El Carnero* purports to be written within the

---

[5]    Other poets whose work, for reasons of space, cannot be treated here are Juan Bautista Aguirre (1725–1786), Miguel de Guevara (1585–1646), Hernando Domínguez Camargo (1606–1656), Jacinto de Evia (1629–?) and Luis de Sandoval y Zapata (1645–1683). For an excellent discussion of the minor poets of this period, see Oviedo, *Historia*, vol. 1, 151–57, 178–81.

chronicle tradition; as its sub-title suggests, it will tell the story of the conquest and discovery of New Granada (now Colombia and Venezuela). It is different from the early chronicles in that it also sets out to record the details of early colonial administration, with emphasis on the military and the ecclesiastical figures who played important roles in that process; the *Real Audiencia* of Bogotá is, according to the foreword, to be provided a privileged place in Rodríguez Freile's account ('Los generales, capitanes y soldados que vinieron a su conquista, con todos los presidentes, oidores y visitadores que han sido de la Real Audiencia'; Rodríguez Freile vi). One could be forgiven for assuming, on the basis of the foreword with its pious stance and the *de rigueur* letter to the King of Spain, in this case Phillip IV, that *El Carnero* will be a dry, academic account of the early years of the colonisation of New Granada. This expectation is confirmed by the first few chapters; chapters I–VII concentrate on the discovery and conquest and offer detailed information on the participants thereof, especially chapter VI, while chapter VIII is concerned with the founding of the *Audiencia Real* and various religious orders in New Granada. The nearer the narrative comes to the days in which Rodríguez was writing, however, the more the narrative veers away from canonical, official history towards the personal, everyday spheres of the inhabitants of the New World, especially the uppers echelons of society (usually the clergy, the military and members of the *Audiencia Real*). The second half of *El Carnero*, thus, consists of self-contained narratives which, while purporting to be moral tales, have an air of the fable about them, and take a keen delight in recounting the various skullduggeries of witches, rogues, murderers, whores, outlaws, priests and judges. Given the importance at the time of expressing allegiance to Christian doctrine, the scenes of roguery are interspersed with long, rather dull sermonizing passages which fulfil the function of an *excursus* which the modern reader is likely to find of little interest (Alessandro Martinengo). Indeed, they fulfil no more than a lip-service function, since the central part of the tales is the depiction of evil in all its nakedness. *El Carnero* exhibits a tension between the canonised history of the *Oidores*, *Visitadores*, and the clergy and an array of micro-narratives based on hearsay, gossip and legend.

*Historia de la Villa Imperial de Potosí* by Bartolomé Arzáns de Orsúa y Vela (1676–1736), like *El Carnero*, offers a series of vignettes of life in the colonies, although it is based on one city, that of Potosí, the source of the greatest wealth in silver that the world had ever seen. It is annalistic and recounts the main events of the year, starting with the year of its foundation (1545) and ending in the year of the author's death (1736). Arzáns's work was not published in his lifetime and this was no doubt because of its satiric nature, and the fact that it names the perpetrators of ignominious deeds; in this sense it is closer in spirit to Caviedes than to the chronicles discussed in Chapter 1. During its heyday Potosí was not only the richest city in the New World, but, according to Arzáns's account, the most violent as well. Arzáns claims that his *Historia de la Villa Imperial de Potosí* is historical and factual, based on real individuals, and derived from a number of printed sources. The picture of Potosí that emerges in the *Historia de la Villa Imperial de Potosí* changes little during the 150 or so years covered annually; consistently, we hear details of family feuds, tribal and racial feuds (typically between the *criollos* and the *peninsular* groups), all of which end in death, adultery, murder, theft, treachery and corruption. The most salient feature of the world depicted in the *Historia de la Villa Imperial de Postosí* is violence. A struggle between the Basques and the *criollos* in 1602 leads to a process of tit-for-tat actions, until there are seventy-nine dead and sixty wounded; in 1657, when a mother finds out that her daughter is with child, she tortures her by stripping her naked, hanging her up by her hair and thrusting a red-hot iron into her private parts until she dies; in 1661 a wife is so disappointed with her husband's reluctance to carry out her wishes that she kills him, tears his heart out of his chest and then, according to one version, eats it (Arzáns 13–19, 81–86, 103–15). Another important feature of these tales is their use of the supernatural: in 1616 eight Indians and a boy emerged from a mine having been trapped for sixteen days, claiming to have been given water and bread and led out of the cave by the Virgin Mary; in 1658 some souls of purgatory appeared in the bedroom of a woman whose lover was under the bed and therefore stilled her husband's suspicions; and in the same year a criminal being pursued by the *Corregidor* was transformed into a blessed corpse at the convent of Santo Domingo (Arzáns 33–36, 86–90, 91–93). Though purporting to be historical, Arzán's tales freely combine the real and the fantastic, and are typical of the hybrid nature of much of the prose writing of this period.

*El gobierno eclesiástico-pacífico* (1656–1657) by Gaspar Villarroel (c.1587–1665), also known as *Los dos cuchillos*, like Rodríguez Freile's *El Carnero*, is a collection of vignettes of contemporary life in the Spanish colonies, although in Villarroel's work the setting as well as the theoretical edifice is ecclesiastic. Their tone and touch is lighter, giving a humorous twist to stories of ill-doing, such as the vignettes entitled 'Como los obispos recobran la salud' in which Villarroel tells anecdotes of how bishops are miraculously revived on their death-beds by servants intent on robbing them and who inadvertently puncture abcesses and thus revive them (Flores 29–30). Others tell tales of saintly intervention in the lives of men (such as 'San Luis ayuda a los cazadores', Flores 32). *El gobierno eclesiástico-pacífico* also contains a description of the life of one Mesa, the *Oidor* of the *Audiencia* who is driven to murder as a result of lust, and whose actions also figure prominently in *El Carnero*. Villarroel's version, however, does not involve a third party, but simply recounts how Mesa killed the husband of a woman he desired; no third party, such as occurred in Rodríguez Freile's version, is in evidence. Though designed to explicate the rules of ecclesiastical government in colonial New Spain, Villarroel's text offers a down-to-earth insight into the customs of everyday life in the Spanish colonies of the late seventeenth century.

An example of first-person narrative recounting personal adventure was *Cautiverio feliz* (1673) by Francisco Núñez de Pineda y Bascuñán (1607–1682?), which recalls the author's experience as a 'happy captive' of the Araucanian chieftain, Maulicán, by whom he was held from May to November of 1629. This work, like Ercilla's, shows immense respect for the Araucanian Indians. During the course of the narrative, the author and his enemy, Maulicán, end up the best of friends. Núñez de Pineda eventually feels a degree of allegiance to his captor which stretches verisimilitude; when an opportunity to escape presents itself in Part II, as he is crossing a turbulent river and finds himself separated from the rest of the tribe, he refuses to flee and returns to his captor. This loyalty is clearly mutual, since Maulicán is prepared to endanger his own life and that of his tribesmen in order to protect Núñez de Pineda from hostile Araucanian tribes. But the greatest danger, as Núñez de Pineda sees it, came not from without but rather from within in the guise of the young nubile bodies of the Indian girls who repeatedly offer him their sexual favours. With great strength of will, Núñez de Pineda refuses them all, even Maulicán's daughter, the sight of whom makes Núñez de Pineda's knees tremble; his respectful distance could not be more at variance with the devil-may-care attitude of the conquistadors who had invaded the New World a century earlier. Núñez de Pineda's text stands as an important stepping-stone between the artless earthiness of the chronicles which preceded it and the artful grace of the novel which came later.

Another important example of the stirrings of the genre of narrative was *Infortunios de Alonso Ramírez* (1690) by Carlos de Sigüenza y Góngora (1645–1700), nephew of the Spanish poet Luis de Góngora (1561–1627), holder of the Chair of Mathematics and Astrology at the University of Mexico, and Chief Cosmographer of the Realm. This text has been sometimes referred to as the first novel of Latin America, but it is perhaps best described as a more sophisticated version of the type of personal adventure chronicle typified by Cabeza de Vaca's *Naufragios*. It is not coincidental that the first true precursor of the Realist novel was written by a scholar who favoured the new scientific method of empirical observation rather than the hide-bound scholasticism which still held sway at the time. *Infortunios de Alonso Ramírez* describes the misadventures of a young Puerto Rican boy, Alonso Ramírez, who ran away from home before his thirteenth birthday for a life at sea. His search for personal wealth leads him around the Caribbean, Cuba, to New Spain, the Phillipines (where he is captured by English pirates), Guadalupe Island, and finally back to Mexico. During his travels he suffers shipwreck, hardship, illness and hunger. His story has all the verve of Cabeza de Vaca's *Naufragios*; he experiences the same kind of fears but the historical frame has changed. Now the enemies are not the Amerindians; they are the English who roam the Caribbean looking for plunder. The story has a type of happy ending, which is provided by the young boy's recognition for services rendered by the Viceroy of New Spain, who orders that his adventures be compiled by none other than Carlos de Sigüenza y Góngora. In retrospect the ending of *Infortunios de Alonso Ramírez* may seem no more than a naive ploy to bring the narrative full circle back to the author's direct remit, but it is an early indication of the self-reflexive and ludic route that the novel would subsequently take in Latin America (Lagmanovich 411–12).

One other significant prose writer of this period who deserves mention is Francisca Josefa de la Concepción de Castillo (1671–1742), the 'Colombian Santa Teresa' as she is sometimes known, famous for her *Afectos espirituales* (written between c.1694 and c.1716). Sor Francisca took the veil in 1693 after two years as a novice, and became a nun the following year, when she was twenty-three years old (Castillo 48). The *Afectos espirituales* consist of forty-four prose passages followed by one poem, all of which have a mystic intent, and are best understood as a record of the trials and tribulations of Sor Francisca's personal pilgrimage to God. They fall roughly into two groups, with the first half of the 'Afectos' concentrating on the nun's emotional affliction and remorse as caused by a sense of separation from God, and the tone bears much similarity with the Old Testament Psalms in their anguished petitions to God (roughly 'Afectos' 1–20), and the remainder ('Afectos' 21–45) which speak with more confidence and authority of God and His will in the world, suggested by the frequent use of verbs of knowing such as 'entendí' and 'conocí'. Taken as a whole, the 'Afectos' evolve, gain in spiritual depth and insight, and reach their culmination in 'Afecto 37', an extraordinary text with numerous similes (including comparisons to clouds, iron, musical instruments, streams of water, and a golden ring) which build up the vision of the difference between the soul who turns to God and the damned. It is clear from the *Afectos espirituales* themselves that Sor Francisca hung on every word of her male confessor, P. Francisco de Herrera, to such an extent that she is emotionally distraught when she finds out that he will no longer be visiting her, as suggested by 'Afecto 5' (Castillo 46–47). The original manuscript of 'Afecto 41' contains a written note to her confessor which describes her affliction and concludes with the following sentence: 'Esto es darle cuenta de lo que me pasa, para que vea si será bueno quemar estos papeles; pues, mientras más me esfuerzo a tomar sus consejos, es más la guerra' (Castillo 353, n. 1). What the *Afectos espirituales* reveal, thus, is not only a seventeenth century Colombian nun's struggle with God but also her tussle with the authority of her male confessor. The Castillo-Herrera relationship makes abundantly obvious the overpowering control the Church had, not only over publishing but also writing and, indeed, thought itself during this period.

The most significant prose work of the colonial period was *El lazarillo de ciegos caminantes* (1775 or 1776) by Concolocorvo, alias Alonso Carrió de la Vandera (1715?–1783), a native of Gijón who went to New Spain at the age of twenty, where he worked for ten years as a merchant. He later worked as a *Corregidor* in the 1750s and simultaneously as Captain General, General Mayor of Mines and Subdelegate of the Goods of the Deceased. In 1771 he was promoted to Second Commissioner of the postal system between Montevideo, Buenos Aires and Lima; José Antonio Pando, one of his rivals, was nominated *Administrador de Correos*; this antagonism would be one of the motives behind Carrió de la Vandera's decision to write and publish his travelogue, *El lazarillo de ciegos caminantes*, copies of which were sent to the head office of the postal service in Madrid (Lorente Medina xii). The journey from Buenos Aires to Montevideo to Lima on which he based his travelogue took place between May 1771 and June 1773. *El lazarillo de ciegos caminantes* is an intriguing, hybrid work, halfway between personal account and public census, between autobiography and novel. In some ways it fits the expected mould of those works commissioned by the Viceroy and which concern such subjects as portrayal of the land, description of the mine industry, or a census of a particular city, of which there are many examples throughout the colonial period. If these works were to the Viceroy's satisfaction they were sometimes published and often led to public office, sometimes even a sinecure. Thus, Carrió de la Vandera has separate sections on the cities of Montevideo and Buenos Aires, their population, the customs of their inhabitants, the important families who reside there (Carrió de la Vandera 20–23, 25–29); he describes minutely the vagaries of transport by cart between Buenos Aires and Carcarañal (Carrió de la Vandera 33–36). The subsequent sections on Córdoba, Santiago del Estero, San Miguel de Tucumán, Salta, Jujuy, Porco, Potosí, Chuquisaca, and Cuzco, for example, all follow a similar pattern in that they describe the topography of each region, the highlights of the main cities and towns there, as well as the customs and commerce of their inhabitants. All of these elements make *El lazarillo de ciegos caminantes* like an 'informe' commissioned by the office of the Viceroy. But there are other elements which reveal to what extent Carrió de la Vandera's work is transitional and deviates from the state sponsorship pattern of publication normal during the colonial era. Most notably the author is introduced in section XI of Part II by the outlandish name of Concolorcorvo: 'Ya, señor Concolorcorvo, me dijo el visitador, está Vm. en sus tierras' (Carrió de la Vandera 109), and the work is dedicated not to 'hombres sabios, prudentes y piadosos' but rather to those 'de la Hampa o Cáscara amarga, ya sean de espada, carabina y pistolas, ya de bolas, guampar y lazo'. The importance of *El lazarillo de ciegos caminantes* lies not only in the invaluable insight it offers into cultural customs of colonial Spanish America but also its place as a transitional text between viceregal patronage and the republican energy of print capitalism.[6]

---

6  For a good background discussion of other prose writers of the colonial period which emphasizes the porousness of fiction and history during this period, see Pupo-Walker, 'El relato virreinal'.

## Essay

The most important essayist of the Enlightenment during the colonial period was the Peruvian Francisco Javier Eugenio de Santa Cruz y Espejo (1747–1795). He published three significant essays, all of which are expressed in dialogue form: *El Nuevo Luciano de Quito* (1779), *Marco Porcio Catón* (1780), and *El Nuevo Luciano de Quito o Despertador de Ingenios Quiteños (Ciencia Blancardina)* (1780). The first dialogue sets the blueprint for what is to follow; *El Nuevo Luciano* consists of nine dialogues between Dr Murillo, a doctor of the old school much enamoured of Thomism, and Dr Mera, clearly a projection of the author Santa Cruz y Espejo, who argues against the rhetorical excesses of scholasticism and shows awareness and admiration for the knowledge and scientific method of the Enlightenment. The nine conversations ostensibly focus on different themes – the first explains how the dialogue itself was inspired by Dr Mera's disappointment at a recent sermon given by one Dr D. Sancho de Escobar, the second discusses the use of Latin in church, the third deals with rhetoric and poetry, the fourth with good taste, the fifth with philosophy, etc. – but the same pattern emerges during each conversation: Dr Murillo is wedded, with some misgivings, to the status quo, while Dr Mera attacks the educational system as well as the deplorable state of science and philosophy of his day in Ecuador. For example, Mera rejects the blandly over-formalistic citation of classical texts such as those of the Church Fathers, instead arguing for a more critical treatment of the text. He champions the deductive method of the scholars of the Enlightenment, and challenges the usefulness of an education system which does not teach the theory of ethics, which looks to Spain as its paragon even though Spain is so backward, where lawyers learn their trade by rote and have no historical knowledge of their discipline, and where churchmen cease to study once they have graduated from college (Santa Cruz y Espejo 53, 54–55). Santa Cruz y Espejo's use of the dialogue form in his essays is, indeed, itself an example of an inductive rather than by-rote attitude towards knowledge and learning. Rather like the Spanish philosopher Feijoo (1676–1764), with whom he has much in common, Santa Cruz y Espejo deplores the dangers caused by an intransigent scholasticism, as typified by speculative theology, and respects the scientific method of the Enlightenment as epitomized by the work of scientist/philosophers such as René Descartes and Isaac Newton; he is, however, not prepared to embrace the atheism which some of the *Encyclopédistes* proclaimed to be a necessary ingredient of the New Science.

## Theatre

Theatre during the colonial period centred around the viceregal court which was the self-conscious hub of artistic, musical and dramatic activity (Weiss 92). Gradually theatrical culture had moved out of the Church into the opera house; the Nuevo Coliseo of Lima, built at the height of the Baroque period, with the latest in stage machinery and sets, was inaugurated in 1662 by the departing Viceroy Guzmán, who had made its construction possible. Many guilds were directed by executive fiat to commission plays; in 1630 in Lima, for example, the birth of Prince Baltasar Carlos was celebrated with a series of plays sponsored by various guilds: the candymakers (6 November), the *pulperos* (grocers or tavern-keepers; 8 and 9 November), the blacksmiths (22 November), and the meat suppliers (10 December) (Weiss 101). Most coliseums, opera houses, and playhouses were built in the eighteenth century, under the enlightened aegis of the Bourbons, but largely by private capital (Weiss 97).

Indeed, it is the genre of theatre which reveals most clearly the cultural dependence the Spanish colonies experienced with regard to the mother country. The playhouses (*corrales*) in Mexico City were modelled on those in Spain, and the playwrights, plays and troupes came from Spain. Their popularity is suggested by Balbuena's observation in his *Grandeza Mexicana* at the beginning of the seventeenth century that Mexico City enjoys new plays and *entremeses* every day: 'fiestas y comedias nuevas cada día,/ de varios entremeses y primores/ gusto, entretenimiento y alegría' (Balbuena 41). The most popular dramatists whose works were staged in Mexico during the colonial era were, as in Spain, Lope de Vega (1562–1635), Calderón de la Barca (1600–1681), and Pérez de Montalbán (1602–1638). The latter's play based on the bizarre adventures of one Catalina de Erauso, who escaped as a young girl from a nunnery in Spain and fled to the New World, dressed as a man, *La monja-alférez*, was a great local success.[7] The case of Juan Ruiz de Alarcón (1581?–1639) is symptomatic. Though born in New Spain he sought fame and fortune in Spain, his plays were staged in Spain, and often set in the mother country as well. His masterpiece is *La verdad sospechosa* (1634), which tells the story of a young man, Don García, whose mendaciousness eventually leads to his own discomfiture. The tale is very skilfully told, and its staging shows a well-attuned sensitivity to the opportunity for humour arising from mutual misunderstanding, particularly in the use of the device of the aside.

There was, however, some homegrown dramatic talent in the colonies. One play, which enjoyed some success during the early colonial period,

---

[7] The Inquisition was, as always, alert to any hint of blasphemy or irreverence expressed in the public space of theatre. Montalbán's play, *El valor perseguido y traición vengada,* was banished from the Mexican stage in 1682 (Leonard, *Baroque* 109–16).

ought to be mentioned here, and that is the *Comedia de San Francisco de Borja* (1641) by the Jesuit Mathias de Bocanegra (1612–1688). A lively, witty drama, it was written to commemorate the arrival of Viceroy Marqués de Villena in Mexico City. The first act is a wonderful piece of art, showing a good sense of the dramatic potential of events on the stage, such as when Flora and Belisa, unbeknownst to each other, both approach Borja at exactly the same time (*Tres piezas* 263–65), as well as a masterful use of the omen (the Emperatriz's dream that she is going to die proves to be a true prediction of the future), and, finally, a lively use of the poetic joust *topos* when Borja, Carlos V and Sansón compete with each other in order to see who can best express the dilemma as to whether man is easier to control than a beast (*Tres piezas* 247–50). The second and third acts, however, which describe how Borja gradually disentangles himself from the world and achieves sainthood, are wooden by comparison.

As might be expected with a genre as socially sensitive as drama, the plays of this period, which were mainly from Spain, had a profound effect on the culture of the times; *sueltas* (single plays in pamphlet form) and *partes* (collections of plays) were imported from Spain and purchased in surprisingly high quantities. Irving gives two examples of how influential this literature was on the creation of a culture of love; he quotes a contemporary observer who notes that 'the reading of books of plays was so general in ladies' drawing rooms and in maidens' chambers that women could only feel sophisticated when they talked about a love affair, an amorous difficulty, the vanquishing of male indifference, or the humble devotion of a swain'. The other example concerns the indifference of a woman who impassively carried on reading a volume of plays while the two men who had fought for her love were hanged on the other side of the street (qtd. in Leonard, 106–107). While the Spanish dramatists had their works as the main feature in any dramatic performance, the native-born Spanish Americans had to be content with having their works performed as the *entremés*. By the end of the seventeenth century, however, it appears that drama had fallen on bad times. An Italian traveller, Gemelli Careri, commented, after seeing a local performance of *La dicha y desdicha del nombre*, that '[i]t was so badly played that I would gladly have given the two *reales* it cost me to go in and take a seat not to have seen it' (qtd. in Leonard, *Baroque* 106).

The late colonial period presents a slightly different picture, in the sense that the models used were not Spanish (they were often French or Italian), but the similarity in the sense of derivativeness remains. All three plays known to have been in the repertoire of the Peruvian dramatist Pedro de Peralta y Barnuevo (1664–1743) were derivative in some sense. *La Rodoguna* (1708) was an adapted translation of Corneille's play of the same name, *Triunfos de amor y poder* (1711) was a Baroque-mythological piece, and *Afectos vencen finezas* (1720) was a play of impeccable Calderonian pedigree; Peralta y Barnuevo also translated for the stage an Italian play, *Bersabé* by Ferrante Pallavicino (1616–1644) (Estuardo Núñez 22–23), as well as a number of other short occasional pieces to accompany these works (Tamayo Vargas).

Another important dramatist of this period is Pablo Olavide y Jáuregui (1725–1803); his contribution can be seen mainly in terms of his translations of French plays for the stage which served to revitalize the theatre of his day. Though born in Peru, Olavide spent much of his adult life in Spain and there established his reputation as a dramatist. His translations included works by Racine (*Phèdre, Mithrydate*) and by Voltaire (*Zayre, Cassandre et Olympie,* and *Merope*), although his best work in translation is probably *El desertor* (1775), based on the French dramatist Mercier's *Le déserteur* (1769) which, in elegant octosyllabic verse, tells the story of a young couple in love whose marriage is ruined by the discovery that the prospective groom is an army deserter, but which, by virtue of the use of the *deus ex machina* device, ends happily. Olavide's sensitivity to the social and particularly national value of theatre is evident in the only play known to be an original work composed by him, *El zeloso burlado* (1764), a lively one-act *zarzuela*. Set in the Paseo del Prado, Madrid, on the evening of a much-anticipated firework display to be held nearby in the Parque del Retiro, this play is very much a circumstantial piece. The opening scene alludes in glowing terms to the royal members of the audience, including Queen Luisa, who is described as 'pasmo/ De talento y discrecion' (Olavide, *Obras dramáticas* 2), as well as to the sovereigns ('Dichosos Pueblos, que tienen/ Tan amables Soberanos'), and other members of the royal family (Fernando, Gabriel, Antonio and Xavier; Olavide, *Obras dramáticas* 3). The plot focusses on the comical aspects of the jealous possessiveness of an older man for a young woman, and is similar in terms of comic wit to Cervantes's short story, *El celoso extremeño*. It is important to note that the overriding ethos of theatrical production during this period centred on the imitation of foreign models which, while serving an important nationalist purpose, also ultimately stunted any possible growth of an intrinsically national theatrical tradition.

Some Amerindian-language plays were also written and performed during this period. In Cuzco the cleric Gabriel Centeno de Osma is credited as the author of the Quechua-language adaptation of a parable of spiritual versus earthly riches, *Yauri Titu Inca o El rico más pobre* (manuscript dated 1701). But the first truly major native-language work is *Ollantay* (anonymous, dating from the end of the eighteenth century), which is based on a pre-conquest legend, embroidered with the addition of a Romantic intrigue between the hero and his beloved, a vestal virgin (Weiss 117). The manuscript of the play, in Quechua, was found among the papers of a *mestizo* priest, one Antonio Valdés, on his death (Luzuriaga & Reeve 167). Although some critics have argued that the mixture of a Romantic love narrative with the story of a struggle for political power is incongruous, what is notable about *Ollantay* is the way in which the discourse of love and the narrative of nation-building are projected as intimately connected (for more discussion of this theme, see Sommer). Ollantay's desire to marry Estrella, the daughter of Pachacutic, King of Cuzco, is also in effect a desire to ascend to the throne. Likewise the period when Estrella is locked away in a cave in a vestal virgin nunnery coincides with the time that Ollantay becomes a rebel fighting against the state, now in the person of King Yupanqui, Pachacutic's son. Pointing in a similar direction, the *desenlace* of the play – in which, contrary to all expectations, Yupanqui elevates Ollantay to the throne and offers him Estrella to be his wife – underlines how successful statehood and blossoming love are interlocking discourses. The distinctive characteristic of the play, which makes it so different from the Maya play, *Rabinal Achí*, which concludes with the sacrifice of the enemy, is that it ends on a note of political harmony within the Incan state; brother and brother-in-law share the kingdom. The projection of a harmonious state is, of course, in direct contradistinction to what had actually occurred some 250 years before when the two sons of Huayna-Capac, Huáscar and Atahualpa, were engaged in a civil war, and as a result were conquered by Pizarro. *Ollantay* should, thus, be interpreted as an important political gesture bodying forth the dream of an Incan state united against Spanish oppression, and which uses the metaphorical symmetry of love to do so.[8]

## The Multi-genre Writer

The most significant poet, and indeed writer, of the colonial era was undoubtedly Sor Juana Inés de la Cruz (1651–1695). The narrative of her life is straightforward enough; born of a poor but honourable family in the village of Nepantla and learning to read at the age of three, learning became her true passion. Barred from attending the University in Mexico City because she was a woman, her plan to attend dressed as a man failed. Sor Juana's intellectual precocity attracted the interest of the Viceroy himself and for a while she served in his palace. In 1669 she took vows as a nun and entered the Convent of San Jerónimo. While there she wrote plays, poetry and prose. Her life of intellectual pleasure was ruined, however, with the publication of her reponse to the sermon of the Brazilian (of Portuguese descent) Jesuit Antônio Vieyra, and her subsequent *Respuesta de la poetisa a la muy ilustre Sor Filotea de la Cruz*, written in response to the Bishop of Puebla's recommendation that she turn her mind to spiritual rather than mundane, literary matters. The authorities silenced her, she sold her library, which for the time was an extremely rich one, having over four thousand books, and distributed the profits to the poor. She died while tending the sick in Mexico City. While she is best known for her poetry, she was also the author of a number of plays, such as *El divino Narciso* and *Empeños de la casa*.

[8] For a discussion of other dramatists of this period, such as 'El Ciego de la Merced', see Oviedo, *Historia*, vol. 1, 291–92.

Sor Juana's essay, *Respuesta de la poetisa a la muy ilustre Sor Filotea de la Cruz*, is an exercise in ingenuity. It opens with an elaborate modesty *topos* and then proceeds to a devastating attack of her opponent's argument. In this essay she made the famous declaration that she joined the nunnery in order to avoid marriage (Cruz 446). The aim of Sor Juana's argument is to turn the tables on her phallocentric audience; this is evident on one level in that she retains the feminine pseudonym of her interlocutor in the title of her essay (Sor Filoteo, the Bishop of Puebla, becomes Sor Filotea), but, more importantly, she continually underlines the injustice of the roles ascribed to men and women.

Much of Sor Juana's poetry makes more sense when put in the context of her *Respuesta* since it invokes the rhetoric of the day but recasts it in an iconoclastic way. Her poetry is normally described as Baroque, in the sense of being marked by complexity and elaborate form, calculatedly ambiguous imagery, and a penchant for the creation of dynamic intellectual oppositions and contrasts. Like many poets of her age, Sor Juana felt the influence of the great contemporary Spanish Baroque poets, Francisco de Quevedo and Luis de Góngora (1561–1627).[9] Her most famous work, *Inundación castálida* (1689), gives a good indication of the type of literary work published at the end of the seventeenth century in Spain and the colonies. It was dedicated to Vicereine Luisa Gonzaga Manrique de Lara (whose full title made her also Countess of Paredes and Marchioness de la Laguna), who was so impressed by its contents that she took it upon herself to take the manuscript to Madrid to have it printed. The contents of *Inundación castálida* can be divided into four categories, the *loas* (introits, or mini plays which acted as a preface to a play), the *villancicos* (roughly equivalent to Christmas carols), the lengthy poem *Neptuno* (an allegorical description of the triumphal arch built for the Viceroys de la Laguna on their arrival in Mexico in 1680), and the lyrical poems with a personal focus. Whereas the first three categories of work were commissioned and fit the Maecenal model, the fourth was not; it is not coincidental that it is for her poems with a personal focus that Sor Juana is now remembered.[10] Some of her most witty poems, written it must be assumed

---

9 The *Encyclopedia Britannica* mentions two possible sources for the term Baroque, both of which are apposite descriptors of Sor Juana's work. The first is the Italian 'barroco', a term 'used by philosophers during the Middle Ages to describe an obstacle in schematic logic', while another source is that of the Portuguese word 'barroco', which is used to describe 'an irregular or imperfectly shaped pearl' (*EB*, I, 910).

10 This is part of the funnelling process whereby over time the notion of literature has been refined, such that 'letras' (which once included creative literary works as well as philosophical, historical, scientific, legal and medicinal works) has been replaced by 'literatura' which in turn came to mean, largely as a result of the paradigm shift brought about by the Romantic movement, imaginative writing written for aesthetic effect. Terry Eagleton has argued that this paradigm shift was accompanied by a change in the patronage system; thus, during the Romantic movement, art became its own patron (Eagleton 27; for

before she took her vows, expose herself as caught in an unbearable love-triangle. Using a device called 'encontradas correspondencias' the poems express how she loves a man who does not love her, and is loved by another man whom she does not love. The first stanza of 'Al que ingrato me deja, busco amante' is a fine example of the Baroque conceit: 'Al que ingrato me deja, busco amante;/ al que amante me sigue, dejo ingrata;/ constante adoro a quien mi amor maltrata;/ maltrato a quien mi amor busca constante' (Campa & Rodríguez 261). The repetition of words, such as 'ingrato/ingrata', 'busco/busca', and 'constante' serves to underline how she is at once dishing out and at the receiving end of spurned love. 'Feliciano me adora y le aborrezco' treats the same theme and shows the same skill in producing opposing semantic units expressed by phonetically identical words in the last tercet of the poem: 'pues ambos atormentan mi sentido:/ aquéste, con pedir lo que no tengo;/ y aquél, con no tener lo que le pido' (Campa & Rodríguez 260–61). Sor Juana's most famous poem is the *redondilla* entitled 'Hombres necios que acusáis' in which she uses the rhetorical baggage of the Baroque to express the double values attached to the sexes in the Mexico of her time. The sixth stanza of this poem, for example, refers to the irony of the man who breathes on a mirror (by which we are to understand takes a woman's virginity) and then complains he cannot see (by which we are to understand he complains that her honour is besmirched): '¿Qué humor puede ser más raro/ que el que, falto de consejo,/ él mismo empaña el espejo,/ y siente que no esté claro?' (Campa & Rodríguez 254).

Sor Juana's most significant single poem is her *Primero sueño*. It is a 950-line self-averred imitation of Góngora's poetry written in honour of D. Gaspar de Sandoval Cerda Silva y Mendoza, the Viceroy of Mexico and Count of Galve, on whose orders French forces attempting to invade the Spanish part of Hispaniola were defeated at the mouth of the Guarico, Hispaniola, on 21 January 1691 by an expeditionary force sent from New Spain. It is written in the poetic form of the *silva*, perhaps as a witty reference to the Viceroy's third surname. Like Góngora's verse, the *Primero sueño* makes liberal use of the hyperbaton, mythological culturalism and a Latinate syntax and vocabulary. However, Sor Juana's poem is unlike Góngora's *Soledades* in that it describes an ontological enquiry into the nature and function of the universe.[11] The poem opens describing the arrival of nightfall, and how the world, including the human body, gradually falls asleep (lines 1–265). The

---

further discussion see Introduction). Quite clearly, the sonnets in *Inundación castálida* are closer to the post-Romantic sense of literature than the commissioned poem, *Neptuno*, is.

[11] Octavio Paz describes the difference between the two poets effectively: 'Por genio natural, sor Juana tiende más al concepto agudo que a la metáfora brillante; Góngora, poeta sensual, sobresale en la descripción – casi siempre verdera recreación – de cosas, figuras, seres y paisajes, mientras que las metáforas de sor Juana son más para ser pensadas que vistas' (*Trampas* 470).

second part of the poem, which is the most substantial, describes how Fantasy begins to copy the things of the phenomenal world showing them to the soul ('las representaba/ y al alma las mostraba'; lines 290–91; Sor Juana 342), and includes a section on two pyramids used as figures of the human soul (Sabat de Rivers, *Sueño* 105–109), a disquisition on the great chain of being followed by an anguished awareness of the limits of human understanding as compounded by the proliferation of diverse human languages and diverse species (lines 266–826). The final section describes the human mind waking up and returning to the phenomenal world of everyday life (lines 827–975). *Primero sueño* is a poetic *tour de force* without equal in the literary scene of the colonial period. The conclusion of the poem, in particular, is remarkable in that it suggests that, through the dream knowledge engendered by her poem, the world has become brighter and she more awake (lines 967–975; Sor Juana 359).

Sor Juana was not only the foremost poet of her day but also an outstanding dramatist. Her play *El divino Narciso* is a Calderonian *auto sacramental* which, as Alexander Parker has pointed out, takes the idea of applying a Christian dogmatic principle to a mythological story from Calderón's *El divino Orfeo* (Parker). The central part of *El divino Narciso* follows the classical story of Narcissus closely: spurning all women and even the loveliest of nymphs, Echo, Narcissus is punished by falling in love with his own image, at which point Echo becomes mute, or rather, unable to do anything other than repeat what has been said to her, a technique adopted with some verve in the play (Act IV, Scene XI; lines 1480–1691; Sor Juana 66–78). Other characters are added, such as Naturaleza Humana, Soberbia, Amor Propio and Gracia, who serve to turn the play into a Christian allegory play. Narciso's last words ('Este es Mi cuerpo y Mi Sangre/ que entregué a tantos martirios/ por vosotros. En memoria/ de Mi Muerte, repetidlo' (lines 2187–2190; Sor Juana 95) echo Christ's words at the Last Supper. At this point of transfiguration of human nature, Eco, Amor Propio and Soberbia die, allowing Naturaleza Humana and Gracia to embrace. Lest one should see this as simply a rewriting of the Calderonian code, attention is focussed on Eco's feminine plight, which is seen as more serious than that of the others. Amor Propio and Soberbia simply commit suicide (line 2201; line 2204), while Eco is condemned to eternal torment: 'Y yo, ¡ay de mí!, que lo he visto,/ enmudezca, viva sólo/ al dolor, muerta al alivio' (lines 2196–2198; Sor Juana 95). Eco will continue to 'live' to pain, which tends to suggest perhaps a feminised consciousness barred from the patriarchal economy of death and sacrifice. In Sor Juana's world vision, thus, a harmonious relationship between the sexes is impossible and can only be transcended through the transfiguring role of Christianity's redemptionism.

## Chapter 3

# NINETEENTH-CENTURY LITERATURE: PART I

The nineteenth century is remembered as the century of independence, even if it was a freedom movement in which the Indian population of Latin America had little voice. It is not coincidental that the two areas where the independence grew, the viceroyalty of New Granada and that of Río de la Plata, were also areas where the printing press burgeoned late on in the seventeenth century. By the time printing came to those areas outside the capitals of the two pre-eminent viceroyalties, Mexico City and Lima, the time was ripe for its use to fan the flames of independence which would sweep across the Sub-Continent in the first two decades of the nineteenth century.[1] By the end of the eighteenth century, for example, the need to seek royal permission for the establishment of a printing press seemed less urgent. Thus Vertiz, Viceroy of the Río de la Plata region from 1778–1784, gave permission for a press to be set up in Buenos Aires in 1779, and the crown gave formal approval in 1782, after some 150 items had already been printed (Thompson 61). The turn of the eighteenth to the nineteenth century was, in terms of history of the printing, as Steinberg argues, 'not a break but rather a sudden leap forward' (Steinberg 275). As he goes on: 'Technical progress, rationalised organisation, and compulsory education interacted one upon another. New inventions lowered the cost of production; mass literacy created further demands, the national and international organisation of the trade widened the channels and eased the flow of books from the publishers' stock departments to the retailers' shelves' (Steinberg 275).

It is furthermore clear that the establishment of the newspaper press, at the end of the eighteenth century, was closely linked to the growth of the emancipation movements in Latin America, early influential examples of the newspaper press being *El Diario Erudito, Económico y Comercial de Lima* (1790–1792) directed by Jaime Bausaute, and the *Mercurio Peruano de Historia, Literatura y Noticias Públicas*, founded in 1791 and published by Jacinto Calero Moreyra. In Bogotá towards the end of the seventeenth

---

[1]  In what follows I follow broadly the categories suggested by Pierce and Kent to describe the growth of the press in Latin America: Pre-Journalism, 1539–1790; Founding Period, 1790–1820; Factional Press, 1820–1900; Transition to Modernism, 1900–1960; and the Modern Period, since 1960 (Pierce & Kent 230).

century, for example, the printing press served the political objectives of the revolutionaries; in 1793 one Antonio Nariño set up a printing shop named La Patriótica, which proved to be short-lived since he was later persecuted for publishing the pro-independence essay, *Derechos del hombre* (based on the seventeen articles of the new French constitution) in the following year (Foreno Benavides 21–38). Printing flourished in Colombia during the revolutionary decades; the new presses were often allied with the pro-independence movement (Thompson 77). In almost all of the urban centres in Spanish America gazettes were established by the newly-independent governments: the *Gaceta del Gobierno de Mexico* in Mexico City (established 2 January 1810), the *Gazeta de Buenos Ayres* in Buenos Aires (7 June 1810), the *Gaceta del Gobierno* in Lima (13 October 1810), and the *Gazeta del supremo gobierno de Chile* in Santiago (26 February 1817) (Charno 348, 14, 533, 127). In some cases, as for example in Upper Peru and Chile, the first newspaper printed coincides almost exactly with the proclamation of independence. Thus, the University of Chuquisaca began to publish the newspaper *La Gaceta de Chuquisaca* on 30 July 1823, and on 8 August of the same year published the Act of Independence of Upper Peru (Quesada 85). Likewise, the newly-independent government of Chile purchased a technologically advanced printing press from the United States in 1811 specifically in order to promulgate the advantages of independent government (Quesada 88–89).

In terms of emerging ideology as well as mode of production (a specific example of which was the new gazette), the new era ushered in by the nineteenth century was one in which the previous indissoluble link between the published word and royal privilege was actively challenged. The democratisation of the written word through the newspaper press was accompanied by a burgeoning capital-based democracy based on individual freedom. In particular, the growth of newsprint was directly linked to the growth of nationalism for the newspaper, as Benedict Anderson suggests, like the novel, 'provided the technical means for "re-presenting" the *kind* of imagined community that is the nation' (Anderson 30). This new print-capitalism allowed the notion of nationhood to flourish since it made it possible for growing numbers of people to think about themselves in new ways, and particularly in terms of a new cross-national simultaneity. While it is true, as Checa Godoy points out, that the nineteenth century was dominated by politically-driven rather than literature-driven newspapers (Checa Godoy 11), the literature produced during this period, as Angel Rama rightly points out, needs to be seen as foundational texts which built identity for the newly emergent nations of Spanish America: 'la literatura se formula inicialmente como una parte, pequeña aunque distinguida, de la construcción de la nacionalidad' (*Crítica* 67). As Thomas Carlyle succinctly put it: 'Literature is our Parliament too' (Carlyle 219).

## Romanticism

Arguably the most important literary movement of the nineteenth century in Europe and the Americas, Romanticism had an important role to play in the evolution of Spanish-American literature. Romanticism swept through Europe in the last half of the eighteenth century and the first half of the nineteenth, originating in Germany and spreading thence to England, France, Spain, Italy and the Americas. It is a literary movement which promotes the transcendance, necessity and centrality of love, which sees the individual as more important than the society in which (s)he lives, which emphasises the imagination and the emotions at the expense of logic and reason, and which values nature rather than culture or the urban environment. Other features which recur in Romantic literature are: subjectivism, uncertainty about identity, the religious instinct (often associated with pantheism), forbidden love (especially incest), medievalism, nationalism, religion and superstition, liberalism, and literary devices such as melodrama, fantastic coincidence, and the *deus ex machina* technique.

Romanticism came to Spanish America in the 1830s; Río de la Plata was more influenced by French Romanticism while Mexico, Peru and Colombia fell under the influence of Spanish Romantic writers (Carilla, I, 42–45).[2] The first authentic Romantic work is normally given as Echeverría's *Elvira o la novia del Plata* (1832), and the most significant Romantic works were centred in the genre of poetry. The European writers who made the greatest impact in Spanish America were Hugo, Byron, Chateaubriand, Walter Scott, Larra, and Espronceda (Carilla, I, 59). The more colourful polemics about Romanticism were centred in the Southern Cone, particularly in the Buenos Aires Salón Literario (1837), the Montevidean Certamen de Mayo (1841) and the polemic in Santiago de Chile in 1842 expressed in the local press, and especially the articles of Vicente Fidel López and Sarmiento (Carilla, I, 134–41). Jotabeche, for example, was scathing about the facile imitation of Hugo's work (qtd. in Carilla, I, 141). There were also those writers who may be grouped in terms of a social Romanticism movement, such as Alberdi and Sarmiento; as Alberdi wrote: 'Queremos una literatura profética del porvenir, y no llorona de lo pasado' (qtd. in Carilla, I, 155).

---

2   A French traveller, Xavier Marmier, who visited Buenos Aires in the mid nineteenth century, was struck by its French ambience. Booksellers stocked Dumas and Musset but not Garcilaso de la Vega (Carilla, I, 62–63).

## Civic/Romantic Poetry (1820–1830)

The three poets studied in this section, José Joaquín de Olmedo (1780–1847), Andrés Bello (1781–1865), and José María Heredia (1803–1839), called 'transition poets' by one critic (Carilla, I, 53), have been placed together since their work demonstrates, firstly, the links that existed at this period between art and politics and, secondly, the differing ways in which the components of a *criollo* national consciousness were arranged in post-independence Spanish America.[3] All three men moved in a tight circle of powerful men who were the intellectual engineers of the independence and avid supporters of nationalism. The nationalism that they experienced and expressed was necessarily hybrid given the recent emergence of nationhood in Spanish America. David Lloyd has described the problems confronted by intellectuals of the post-colonial nation in using a term – 'perpetually split consciousness' (Lloyd 112) – which is eminently applicable to this trio of writers, the first generation of *criollo* intellectuals. Olmedo, Bello, and Heredia, as their works and their biographical itineraries show, were gripped by a nationalist fervour which used the language of the oppressor, both literally and in terms of its institutional culture, to find expression.

In Olmedo's 'La victoria de Junín' (1825) we have the first poem which celebrates the independence of Spanish America. Like the many examples of civic verse designed to commemorate this event it had its ideological inconsistencies. The most significant of these was one identified by Simón Bolívar in his *Carta de Jamaica* (1815), that the *criollos* have as little right to the land they inherit as the Spaniards who arrived some three hundred years before: 'no somos indios ni europeos, sino una especie media entre los legítimos propietarios del país y los usurpadores españoles: en suma, siendo nosotros americanos por nacimiento y nuestros derechos los de Europa, tenemos que disputar éstos a los del país y que mantenernos en él contra la invasión de los invasores; así nos hallamos en el caso más extraordinario y complicado' (Bolívar 46). It was the elements within this 'most extraordinary and complicated case' that the poets writing about the independence movement attempted to reconcile. It is important to note that the notion of Spanish as language-of-state was never questioned by the *criollo* writers; it was only many years later, and particularly in Fernández Retamar's *Calibán* (1971), that the language itself would be seen as the bedrock of the post-colonial dilemma rather than an unpleasant side-effect. Spanish as language-of-state was, in those years immediately after independence, not seen as problematical, but a political unease was, nevertheless, evident in the work of *criollo* writers. Olmedo responded to this dilemma by having much of the narrative

---

3   In this context Ricardo Palma's words are telling: 'Casi no hay en toda la cadena de repúblicas que baña el Pacífico un solo nombre literario que no sea al mismo tiempo un nombre político' (qtd. in Carilla, I, 20).

of his poem spoken by an Incan emperor, Huayna-Capac, thereby giving greater authority to the sense of justice involved in emancipation from Spanish rule. 'La victoria de Junín' is, thus, a good example of the Indianist mode.[4] In a review of Olmedo's poem, Bello referred to the Incan emperor's speech as 'la parte más espléndida y animada de su canto' (Bello 267), since it was an ingenious way of resolving the contradiction between the desire, on the one hand, of presenting Bolívar as the author of independence in Peru and the historical fact, on the other hand, that Bolívar was absent from the decisive battle which sealed independence, namely, the battle of Ayacucho (1824). Bolívar was present at the battle of Junín which took place earlier on that year; to solve this problem, as Bello points out, in a *leger-de-main* Olmedo fuses the two battles together (Bello 268). Yet, despite the favouritism this rhetorical gesture accorded Bolívar, the latter was not impressed. Having read the copy of the copy which Olmedo sent him, Bolívar replied in a letter to the author of 'La victoria de Junín' that he found the Inca in the latter's poem 'un poco hablador y embrollón' (Espinosa Pólit 538). As the above quote suggests, Bolívar knew that to view his great deeds as somehow justifying the Amerindian heritage of South America was a distortion. In his reply to Bolívar, Olmedo basically defended his poem in terms of poetic licence, while skirting around ideological matters (Espinosa Pólit 538–39).

Nevertheless, and despite Bolívar's own quibbles, Olmedo chose not to revise his poem; thus Bolívar is hailed by the Incan emperor in the following terms: '¡Oh predilecto/ Hijo y Amigo y Vengador del Inca!' (Olmedo 136). The Spaniards, predictably enough, are seen as cruel usurpers and, through Bolívar's and Sucre's efforts, the Incas have finally been justified: 'Esta es la hora feliz. Desde aquí empieza/ la nueva edad al Inca prometida/ de libertad, de paz y de grandeza' (Olmedo 136). Echoing Bolívar's dream of a united Spanish-American republic, Olmedo naturalizes its proportions by tying it to the geographics of Latin America, and specifically the Andes. Like much of the civic verse of its day, thus, Olmedo's poem predicates its political dream for the future on an organicist faith in the interchangeability of nature and culture, a *topos* which, as we shall see, played an even more significant role in Andrés Bello's civic verse.

Both 'Alocución a la poesía' (1823) and 'La agricultura de la zona tórrida' (1826) by Andrés Bello, despite their non-political titles, are what might be called civic poems which extol the American way of life, its culture and its flora and fauna. Like Olmedo's poetry, they speak on behalf of an educated elite; his poems were certainly not literature for the masses. In a letter to Fray Servando Teresa de Mier, Bello reproached him for having sent 750 copies of one of his books to Buenos Aires; as he suggested, '50 ejemplares hubiera

---

[4] Carilla makes a further helpful distinction between 'indianismo' and 'indigenismo': 'Indianismo, como evocación, idealización, proyección hacia el pasado; indigenismo, como realidad concreta e inmediata, como realidad social' (Carilla, II, 19).

sido un exceso y estoy seguro de que no se habrán vendido 20' (qtd. in Rama, *Crítica* 69). Though not having a massive popular impact, however, Bello's work, and particularly his poems, are noteworthy in that they demonstrate the ideals about nationhood epitomized by the new elite *criollo* intelligentsia produced after the Wars of Independence. In its markedly inclusivist way, Bello's poetry defines culture as nature and vice-versa, and reveals an impeccable Rousseauesque pedigree. It could be argued that this use of nature as the pointer to cultural identity in Latin America is an ideological cul-de-sac since it belies a facile organicism (to use Terry Eagleton's term) which does not face the challenge of history squarely.

'La agricultura de la zona tórrida' is written in *silvas*, that is, a mixture of seven-syllable and eleven-syllable lines, a traditionally appropriate *culto* verse form for the epic description of nature. Part I of the poem stresses the unbounding creativity of the natural world, while Part II extends this theme, and underlines in particular the different ways in which nature *clothes* the earth (an important metaphor in this context since it stresses culturalism; 'Tú vistes de jazmines/ el arbusto sabeo'; lines 16–17; Bello 41). In Part III the *locus amoenus* is given a political edge, as Bello rejects 'el ocio pestilente ciudadano' (line 11), in favour of the blissful peace of the farm-labourer's lot. City dwellers are goaded, so Bello suggests, by greed, ambition and patriotism: 'y en el ciego tumulto se aprisionan/ de míseras ciudades,/ do la ambición proterva/ sopla la llama de civiles bandos,/ al patriotismo la desidia enerva' (lines 81–85; Bello 42). It is intriguing that patriotism should be included in the bag of many ills contingent upon urban life which suggests, on the face of it, that Bello's discourse is anti-political. Given that the poem was written and published in the midst of the Wars of Independence, it may indicate that Bello was tired of political violence. True liberty, as Bello suggests in Part IV of the poem, inhabits the countryside: '¿Amáis la libertad? El campo habita:/ no allá donde el magnate/ entre armados satélites se mueve,/ y de la moda, universal señora,/ ve la razón al triunfal carro atada . . .' (lines 148–152; Bello 44). The 'magnate' referred to here who moves 'between armed satellites' exposes Bello's notion of what Spanish colonial rule essentially meant for the people of New Spain, since 'satellite' itself suggests how the pockets of Spanish power were simply supervising from afar. This type of government, as Bello suggests, is part of the political trend ('moda'), rather than based on reason. Part V of the poem reiterates this idea, and calls upon the natural world to heal the political wounds that the fratricidal war with Spain created: 'Abrigo den los valles/ a la sediente caña:/ la manzana y la pera/ en la fresca montaña/ el cielo olviden de su madre España' (lines 213–17; Bello 45). It becomes clear in Part VI that Bello is speaking from a specifically *criollo* perspective in that he neither speaks on behalf of the Spaniard or the Amerindian: 'Asaz de nuestros padres malhadados/ expiamos la bárbara conquista' (lines 302–304; Bello 47). The emperors of the Incas and the Aztecs are recalled as mere shadows put to rest by the Spanish: 'Saci-

adas duermen ya de sangre íbera/ las sombras de Atahualpa y Moctezuma'
(lines 311–12; Bello 47). Unlike the Spanish 'fathers', or the Amerindian
'shades', the *criollo* 'sons' hold the key to the future (lines 366–73; Bello
49). As the conclusion of the poem makes quite clear, the new culture which
is destined to emerge from the slaying of Spanish imperialism will be based
on the laws of the natural world.

    José María Heredia's poetry, like Olmedo's and Bello's, combines the
personal with the civic levels. By far his most famous poem is 'En el teocalli
de Cholula' (1820), written when Heredia was only seventeen years old, and
acknowledged to be one of the finest nineteenth-century poems of Spanish
America. Like many of the poems of the time celebrating independence from
Spain, Heredia's poem takes its point of reference from the Amerindian
world, in this case the Cholultecans and specifically the impressive Great
Pyramid of Cholula, which, at 425 metres square and 60 metres high, ranks
as the largest ancient pyramid in the Americas. But Heredia takes a different
approach to Olmedo, for example, since the Cuban poet uses Cholultecan
culture as a lesson from which the future republics of Spanish America need
to learn. He describes the 'teocalli', the main temple at Cholula, as an
immense structure which 'vio a la superstición más inhumana/ en ella
entronizarse' (ii. 134–35; Flores 160). Superstition is a key word in the poem,
since it is associated in Heredia's personal conceptual network with war, and
specifically the internecine war which had gripped the Sub-Continent. The
present silence of the scene as the poet sits looking at the ruins contrasts with
these visions of war:

> ¡Qué silencio! ¡Qué paz! ¡Oh! ¿Quién diría
> que en estos bellos campos reina alzada
> la bárbara opresión . . .?    (lines 42–44)

Heredia is thus writing a type of palimpsest in which the violence of the War
of independence is superimposed on the violence and superstition of the
Mesoamerican rite of human sacrifice. The Cholultecan rite and war are
linked terms in an equation of something Heredia specifically rejects. As in
Bello's 'La agricultura de la zona tórrida', Heredia's poem places its faith in
nature, as the opening stanza eloquently suggests (lines 1–23; Flores 158), for
which Heredia felt a deep affinity, as his poems 'En una tempestad', 'A la
estrella de Venus', and 'Niágara' in particular show. Like the other poems
studied in this section, 'En el teocalli de Cholula' is a poem which strives to
promote a notion of *criollo* nationalism through an uneasy balance mediated
on the one hand by a rejection of the external accoutrements of Spanish culture and on the other by an ambivalent evocation of the grandeur of pre-
Columbian culture.

## Post-Independence Poetry: Melgar and 'Placido'

The work of two poets stands out in this era, that of the Peruvian Mariano Melgar (1790–1815), and the Cuban 'Plácido', aka Gabriel de la Concepción Valdés (1809–1844). Mariano Melgar is mainly remembered for his *Yaravíes*, Quechuan lyrics translated into Spanish. They describe the author's pangs of unrequited love for María Santos Corrales, who is provided with the pseudonym Silvia in the poems (Melgar 19–23), and their use of a refrain as well as a simple idiom assured them instant popularity. The *Yaravíes* are sparse in the use of metaphor and simile, and they possess as a result a transparency which verges on the colloquial. But the apparent simplicity of these poems is deceptive. The use of short, punchy lines, introducing a staccato effect, shows skill in the use of rhythm which is refreshing when compared to the turgid formalism of much poetry of the early nineteenth century in Spanish America. 'Lágrimas que no pudieron', for instance, is a powerful five-stanza poem built around the comparison between the salt of the sea and the saltiness of the tears of unrequited love: 'Lágrimas que no pudieron/ Tanta dureza ablandar,/ Yo las volveré a la mar,/ Porque de la mar salieron' (Melgar 101). The use of the octosyllabic metre here, in its brevity, an impression heightened by the use of *acento agudo* in the infinitives ending the two internal lines of the stanza, shows Melgar as the master of the short line. Melgar was a fervent Republican (he was captured and executed for fighting against the Spaniards at the battle of Humachiri, Peru, in 1814), and this is clearly evident in his earnest poem, 'A la libertad'. Given his pro-Indian sympathies, it is perhaps not surprising that he takes the side of the Amerindian populace in his depiction of the struggle for independence, notably in his poem 'A la libertad' (Oda II, lines 7–12; Melgar 124). Unlike Heredia, who simply used the Amerindian heritage as a negative point of reference, Melgar saw independence as ushering in a new era of Incan culture, although it is presided over by Spain's spirit in the form of Iberia. Political independence, of course, led to no such thing in an empiric sense (the indigenous populations were as bad if not worse off after the Wars of Independence), but the fact that poets continued to visualize independence in these terms suggests a groundswell of (theoretical) support for the idea.

'Plácido' (1809–1844), the son of a Spanish barber and a mulatto woman, was put to death on the orders of the Captain General of Cuba, Leopoldo O'Donnell, in 1844 for his involvement in the anti-slavery movement in Matanzas. Called 'the Strauss of Havana' by the Countess of Merlin (Meyer 15), Plácido has since become an icon of Afro-Cuban culture. The vicissitudes of his life have inspired a number of literary works: two novels, Cirilo Villaverde's *La peineta caleda* (1843), and Joaquín de Lemoine's *El mulato Plácido* (1875), as well as a play, Diego Vicente Tejera's *La muerte de Plácido* (1875) (Plácido 10, n. 2). Plácido

wrote many different types of verse, ranging from historical poems such as
'Jicotencal' based on the Tlaxcaltecan chief who first fought against Cortés
and then joined forces with the Spaniard, to political poems such as '¡Haban-
eros, libertad!', religious verse such as 'Muerte de Jesucristo', and fable-type
poems such as 'Los dos perros' (Plácido 85–87, 112–13, 123, 68–69), but his
fame rests now with his satirical verse and, especially, his 'flora cubana'
poems. The association made throughout these latter poems is that between
womanhood and the flower. Again, like Melgar, the 'flora cubana' poems
have a poetic transparency which verges on the colloquial. As 'La flor del
café' opens:

> Prendado estoy de una
>    hermosa
> Por quien la vida daré
> Si me acoge cariñosa;
> Porque es cándida y hermosa
> Como la flor del café.   (Plácido 34)

Each of the following eleven stanzas ends with the refrain 'Como la flor del
café' and builds on the poetic association between coffee blossom and the
object of the poet's desire. One of Plácido's most elegant pieces is 'La flor de
la caña', a poem of nine verses each with twelve six-syllable lines, the twelfth
containing the refrain 'flor de la caña'. One important feature of Plácido's
verse, evident in this poem, is its re-moulding of the tradition of amatory
verse, the object of which was normally a white woman with blond hair.
Plácido's beloved, however, is a mulatto ('Veguera preciosa/ De la tez
tostada'; Plácido 39).[5] Some of the poems have a ribald tone. 'La calentura
no está en la ropa', for example, is an ironic, humorous poem about a local
prostitute, which is redolent of the caustic wit of Caviedes (Plácido 55).

## The Novel

It is often said that the Spanish-American novelists of the nineteenth
century do not compare well with some of the European masters such as
Tolstoy and Balzac, Stendhal and Dickens. One reason that has been adduced
is the lack of large cities in Spanish America in the nineteenth century; as
Sarmiento argued, it was in the large city that the artist had at his disposition
'esa multitud de acontecimientos de las grandes y poderosas ciudades, donde

---

5   Other poets of this period whose work cannot be studied here in any detail for reasons of space are Manuel Acuña (1849–1873), Rafael García Goyena (1766–1823), and
José Batres Montúfar (1809–1844). For a discussion of these and other minor poets of this
period, see Oviedo, *Historia*, vol. 1, 367–71, and Franco, *An Introduction to Spanish-
American Literature*, 74–77.

la especie humana aglomerada, oprimida, despedazada, deja oír a cada momento gritos tan terribles de desesperación, de dolor' (qtd. in Carilla, II, 72). But probably more compelling is the role of the intellectual influence that Europe exerted throughout the nineteenth century on Spanish-American writers. The artistic dilemma for the nineteenth-century novelist centred around the tension between describing a reality (the new post-independence reality) with an artistic medium (the Realist novel form) designed and implemented elsewhere (Europe).[6] The results, predictably enough, were mixed in success.

El Periquillo Sarniento (1816) by José Joaquín Fernández de Lizardi (1776–1827) is generally credited with being the first Spanish-American novel. The novel echoes the structure of the picaresque novel, as epitomized by Lazarillo de Tormes, in that it describes the misadventures of a young man driven on by hunger and poverty to make a way in the world, in which he must cheat to survive, and has a liberal amount of slap-stick humour (good examples of which occur during his residency as a doctor's assistant in Tula, and the episode when he attempts to steal jewelry from a corpse). Like the protagonist of Lazarillo de Tormes, Periquillo experiences a series of apprenticeships – in a ranch, a monastery, a barber's shop, a pharmacy – thereby learning a variety of trades which range from the socially prestigious (doctor's assistant, sacristan's assistant) to the dubious (croupier, cardsman) to the illegal (thief). The important part of these learning experiences is that they are all based on deception. The novel also describes Periquillo's marriage to one Mariana and his discussion, which takes up most of the third volume of the novel, with a Chinese chieftain, as a result of which he decides to give up the error of his former ways. Those elements which El Periquillo Sarniento shares with the great Spanish classic (i.e. those just described) are effective. But, unlike Lazarillo de Tormes, Fernández de Lizardi's novel inserts long, moralizing passages which expound on the moral meaning of the events described and, for the modern reader at least, reduce their impact. Another important influence, evident to good effect in the prologue to the second volume is Cervantes; like Don Quijote, the second volume opens with a discussion between the editor and a personage called Conocimiento about

---

6  I am using Realism here to mean a literary work which aspires to create 'the objective representation of contemporary social reality' (Wellek 241–42), and which shows man as embedded within a specific social fabric (Auerbach 431). There are a number of accompanying characteristics associated with the Realist style which (summarized from Ian Watt) are: (i) the use of non-traditional plots, either wholly invented or based in part on a contemporary incident, (ii) the plot is acted out by particular people in particular circumstances, (iii) characterization and presentation of background become essential elements, (iv) characters have ordinary contemporary proper names, (v) characters are rooted in the temporal dimension, (vi) the action takes place in an actual physical environment, (vii) the novel works by exhaustive presentation rather than by elegant concentration, and (viii) the novel's mode of imitating reality is similar to that of the jury in a court of law (Watt 15–31).

the reputation that Periquillo now has as a result of the publication of the first volume, as if to underscore that Periquillo is a real-life person.

The society which *El Periquillo Sarniento* describes is one which is in flux, particularly as far as the professional classes were concerned. The growing production for export made possible by expanding metropolitan markets and the faster ships employed in ocean trade in the eighteenth century led to new needs for intermediaries, credit facilities, and suppliers in urban centres, which was accompanied by the growth of a new class made up of doctors, lawyers, and merchants. Especially the second half of the seventeenth century in the Spanish colonies saw a displacement of power from the hands of the Church, the monarchy, and the landowning elite to this new self-aware professional class. A key date is 1778 when Charles III's Decree of Free Trade allowed the twenty-four ports of Spanish America to trade between themselves directly without any need for Spain as an intermediary. *El Periquillo Sarniento* is sensitive to these changing social phenomena and gives a vivid picture of a society under the Bourbons (whose family succeeded to the throne in 1713) which, gradually, was becoming more economically and politically independent from Spain. An indication of this change of ambience is evident in the opening pages of the novel. Some mention has already been made at the beginning of this chapter of the growth of a capital-based democracy which accompanied the democratisation of the written word at the turn of the eighteenth century, and the novel's prologue describes an imaginary conversation between the author and a friend who tries at first to persuade the former to dedicate his work to a wealthy patron, preferably a count, but then advises him to dedicate it to his readers since 'ellos son los que costean la impresión, y por lo mismo sus mecenas más seguros' (Fernández de Lizardi 3). In *El Periquillo Sarniento* we see at work what Anderson calls the 'national imagination' as encapsulated by 'the movement of a solitary hero through a sociological landscape of a fixity that fuses the world inside the novel with the world outside' (Anderson 35). It is not by chance that the first Spanish-American novel should refer to a new mode of production (capital-based entrepreneurial book production) and, by implication, to the new class from which it sprang, since the nineteenth-century novel is an outgrowth of the bourgeoisie. In Spanish America, as elsewhere, the growth of the new professional classes, including doctors, lawyers, merchants, suppliers, and, indeed, printers, was accompanied by a parasitical group of unqualified and dishonest professionals; it is these latter that *El Periquillo Sarniento* sets out to satirise.[7]

José Mármol (1817–1871) had the dubious distinction of experiencing at first hand the iron grip of Manuel Rosas's dictatorship and, in more senses

---

[7]  Other writers whose works can broadly be characterised as Realist during this period but which cannot be treated here are Alberto Blest Gana (1830–1920) and Ignacio Manuel Altamirano (1834–1893). For discussion of these and other minor Realists of this era, see Franco, *An Introduction to Spanish-American Literature* 70–73, 113–15.

than one, his work can profitably be studied in parallel with Echeverría's *El matadero* (see pp. 65–66). Mármol's claim to fame largely rests on his novel, *Amalia* (1851), which is normally remembered as the first Spanish-American dictator novel, being based on the life and regime of Juan Manuel Rosas who ruled Argentina with an iron fist for more than twenty years in the early nineteenth century. But perhaps more remarkable is the novel's uneasy mix between the fictional and the purportedly real, since it brings together within two covers an historically real individual, Rosas, and the conspicuously fictional, Eduardo (the archetypal *unitario*) and Amalia (the Romantic heroine and Eduardo's lover). The text strives to blur the distinction between the two realms; at the beginning of chapter X, for example, the omniscient narrator refers to 'escenas de que la imaginación duda, y de que la historia responde' (Mármol 107). History is thereby the guarantor of the events which appear in the novel. The whole of the political struggle between the *federales* and the *unitarios* which tore Argentina apart in the civil unrest of the first few decades of the nineteenth century is focussed on the competing wills of Rosas and the archetypal *unitario*, Eduardo, who is wounded badly in a street brawl early on, nursed back to health by Amalia (who promptly falls in love with him), and forced into exile at the conclusion of the novel; the ideology of the struggle is thus reduced to a more manageable scale, revolving around the competing wills of two men, and a love affair is added to spice up the ingredients. *Amalia* is very much a thesis novel in that we are left in no doubt whom to love and whom to hate; the *unitarios*, Eduardo and Amalia, are struggling to fall in love in a world hostile to them, while the *federales* are variously described as sadistic (Rosas who forces his daughter to kiss the priest against her wishes, chapter IV, and his sister-in-law, Doña María Josefa Ezcurra, who in the course of a surprise visit deliberately leans on Eduardo's injured thigh in order to cause him as much pain as possible, chapter XII) and physically repulsive (Mármol 122). Perhaps most tellingly of all, the threat of the *federales* is presented as an invasion of the domestic sphere; one of the results of Rosas's violence was that 'El hogar doméstico era invadido' (Mármol 126). Pointing in a similar direction, the title of the novel, which focusses on Amalia and her associations with receptive domesticity, shows Mármol's ideological affiliations to be Eurocentric, pro-urban and pro-bourgeois.

Jorge Isaacs (1837–1895) is celebrated in Colombia as much as elsewhere in Spanish America as an icon of the Romantic movement. His authorship of *María* (1867), the most famous of the nineteenth-century Romantic novels published in the Sub-Continent, certainly helped to foster this image. As a result of political instability, Isaacs's father lost his estate, which reduced his family to penury. His son, Jorge, was very much part of a moneyed generation forced to earn a living in the newly emerging capitalist society of his day as a result of circumstances beyond his control. In effect, it was that world of inherited rather than independently created wealth that Isaacs would look back to nostalgically, and was to form the emotional matrix of the nostalgia which coloured the literature he would one day write. It is for *María*, of course, that Isaacs is now remembered; essentially a Romantic novel set in rural Colombia, it describes in poignant detail the ill-starred love between the protagonist and first-person narrator, Efraín, and María.[8] Typical of many nineteenth-century Romantic novels, the protagonists spend much of their time not earning a living, marrying, and raising children; instead they spend their days being in love and, particularly evident in this novel, breaking down into tears at the slightest provocation. The plot is skimpy; Efraín, for as long as he can remember, has been in love with María; she has lived in the family home since the age of three when she was adopted by Efraín's father from a close friend, Salomón, whose wife had recently died. María is diagnosed as suffering from epilepsy but, despite this, Efraín's parents agree to the couple's desire to marry, although Efraín is sent away to London to finish his studies and thereby launch his career before the marriage takes place. In the two years that Efraín is away María gradually wilts; she dies before he returns. The emphasis in the novel, as the above suggests, is on what Freud identified as 'obstacle-love', that is, a sexual love which is characterised by repeated deferral and, eventually, non-consummation (Tanner 88). The love as projected in the novel as quiveringly platonic. The parting scene epitomises this; there is no verbal language, much body language, and many tears. María is sitting praying in the oratory and utters a 'weak cry' when she hears Efraín approach (chap. LIII; Isaacs 131). Efraín subsequently kisses María's forehead and the three suspension points which follow this statement ('Mis labios descansaron sobre su frente . . .') underline how momentous the occasion is felt to be. Also important in this scene is the religious motif; details such as Efraín's kneeling posture, María's parting gesture in which she points towards the altar ('extendió uno de los brazos para señalarme el altar') make very clear, if the name were not enough, that María is being explicitly conflated with the Mother of Christ (an image that occurs later on when María, already dead, is described as wearing 'un delantal azul como si hubiera sido formado de un jirón de cielo'; chap. LXIX; Isaacs 153). This becomes a highly-charged image given that the motif of incest occurs not only in the son-mother but the brother-sister paradigm; by the time María is nine years old, for example, she is seen as indistinguishable from Efraín's sisters (chap. VII; Isaacs 12). On one level this incestual pattern in *María* is to be understood as an allusion to the fascination with incest which characterised

---

8   Numerous editions of the novel abounded thoughout Spanish America in the second half of the nineteenth century. A play based on the novel, written by E. O. Palencia, was staged in the Teatro Baranquilla on 21 January 1892, and published the same year. *María: leyenda dramática tomada de la novela del mismo hombre, de don Jorge Isaacs.* Baranquilla: Imprenta Americana, The Old Reliable, E. P. Pellet, Proprietario, 1892. Miscelánea, No. 90, Biblioteca Nacional, Santafe de Bogotá. A movie version of the novel was made and shown in Bogotá in 1922; unfortunately the film has been lost.

Romantic literature; we may recall here Byron's contention that 'great is their love who live in sin and fear' (qtd. in Praz 73). It is also a specific allusion to Chateaubriand's *Le Génie du Christianisme* which describes the socially impossible love between a brother and sister and which Efraín and María read together ecstatically and mournfully (chaps. XII–XIII).

The form of Isaacs's novel is striking since it gives less the impression of being a polished work and has that disregard for form which is the hallmark of the epic. Thus, the novel is constructed around a series of interludes which fill out the resonance of the main action (Efraín's love for María), such as the hunting expedition during which Efraín shoots a tiger (chap. XXI), and the story of how Feliciana came to America from Africa (chaps. XL–XLIII). Even the *post facto* blow-by-blow description of María's death is introduced as a transcription of the account given to Efraín by his sister, Emma (chap. LXII). This, indeed, underlines the future perfect atmosphere of the novel, its insistence on the importance of memory. The continuity of the love theme and the use of recurrent symbols, however, manage to ensure that *María* is a unified work of art. The two most significant examples of symbolism are the flowers which María repeatedly places in Efraín's bedroom as a sign of her love (the devotional resonances are clear here too), and the sinister blackbird which appears in the narrative on three crucial occasions – when the first clear sign of María's illness appears (chap. XV; Isaacs 20), when the fatal letter arrives which announces the bankruptcy of Efraín's father's business (chap. XXXIV; Isaacs 74), and, at the end of the novel, as an emblem of María's death when it lands on her tombstone (chap. LXV; Isaacs 154).

## Short Story

With *El matadero* (written 1838; published 1871) by Esteban Echeverría (1805–1851) came the birth of the short story in Latin America. It is an effective if at times over-obvious allegory of the struggle between the Unitarians and the Federalists in Argentina in the second quarter of the nineteenth century. In an essay, 'Ojeada retrospectiva', written in exile in Montevideo in 1848, Echeverría described Argentina during those years as characterised by 'dos facciones irreconciliables por sus odios' (Echeverría 155). *El matadero* employs the slaughter-house as a symbol of Argentine society under Rosas's despotic rule, and the allegory shuttles between the image of the human body and that of the body politic. The local level of the image of the slaughter-house involves reference to the greatest source of capital over which the Federalists, a loose federation of ranch-owners and Rosas's die-hard supporters, had direct control: beef livestock. Echeverría also manages to use this image to poke fun at the Catholic Church of the time, stressing the Church's connivance with the Federalists in forcing beef prices up when prohibiting the consumption of meat during Lent (Echeverría 427–28). The Church is projected as a restrictive organization better suited in Echeverría's eyes to pre-independence days (Echeverría 432). Throughout the story the connections between the slaughter-house and Rosas's regime are underlined, at times in an over-obvious way. When the slaughter-house workers turn on a bull, as if the political metaphor were not clear enough already, one of them remarks: 'Es emperrado y arisco como un unitario' (Echeverría 436). Some details are a little more subtle. When chasing the bull, which is as we have seen a symbol of the Unitarian cause, there are two casualties; the first is the child who is decapitated (destruction of innocence) and the second is the 'gringo' who is knocked down in the rush (destruction of the good will of foreign investors). Though a seemingly insignificant detail, the allegory is loaded from a Unitarian perspective. The Unitarians espoused the doctrine of free trade based on the harbour of Buenos Aires, and were bitterly opposed to what they saw as the Federalists' closed-market philosophy and use of high protectionist tariffs which frightened foreign investors away. This much is hinted at in the detail.

*El matadero* is curious in that the use of allegory (sacrifice of the bull) then leads into a stretch of Realist narrative (an actual Unitarian appears on the scene). Rather than being killed by the Federalists, however, as might have been expected giving the allegorical playing-out of a Federalist execution just before, the Unitarian explodes into a pool of blood caused by the outrage of being undressed, which is probably to be understood as denoting allegorically the divestment of his Unitarian culture: 'Entonces un torrente de sangre brotó borbolloneando de la boca y las narices del joven y exten-diéndose empezó a caer a chorros por entreambos lados de la mesa' (Echeverría 442). The final image is one of political defiance on the part of the Unitarian in the face of inevitable destruction by the Federalists: suicide is preferable to defeat, the metaphor suggests. The image of the body is crucial here since it acts as an allegory mediating between the national and the personal drama. Although bodily violation (either in the form of castration or rape) is not explicitly mentioned in the second scene in which the Unitarian has his clothes pulled off, its potency is evoked through associative juxtaposition with the earlier scene in which the testicles are cut out of the dead bull's body ('¡Aquí están los huevos!'; Echeverría 438), and details of the scene which operate as displaced images of rape (scissors are mentioned repeatedly, the Federalists cut off the Unitarian's sideburns, they expose his buttocks for punishment, etc.). This adds a further level of association which helps to explain the artistic logic behind the image of the Unitarian's exploding body. Just as the body politic is violated and confined by Rosas's dictatorship, both of which ideas are suggested in the slaughter-house image, so the only appropriate image of escape is one of bodily explosion which defies the confinements of forced bondage.[9]

---

[9] Another significant short-story writer of this period whose work is not discussed here is the Chilean Daniel Riquelme (1857–1912).

## Theatre

Nineteenth-century Spanish-American drama has little of the vigour of its European counterparts. There were flourishing theatre houses in the major Spanish-American cities, but most of the works put on derived in the main from Spain and France. The most popular works staged were by Alexandre Dumas, Victor Hugo, Larra, García Gutiérrez, Ventura de la Vega, Zorrilla, Bretón de los Herreros, Hartzenbusch, and Ducange; plays by Shakespeare, Schiller, Martínez de la Rosa and Moratín also enjoyed some popularity (Carilla, II, 40–41). The three most memorable dramatists of the mid nineteenth century were the Mexican, Manuel Eduardo de Gorostiza (1789–1851), born in Veracruz, and the two Peruvians, Felipe Pardo y Aliaga (1806–1868), and Manuel Ascensio Segura (1805–1871). The work of these dramatists concentrates on the nodal point of the middle-class way of life in the nineteenth century, namely, the family. In the nineteenth century, as Tony Tanner has pointed out, middle-class society viewed marriage as sacrosanct, the 'all- subsuming, all-organizing, all-containing contract' (Tanner 15). The most well-known plays by these three authors focus, indeed, on the centrality of marriage, and specifically on the struggle, common in Spanish Romantic drama, between the will of the parents and the desire of the daughter as to the latter's marriage partner. What makes these plays different from their Spanish counterparts – plays such as Duque de Rivas's *Don Álvaro o la fuerza del sino* (1835), Antonio García Gutiérrez's *El Trovador* (1836) and José de Zorrilla's *Don Juan Tenorio* (1844) – is that the Spanish plays typically end in death for one or both of the lovers, while the Spanish-American plays tend to express more pragmatism with regard to the dilemma of choice between a marriage based on romantic love or one based on social pedigree; they often conclude voting on the side of happiness rooted in domesticity.

Gorostiza's play, *Contigo pan y cebolla* (1833), for example, has all the classic ingredients of a Romantic play: Doña Matilde is in love with Don Eduardo de Contreras and, against the wishes of her father, Don Pedro de Lara, she plans to elope with her lover. The play is careful to point out that Doña Matilde's views about love have been created by her literary readings. In the opening scene of the play, the servant, Bruno, scolds her for staying up too late reading (Luzuriaga & Reeve 204). And when Matilde first sees Eduardo, it becomes clear that she is dramatising the events of her own life and attempting to fit them into a preconceived literary stereotype; Eduardo says he is late because he had to shave and she replies that she would have expected him to arrive without having shaved if he had travelled non-stop for three or four days to see her, but, since he only lives down the street, his excuse seems reasonable (Act I, Scene ii; Luzuriaga & Reeve 206). This amusing interface between Matilde's expectations about her future elopement and the reality continues throughout the play; one of the most comical scenes occurs when she refuses to leave the house through the door, but insists on squeezing through the window instead. Attempting to compress her life into the shape of a Romantic cliché, she refuses Eduardo's offer of marriage once it becomes clear that her father is in favour of such a union (Act I, Scene viii). Bruno subsequently comments that women have changed: 'las nuestras pasaban sus días y sus noches haciendo caleta . . . Pero las de ahora, como todas leen la *Gaceta* y saben dónde está Pekín, ¿qué sucede? Que se le va el tiempo en averiguar lo que no les importa . . . y ni cuidan de casarse, ni saben cómo se espuma el puchero' (Luzuriaga & Reeve 216). It is noteworthy that reading the *Gaceta de México* should be seen as the cause of a paradigm shift in the social behaviour of women. Indeed, Matilde only decides to run off with Eduardo once she 'discovers' (it is, in fact, an elaborate trick) that he has been disinherited. And, once she does elope, she is very much disillusioned by her meagre life in a garret, and is humiliated when one of her friends, the marchioness, comes to visit and lord it over her. As soon as her father asks her to come home, Matilde agrees to do so, much to her lover's chagrin; Eduardo comments wryly that the pleasures of indigence which Matilde is now giving up still have merit in the eyes of 'las jóvenes de diecisiete años que leen novelas' (Act IV, Scene xi; Luzuriaga & Reeve 250).

*Frutos de la educación*, by Felipe Pardo y Aliaga, which was first staged in the Teatro de Lima on 6 August 1829, once more focusses on the generational conflict about the value of marriage. Don Feliciano, because of some business losses, is keen to marry off his daughter, Pepita, to Bernardo, a young man who is soon to inherit a great deal of wealth. The mother, Doña Juana, aided and abetted by her brother-in-law, Don Manuel, favours an English businessman, Don Eduardo, as a better candidate. The struggle between the husband and wife, which also appears (and virulently so) in *Ña Catita* (see p. 69), is intensified by the question of cultural difference; Don Eduardo is English and therefore assumed to be a heretic by Don Feliciano (Act II, Scene iv; Pardo y Aliaga 81). The play is rather slow-moving and has many scenes, such as the description of the marchioness's ball, which are essentially *costumbrista* pieces which have the effect of slowing the play down. The play does not really possess a *desenlace* since, by the final act of the play, Pepita is left with no suitor in sight; Don Eduardo goes back on his word to marry her because he saw her dancing an Afro-Peruvian dance, the *zamacueca*, in an over-suggestive way, while Bernardo decides to marry somebody else. The significance given to subaltern culture as a result of this appears not to be accidental. The play ends with a speech given by Don Feliciano ostensibly to advise his daughter, but which at the same time serves as an assessment of the moral health of the (Peruvian) nation; he advises her, as a *criolla,* to avoid mixing with the lower classes by, for example, dancing the *zamacueca* (Act III, Scene xi; Pardo y Aliaga 164). This echoes the white-aesthetic ideology of the play taken as a whole in the sense that the one Negro who appears, Perico, is treated as a caricature; he is called a savage by

Don Manuel and a devil by Doña Juana (Pardo y Aliaga 130, 161). Yet, more than simply a part of a process of grotesque caricaturing, Africanness seems to exist in *Los frutos de la educación* as the skeleton in the cupboard; it is, after all, Perico who brings news of the identity of Bernardo's intended; she is a *mulatiya* (Pardo y Aliaga 160), whom he met, presumably, in one of his secret nocturnal sallies to the other side of town, and on whose account he lost his reputation in Doña Juana's eyes. These elements, when placed together, point to the prickly nature of the issue of race in the play. Pepita loses one (upper-class) man because she is associated with the lower classes, and loses another man to a woman of a lower class; her intermediary position at the conclusion of the play, stuck in the middle of two social/racial options, portrays perhaps the ideological unease of the middle class of the time with regard to citizens of African descent who were perceived to be encroaching on the 'sacrosanct' space occupied by the social institution of marriage. If anything, thus, Pardo y Aliaga's play speaks out against the social validity of the notion of Romantic love, since the latter involves the risk of racially dangerous liaisons.

A similar distance with regard to the Romantic ideal of love expressed so fervently in a play like Duque de Rivas's *Don Álvaro o la fuerza del sino*, is evident in Ascensio Segura's delightfully well-written play *Ña Catita* (1856) which, again, begins with all the ingredients of a Romantic drama: two lovers, Manuel and Juliana, desire to get married but are thwarted in this by Juliana's mother, Doña Rufina, and her dastardly accomplice, Ña Catita, a hypocritical old maid who will stop at nothing to ruin other people's happiness; instead they propose a young man, Alejo, a pompous pedant who appears to be wealthy. Their plans are dashed, however, when one of Alejo's friends arrives and hands Alejo a letter from his wife (Act IV, Scene xiv). After this *deus ex machina* device the play only has one place to go, and the marriage of Manuel and Juliana is assured. The play concludes on a note of moralism: 'Desconfía, en adelante,/ del que ostenta beatitud,/ y de todo hombre pedante,/ que nunca fue la virtud/ ficciosa ni petulante' (Luzuriaga & Reeve 354). It is quite clear that Ascensio is satirising in this play the middle class's acquisitive and capitalist attitude towards the choice of marriage partners. The moral of *Ña Catita* is that arranged marriages are misguided and that unions based on mutual consent and Romantic love are necessary for the well-being of society.

## Essay

Perhaps the single most important post-independence essay is the *Carta de Jamaica* (1815) by Simón Bolívar (1783–1830). The letter was composed in Jamaica and dated 6 September 1815, when Bolívar was gathering his strength and troops in preparation for his counter-attack on Royalist forces in

Venezuela and New Granada. Though written in response to a letter of enquiry from a sympathiser ('Contestación de un americano meridional a un caballero de esta isla'), the letter is in effect an independence manifesto. It begins by stating that the paths of Spain and its American colonies are now distinct; Spain is no longer the mother country but a 'desnaturalizada madrastra' (Bolívar 38). Bolívar then describes the population of the main political blocks of Spanish America, including Río de la Plata, Chile, Perú, Nueva Granada, Venezuela, New Spain, and the Caribbean (Puerto Rico and Cuba). That his letter is directed to Europe is suggested by his rhetorical question: '¿Y la Europa civilizada, comerciante y amante de la libertad, permite que una vieja serpiente, por sólo satisfacer su saña envenenada, devore la más bella parte de nuestro globo?' (Bolívar 41). Much of the rest of the letter is designed to persuade the Western powers to intervene in the struggle for independence then in full swing. Bolívar complains that Spain is sucking its colonies dry of wealth and, as a representative *criollo*, complains that they have been excluded from office and power, 'ausentes del universo en cuanto es relativo a la ciencia del gobierno y administración del estado' (Bolívar 48). The political position that Bolívar subsequently fleshes out is intriguing; he argues that neither federalism nor democracy are entirely suitable for the newly-independent nations of Spanish America (Bolívar 53), and also argues against the notion of a republic (Bolívar 55). He concludes his essay by suggesting that Spanish America will achieve independence but different parts will do so in different ways (some democratic, some federal, some monarchical). It is clear from his concluding statements that his own political ideal was a strong, unified republic ('una sola nación con un solo vínculo que ligue sus partes entre sí y con el todo'; Bolívar 61). This, however, was not to be and twenty years later Spanish America was already well along the path of division. The *Carta de Jamaica* was by no means the only document that Bolívar wrote during the turbulent years of independence; he wrote eighty-three letters to his allies in the independence movement during the period 1812–1829 (Bolívar, *Documentos*) and most repeat his ideological repertoire: war against Spain, bring the European powers, especially England, into the conflict, and conserve unity after independence. But no letter puts these main points over as forcefully as the *Carta de Jamaica*.

The most celebrated prose work written in Latin America in the nineteenth century was undoubtedly *Facundo o civilización y barbarie* (1845) by Domingo Faustino Sarmiento (1811–1888). Like Echeverría and Mármol mentioned above, Sarmiento fell foul of Rosas's regime; after the Unitarian defeat at the battle of Chañón in 1831, he was forced to flee to Chile, and he was to remain in exile throughout Rosas's dictatorship. *Facundo o civilización y barbarie*, as the title suggests, is primarily about the Argentine *gaucho caudillo*, Juan Facundo Quiroga (1793–1835), but also about the dichotomy in nineteenth-century Argentina between civilisation and barbarism. Sarmiento's basic thesis is that western culture was the only way forward and that the main problem with Argentina was its savage, untamed land. An important after-effect of Sarmiento's text was the policy in the last two decades of the nineteenth century in Argentina of 'gobernar es poblar' which effectively led to the massive immigration of Italian and Spanish workers along with the ruthless decimation of the remaining Indian tribes in the Argentine hinterland, while simultaneously 'whitening' the population. Even though Sarmiento's text promotes Europe and the rapidly emerging United States as the paragons of the social model to be followed by Argentina, it also expresses a sneaking admiration for the 'natural savage' prototype (and here Sarmiento shows his Romantic credentials), typified by ruthless individuals such as Quiroga, known for his ability to trick individuals into confessing their guilt and for confronting man-eating tigers and winning (Chapter V, 1; Flores 203–204). In this way Sarmiento repeats all the anecdotes which led to Quiroga's 'reputación misteriosa' (Chapter V, 2; Flores 206) which in effect does nothing to dampen its power.

## The Multi-genre Writer

Gertrudis Gómez de Avellaneda (1814–1873), although born in Cuba, spent much of her life in Spain. Avellaneda left Cuba in 1836 and, apart from a five-year period when she returned (1859–1864), she resided for the remainder of her days and, indeed, established her literary career in Spain. She is without doubt one of the most significant women writers of the nineteenth century, and she wrote in the three main genres. Despite this her candidacy in 1853 for membership in the Spanish Royal Academy of Letters was denied. Avellaneda's poetry typifies the Romantic mentality, is defiantly related to biographical events, and focusses above all on the themes of death and love and their interconnectedness. For this, in her view, she had a unique perspective as a woman since her gender provided her with the 'title of sovereignty in the immense sphere of the emotions', as she put it (Meyer 25). A frequently anthologised poem, 'Al partir', written, if we accept the poetic convention, on the boat as she left Cuba for Spain, emphasises the sense of fragmentation and loss associated with (self-imposed) exile. Typical of the Romantics, Avellaneda's view of love is of an all-powerful, chaotic and often malevolent force. Her two poems with the same title, 'A él', both dedicated to Ignacio de Cepeda y Alcalde with whom she had a stormy love affair soon after her arrival in Spain, abound in metaphors of nature and transcendance. The first shows the 'él' of the title as produced idealistically within nature before she meets her lover, and compares the fascination that her lover has over her to that of the serpent over the bird, an animal with whom she often compared herself when in love (Avellaneda 69). The second treats their love affair, now over, as guided by divine forces: 'No era tuyo el poder que irresistible/ Postró ante ti mis fuerzas vencedoras/ Quísolo Dios' (Avellaneda

147). The metaphors used in the poem give an indication of the class-value of the backdrop against which their love affair is measured. The sixth stanza opens with the line, 'Cayó tu cetro, se embotó tu espada . . .' (Avellaneda 147), which points to the aristocratic/tragic nature of the love projected in the poem. Avellaneda's most famous poem, however, is 'A la muerte del célebre poeta cubano Don José María de Heredia', dedicated to one of the many Latin-American poets who died in their mid-thirties (Heredia, like Plácido and Batres Montúfar, was only thirty-five when he died, Melgar was only twenty-five!). Like many poems of this type, Avellaneda uses the death of a loved one to inquire into metaphysical matters. As we have already noted, Heredia was a fierce 'independentista' who was condemned to death for his political beliefs; little of this, however, surfaces in Avellaneda's elegy to him. Heredia is remembered as 'el férvido patriota' (line 10; Avellaneda 71), and the ideal for which he fought, his 'patria', is described as '¡Idolo puro de las nobles almas!' (line 28; Avellaneda 72), but the main emphasis of the poem diverts attention away from the political towards the transcendance of his ideal achieved through death. 'A la muerte del célebre poeta cubano Don José María de Heredia', thus, is an important statement of her own political position during the post-independence epoch. While Heredia was forced into exile from his country, Avellaneda accepted the colonial structure which underlay the Spanish monarchy (she wrote a poem of homage to Queen Isabel II, and the Spanish monarchs were godparents at her wedding to Domingo Verdugo y Massieu in 1855; Avellaneda 134–38, 11), and appeared to place her faith in the dispensation of true justice in the next world.

Avellaneda's *Sab* (1841) is often remembered for its historical, anti-abolitionist content but there is more to *Sab* than first meets the eye. Set in Cuba in the early years of the nineteenth century when the Caribbean island was still a Spanish colony, this novel tells the story of a mulatto slave's love for his master's daughter, Carlota, with whom he spent most of his child-hood. When Carlota finally decides to marry the son of a rich English priva-teer, Enrique, son of Jorge Otway, he dies heartbroken, and he leaves evidence of his love in a long, passionate letter he writes to Teresa, Carlota's maid. This letter, whose content Carlota finally becomes aware of five years after Sab's death, is the finale to the novel. Though the story is predictable enough (a Cuban slave who falls in love with a white woman and who dies heartbroken when his love is not returned), the author is not eager to stress the realistic qualities of the plot, showing a fondness for the *deus ex machina* device so dear to the heart of the Romantics. Sab's brother, Luis, for example, dies soon after he is visited by Sab; Sab dies soon after his brother's death and, to underline the supernatural nature of the event, at the precise moment when Carlota and Enrique are pronouncing their marriage vows: 'Sab expiró a las seis de la mañana; en esa misma hora Enrique y Carlota recibían la bendición nupcial' (199). The characters, in a way which is remi-niscent of the Romantic rather than the Realist mode, are larger-than-life types: Enrique Otway, the English villain of the piece, only marrying Carlota because of her money; Carlota, a mindless *criolla* whose mind is only on love; Teresa, a long-suffering maid in denial; Sab, the noble savage who dies of love. Indeed, the stereotyping at times goes rather awry. In the case of Sab, the enigma of this text, this is most in evidence. Sab bears little resemblance to the historical mulatto; he is more like a *criollo* disguised as a mulatto. This is clear when he begins speaking to Enrique Otway in the dramatically charged opening chapter of the novel; Enrique is so impressed by Sab's speech, clothes and demeanour that he assumes he is a landowner. These signals of social, reinforced by spiritual, nobility continue throughout the novel, such that we almost forget that Sab is a mulatto. In this sense we can agree with Richard Jackson's conclusion about the novel: '[t]hough camouflaged by . . . her antislavery pronouncements, Gómez de Avellaneda's false tears are nevertheless manifest in her apologetic descriptions of other slaves and in her penchant for portraying them as being tranquil, docile, and happy with their lot, indeed, even unaware of their misfortune' (*Black Image* 27).

If we look more closely at Sab as the symptom of a dilemma, his role becomes clearer. On one level the novel projects the personal anguish the author felt as a result of unrequited love but, on another level, it allegorises the national dilemma. Cuba, throughout the nineteenth century, was torn between two power factions, the *criollos* who wanted independence from Spain and the *peninsulares* who opposed such an idea. We only find reference to this historical dilemma in the novel if we assume that the veiling process has gone one step further to include the main characters, such that Sab stands for the *criollo* option just as Enrique stands for the *peninsular* option (in this scenario Carlota, standing for Cuba, would be the prize to be won as a result of this historical struggle). What makes this allegory stronger in the novel is that Sab's testament appears in the form of a letter; 'Carta de Sab' is the title of the last chapter of the novel. This letter reads like a reworking of Bolívar's *Carta de Jamaica*, since there are manifold references to Sab's desire to die for his country, although this was not exactly a theme raised in the rest of the novel, and strikes the reader as oddly inopportune. The veiling hypothesis also works here, since Avellaneda was in the unusual situation of being a Cuban émigrée living in Spain, and therefore not in a position to bite the hand that fed her. If we see the novel as an example of veiled self-expression, as it undoubtedly is, then the kernel of its meaning lies in its promotion of the female desire for sexual, political and emotional liberation even at the same time that the validity of this desire is negated. *Sab* the novel is itself a kind of post-factum linguistic event, like Sab's letter within its covers, since it is the only means whereby the desire for liberation could be expressed. In a sense, therefore, Avellaneda pronounces a death sentence on herself, since she places herself in a similar position to Sab's, the difference being that Sab dies when he speaks his truth, and Avellaneda distorts the ingredients of her personal narrative in order to avoid the kernel of her desire being openly expressed. *Sab* is, therefore, anything but a transparent anti-slavist novel; it is rather a subtly veiled document which expresses a feminist desire for liberation even while, simultaneously, debunking its validity.

Among Avellaneda's more famous plays are *Saúl* (1846) and *Baltasar* (1858). *Saúl* (completed 1846; first performed 1849), the more significant of the two, recounts in dramatic form the story of Saul, King of Israel who, despite being consecrated by Yahweh, later turns from Him and commits a number of evil deeds, among which is his plotting to kill his son-in-law, David, through jealousy of his fame and military valour (I Samuel 10–31). *Saúl* follows the biblical text in its main outline and even in some of the small details, such as Saul's visit to the medium at Endor and the resuscitation in bodily form of Samuel's spirit (I Samuel 28; Act IV, Scene VII). The few changes made to the plot, such as the suppression of the fact that David had other wives apart from Michal (Abigail and Ahinoam; I Samuel 25: 39–44) and the addition of the murder of Jonathan by his father, Saul (Act IV, Scene XIV; the Old Testament suggests that Jonathan committed suicide after his father; I Samuel 31: 3–4), streamline the play and emphasise the motif, in effect converting a narrative concerned with succession in the Royal House of Israel into a Romantic love story between David and Saul's daughter, who is hardly mentioned in the Bible. The biblical story, however, lends itself very well to this treatment since it includes a 'family romance', namely a generational conflict compounded by sexual love, which is one of the mainstays of the Romantic plot (Hart, *Other* 7–18). Other devices in the play emphasise its Romantic pedigree. Act IV, for example, opens with a scene in which David and Jonathas dramatically reveal their identities by taking their masks off. There are abundant references to a malevolent fate, one example being Jonathas's question to his father (which will be proved correct): '¿La fatal dolencia/ Se anuncia ya con tétricos amagos?' (Gómez de Avellaneda 168), as well as to the supernatural world (Samuel's dramatic appearance as a ghost at the end of Act IV, Scene VII is redolent of the appearance of the statue in Zorrilla's *Don Juan Tenorio*). Yet, despite these Romantic elements, Avellaneda's play is distinct in that it does not exclude the possibility of a happy ending, something which typically Romantic plays could not have countenanced. *Saúl*, indeed, ends with the suggestion that, now Saul has died, David and Micol will ascend to the throne and live happily ever after. Unlike other of Avellaneda's dramas, there is no third party in a love triangle to mar the happiness of David and Micol (Harter 97). This is the reason why the play is called a 'biblical tragedy' by Avellaneda in her prologue (Gómez de Avellaneda 141), which we must assume to mean 'a play with a happy ending'. But, more important for our purposes, *Saúl* refocusses the biblical story from a personal and feminine rather than social and male perspective; in effect Micol gets what she wants and her dream comes true. Avellaneda's play therefore contains glimpses of a feminine perspective in that, unlike the Book of Samuel which narrates the story from the point of view of David and Jonathan, the main drama of *Saúl* is focussed from the feminine perspective of Micol and her maid servant Sela (Act I, Scenes ii–iii; Act I, Scene xii; Act II, Scene v; Act III, Scene i).

Chapter 4

# NINETEENTH-CENTURY LITERATURE: PART II

The second half of the nineteenth century was the period in which the Spanish-American writer saw his craft becoming much more professional-ised, but typically he had to resort to journalism to support his creative writing (see Rama *Crítica* 83–84). The main difference in terms of the writ-er's role in society during this period when compared with the previous century was the absence of an explicit connection between print and state power (normally in the form of a position sponsored by the Viceroy) and the emergence of a new type of social value attached to print in the form of the newspaper article. If there is one thing which characterises the writers of the late nineteenth century it is their social position as a relayer of information about decisions taken by others. Many of the *modernistas*, for example, were journalists or diplomats, and some were both. This is, indeed, what journal-ists and diplomats have in common; one step removed from the decision-making process associated with statecraft, they relay that information on to other members of the society in which they live. The writers of this period, especially the *modernistas*, might be seen as 'diplomats' of the literary Word, using smooth words to relay on truths dictated to them from on high.[1]

*Modernismo*, which should not be confused with its English cognate Mod-ernism, is the first example of a genuinely Latin-American literary move-ment, 'strong' enough in Bloom's phrase, to produce ripples in the Old World. With *modernismo*, and particularly the work of Rubén Darío, Latin America became no longer simply an echo chamber of bigger events happen-ing elsewhere, but was now at the centre of its creative movement. While this is undeniable in artistic terms we would do well to heed Angel Rama when he argues convincingly that *modernismo* was the cultural equivalent of the imperial expansion of capitalism which characterised the relationship between Latin America and Europe at the turn of the century (*Crítica* 19–33), the prototype being the export-import growth of Argentina's economy during

---

[1]  For a short description of the careers of the *modernistas*, see Schulman & Picon Garfield, *Poesía modernista hispanoamericana*, which has a very helpful short biography for each poet included in the anthology. It is striking how similar the careers of the writers of this period are. It is important to note that there is a perceptible paradigm shift from the role of the writer in the Romantic era – epitomised by Bello the legislator – and the *modernista*, typically a journalist/diplomat.

the last two decades of the nineteenth century (Skidmore & Smith 44–48). *Modernismo* was an intrinsically literary movement spearheaded by the Nicaraguan poet, Rubén Darío (1867–1916), and its dates are normally given as emerging in 1888 (with the publication of Darío's *Azul* . . .) and off the literary horizon by 1916 (the year of Darío's death), including a period of decline from 1910 until 1916. *Modernismo*'s gradual movement of crescendo followed by a diminuendo after the apex around the turn of the century is best understood in visual terms (see next page).

The main sources of inspiration for the *modernistas* were not Spanish but French poets, particularly the Parnassians and the Symbolists. The main themes were aestheticism, exoticism, cosmopolitanism, escapism, scepticism, indifference to moral issues, fascination with death, pessimism, and melancholy. The metaphors and symbols of the *modernistas* typically refer to an ideal realm of regal splendour; their favourite symbols of elegance are the swan, the peacock, the lily, precious gems, and the nocturne.

Many writers, and particularly the *modernistas*, however, were not content with their new social role. While they were protective of their freedom to say what they wanted, they were disgruntled by the lack of a stable employment based on that ability. Manuel Gutiérrez Nájera, in particular, was depressed by what he saw as the social demeaning of the writer. Even brilliant writers such as the Greek dramatists Aristophanes and Aeschylus, he argued, would have ended up as third-rate hacks in the nineteenth century (qtd. in Rama, *Crítica* 85). For many of the writers of the period, literature was, in Lafleur's word, a 'pretext', a prelude to greater things (Lafleur 14). This period was also accompanied by an unprecedented growth of literary societies whose aim was to provide a forum for the reading and discussion of literature. One of the most successful of these literary societies was the Ateneo de Buenos Aires, officially inaugurated on 26 April 1893, presided over by Carlos Guido Spano, and which met in a house on the calle Florida, no. 783 (Lafleur 15).

Important precursors of the *modernista* movement were Salvador Díaz Mirón (1853–1928), Manuel Gutiérrez Nájera (1859–1895), Julián del Casal (1863–1893), and José Asunción Silva (1865–1896), and the one thing linking these poets is their attention to the technical art of poetic composition. Díaz Mirón's striking poem, 'Ejemplo', for instance, inspired by the sight of a dead man hanging from a tree, is written in alexandrines which have three 'esdrújulo' rhymes ('patíbulo', line 10; 'turíbulo', line 12; 'Tíbulo', line 14). Despite the stench of the man's corpse, as the poem concludes, the countryside around him is worthy of an elegiac poem by the Latin poet, Tibullus (59–19 B.C.) (Schulman & Picón Garfield 53–55). Gutiérrez Nájera's best poem, 'Mis enlutadas', has sixteen five-line stanzas, each stanza combining different metrical patterns, with the normal pattern being hendecasyllables (line 1 and line 3), heptasyllables (line 2), and pentasyllables (line 5); this descending pyramidal metric structure echoes formally the semantic

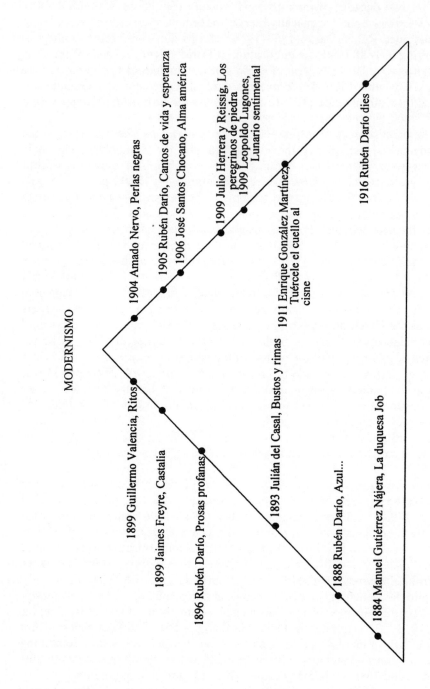

MODERNISMO

1904 Amado Nervo, Perlas negras

1905 Rubén Darío, Cantos de vida y esperanza

1906 José Santos Chocano, Alma américa

1909 Julio Herrera y Reissig, Los peregrinos de piedra
1909 Leopoldo Lugones, Lunario sentimental

1911 Enrique González Martínez, Tuércele el cuello al cisne

1916 Rubén Darío dies

1899 Guillermo Valencia, Ritos

1899 Jaimes Freyre, Castalia

1896 Rubén Darío, Prosas profanas

1893 Julián del Casal, Bustos y rimas

1888 Rubén Darío, Azul...

1884 Manuel Gutiérrez Nájera, La duquesa Job

movement of the poem which searches out the sadness contained within the poet's subconscious, employing a confessional cadre to do so. One of Julián del Casal's best poems, 'Crepuscular', focusses on a seascape at dusk in which images of violence and disharmony abound; the sunset is compared to the sun dripping from a 'split open stomach' (line 1), the noise of seagulls becomes a 'chirrido agudo' (line 6), and the seaweed is described as covered with 'infecto lodo' (line 14). This dissonance is echoed on a formal level by the metric structure of the poem; the five quatrains are dodecasyllables except for the fifth line ('Alzan sus moles húmedas los arrecifes') which has thirteen syllables and introduces a note of barely audible dissymmetry into the poem. Asunción Silva, for his part, in his most famous poem, 'Nocturno' (1894), written to express his anguish at the death of his sister, evinces a bold desire to reformulate the stanzaic structures which had traditionally modelled the expression of poetic thought until then, combining long with short lines and repeating phrases as if they were refrains. Also striking about this poem is its refusal to retreat to the world of Greek mythology or Christian symbolism; its point of reference is the quotidian, itself suggested by the recourse to a conversational tone in opposition to the abstract dignity of rhymed verse and, in this, Silva was more prescient than Darío about the direction that twentieth-century poetry would follow.

Rubén Darío (1867–1916) dominated the literary horizon of Spanish America at the turn of the century. The narrative of his life – born an orphan, perpetually travelling either as a correspondent for *La Nación* or in search for new experiences, a string of unhappy and passionate love affairs on different continents – suggests perpetual displacement and, indeed, centerlessness. This is a motif that binds together what are normally seen as the three stages of his work, which centre around *Azul* . . . (1888), *Prosas profanas* (1896) and *Cantos de vida y esperanza* (1905). *Azul* . . . combines short prose poems in the Baudelairean style with fifteen poems dedicated, in the main, to weather seasons, legendary Greek figures and famous contemporary poets. The opening prose poem, 'El rey burgués', sets the tone for the whole collection in its affirmation of a non-bourgeois, aristocratic type of art which rejects the dictates of commercialism. The most striking characteristic of *Prosas profanas* was, certainly for readers of the time, its innovatory versification. In the collection of poems, Darío mixed half-conventional forms – sonnets whose rhyme was orthodox but had more than the traditional eleven-syllable lines (most were French-inspired alexandrines such as 'El cisne'; Darío 587–88) – with unconventional forms such as the elegy to Paul Verlaine, 'Responso', which followed a syllabic pattern of 14-14-7 throughout (a sort of inflated 'copla de pie quebrado'), the 'Elogio de la seguidilla' (Darío 586) which resurrected an irregular Castilian metre not used since the Renaissance, as well as 'La página blanca' which combines assonant rhyme with a gradually increasing ametricality (Darío 588–89), among many other variations. Darío's 'galicismo mental', as Juan Valera called it, led him to seek an ethnically white poetic ideal; as he suggested in the prologue to *Prosas profanas*: '¿Hay en mi sangre alguna gota de sangre de Africa, o de indio chorotega o nagrandano? Pudiera ser, a despecho de mis manos de marqués; mas he aquí que veréis en mis versos princesas, reyes, cosas imperiales, visiones de países lejanos o imposibles: ¡qué queréis!, yo detesto la vida y el tiempo en que me tocó nacer' (Darío 546). Indeed, many of the poems explicitly follow the blueprint set out here. 'Era un aire suave . . .', for example, describes a utopian social gathering hosted by Eulalia the marchioness and attended by Greek gods and goddesses such as Terminus (Pluto), Diana, Eros, and Philomela. 'Divagación' likewise invites ('¿Vienes?') the reader to accompany him on his travels to a utopian land which is defiantly cosmopolitan: stanzas 1–14 situate us in ancient Greece and France (though the former is refracted through the latter: 'Amo más que la Grecia de los griegos/ la Grecia de la Francia'; Darío 553), stanzas 15–22 turn to Italy and Germany, while stanzas 23–31 turn to the Far East, China, Japan and India. Throughout these visits to far-off places, the emphasis is on exotic love; as stanza 25 begins, 'Amame en chino' (Darío 555). The poet's lover, as the comparison suggests, will feel attracted to the poet because of his wisdom, although the reference to 'mi unicornio cuerno de oro' also points to a sexual latency in the poet's gesture. 'Sonatina' follows a similar line of reasoning, although it is now the poet who arrives from afar to awaken the imprisoned princess of his dreams, like Sleeping Beauty, with a kiss: 'el feliz caballero que te adora sin verte,/ y que llega de lejos, vencedor de la Muerte,/ a encenderte los labios con su beso de amor' (Darío 557). What is important about these poems is the connection they assert between the death implied in the statues which embody culture and the penned-in nature of the female beloved as projected in Darío's dreams, a theme which occurs repeatedly in *Prosas profanas*. In 'Yo persigo una forma . . .', for example, we find a combination of dreamscapes which include an impossible embrace between the poet and the Venus of Milo statue (line 4), and between the poet and Sleeping Beauty (line 12). The swan in the poem operates not only as a symbol of the aristocratic ideal but also as a sign of the ambiguous nature of the poetic universe created by the poet himself. The poem concludes with an image of 'el cuello del gran cisne blanco que me interroga' (Darío 622), indicating a point of crisis in the poet's symbol-creating process.

Three poets – Ricardo Jaimes Freyre (1868–1933), Amado Nervo (1870–1919), and Guillermo Valencia (1873–1943) – are normally considered to be part of the *modernista* inner circle, suggesting their proximity in poetic terms to an ideal epitomised by Darío's poetry. While seeming at first quaint, it is perhaps logical that Freyre should have lighted upon a Nordic environment for his poetic projections since the country in which he grew up – Bolivia – especially in its northern regions such as Lake Titicaca, has cold, bleak weather. But, at the same time, Freyre's rhetorical gesture shows how other-culture-orientated the *modernistas* were. His poem 'El camino de los cisnes' from *Castalia bárbara* (1899), for example, re-focusses Darío's swan within the framework of a Viking burial (Schulman & Garfield 179). Amado Nervo's poem, 'Como blanca teoría por el desierto' from *Los jardines interiores* (1905), in its emphasis on the comparison between his spiritual/writerly emptiness and the vastness of the desert, is ostensibly a re-writing of Darío's poem, 'La página blanca' from *Prosas profanas* (1896) (Darío 588–89), in neo-Catholic terms. Valencia's best poem, 'Cigüeñas blancas', from *Ritos* (1899) is a long, meditative piece of forty-seven cross-rhyme, hendecasyllabic quatrains and one five-line concluding stanza which takes its point of departure from a phrase from Petronius's *Satyricon*, 'ciconia pietatis cultrix'; a group of storks are evoked in a stanza which periodically recurs as 'la augusta calma de mejores días' (line 36; Schulman & Garfield 204). The poem is *modernista* in its evocation of *topoi* such as the pictorial, the melancholic, the musical, cosmopolitanism and the conflict between religion and sex, but striking in its evocation of a Latin culturalist backdrop (of which the *Satyricon* is the centre-piece), and its exchange of Darío's swan for the stork.

The decline of *modernismo* was decisively signalled in 1911 by the publication of 'Tuércele el cuello al cisne . . .' by Enrique González Martínez (1871–1952); as the first line went: 'Tuércele el cuello al cisne de engañoso plumaje . . .' (Schulman & Garfield 197). Two poets whose names are associated with the latter phase of *modernismo* are Julio Herrera y Reissig (1875–1910) and Leopoldo Lugones (1874–1938). In the work of both poets, which ranks among some of the best written by the *modernistas*, the *modernista* ideal is taken to such an extreme that the cracks in its ideological superstructure begin to appear. Herrera y Reissig's 'La vida' (written in 1903 but published in *Las pascuas del tiempo* in 1920), for example, demonstrates precisely a dissonant figure; the poem begins as a fairy-tale narrative about the poet chasing his beloved and ends unexpectedly as the poet's beloved turns into a man and pierces his heart with a sword blow. Likewise 'Solo verde-amarillo para flauta: llave de U' (1901) turns the *modernista* pursuit of musicality into a hodge-podge of sound written in the 'key of U' (Schulman & Garfield 250). Like Herrera y Reissig, though more ostentatiously than his compatriot, Lugones mercilessly unravelled the poetic threads of *modernismo*. In *Lunario sentimental* (1909), for example, Lugones builds upon the ironic and parodic vein of *Los crepúsculos del jardín* (1905); the opening poem of that collection, 'A mis cretinos', effectively sets the tone. The moon is lauded as the inspiration of his verse, but rather than the wistful poetry of the early *modernistas* we meet an aggressive voice which brings all those notions crashing to earth; for greater effect, Lugones shortens the lines of his poetry, making them punchier:

> A ella da en obra pingüe
> poéticos tributos
> por sus dobles cañutos
> mi zampoña bilingüe. (Schulman & Garfield 238)

Rather than Orpheus's lyre, Lugones projects himself as paying tribute to the moon with a rustic flute; his 'zampoña' is 'bilingual', perhaps, since his verse will be using Spanish to refer to an American reality. Lugones's later experiments with free verse, such as in 'La blanca soledad', *El libro fiel* (1912), are important indicators of the mood of the literary times which, within the next decade, would discard the heritage of *modernismo* and, to quote González Martínez's words, give the final 'twist' to the swan's neck.[2]

## Postmodernismo

There is an intriguing group of poets writing at the turn of the century who were not included in the *modernista* group, and were not quite part of the avant-garde movement, and who have, for want of a better title, been labelled members of the *postmodernismo* movement. Ramón López Velarde (1888–1921) is normally listed as a member, and the distinctive feature of his work is its private perspective. In particular, his poetry has a *fin de siècle* feel about it in that Catholicism and sin form the ideological backdrop for the anguished investigation of sexual feelings. Many of the key images – the projection of womanhood as purity, the deliberate palimpsest of the codes of sex and religion, melancholy, the nocturne as backdrop – in his work are culled from the *modernistas*.

While the male poets of this period were busily setting up genealogies for themselves, the female poets of this period, such as Delmira Agustini (1886–1914), Gabriela Mistral (1889–1957), Alfonsina Storni (1892–1938), and Juana Ibarbourou (1895–1938), found themselves ostracised from the literary establishment. Agustini's work is, indeed, an intriguing example of the halfway house of women's writing at the turn of the century, for it is a type of writing in which two ideologies – one female-specific and one male-specific – are vying for supremacy in her discourse. An analysis of the image-universe of her poetry, for example, shows that she rewrites – and, in the process, feminizes – the image-universe of the *modernistas*. 'El cisne', for example, opens with a typical dreamy *modernista* landscape in which an aristocratic swan is pictured swimming around a lake. From the fourth stanza on, however, the swan's sexual nature is emphasised, and, as the final two lines of the poem read: 'el cisne asusta de rojo,/ y yo de blanca doy miedo!' (Agustini 57). Mistral, for her part, is something of an enigma. The first Spanish-American writer to receive the Nobel Prize (1945), school teacher and cultural educator (she was invited to work with José Vasconcelos in his cultural enterprise in Mexico in 1922), her poetry at first glance tends to

---

2    One other significant poet of this period not discussed in this section is José Santos Chocano (1875–1935); for a good overview of his work, see Franco, *An Introduction to Spanish American Literature* 165–67.

confirm the traditional notion of her as a female poet frustrated by her lack of luck in love, and her consequent inability to have children.[3] Poems such as 'El niño solo' and 'La mujer estéril' from *Desolación* (1922), 'Sueño grande' and 'Piececitos' from *Ternura* (1924), tend to underline the traditional image of Mistral as a loving, maternal figure. But there is another side to Mistral's poetry which is much more disturbing. 'Los sonetos de la muerte', for example, opens with an image of Mistral imagining how she will cradle the body of the young man she has lost within the earth (thereby underlying an association common throughout Mistral's work between femaleness and nature). The poem specifically contrasts the togetherness that she and her dead lover will share with that death which is presented as if instituted by 'los hombres'. The final tercet of this sonnet underlines this point even more graphically: 'Me alejaré cantando mis venganzas hermosas,/ ¡porque a ese honor recóndito la mano de ninguna/ bajará a disputarme tu puñado de huesos!' (Chang-Rodríguez 343). There is almost a smug satisfaction in these lines; no woman can take her man from her now, since she is able to hold his bones in her hand. The notion of possession outlined here – one which not even death can dispute – is one which contradicts the homely image of Mistral we derive from other poems. Storni's poetry, for its part, provides a stark contrast with Mistral's; it contains a feminist structure of feeling in that it turns away from Mistral's maternalism and focusses instead on the writer's identity as a new woman of the modern world. Her view of feminism has a suffragette-like wisdom about it; beginning with the premise that 'life is not an equation perceivable by the eyes of men', Storni reasoned that feminism 'is nothing more than man's managerial failure to achieve by legal means the necessary equilibrium of human happiness' ('An Old Story', in Meyer 102). Storni's most famous poem, 'Tú me quieres blanca', turns the tables abruptly on the male stereotype of womanhood. If the man wants his woman to be so perfect then he must be perfect too; she advises him, with tongue in cheek, to go to the mountains, clean his mouth, live in a cabin, eat bitter roots, sleep on the hoarfrost, talk to the birds and get up at dawn. Then, only then, as the poem finishes: 'preténdeme blanca,/ preténdeme nívea,/ preténdeme casta' (Chang-Rodríguez 352). The short verse form Storni uses for this poem – the hexasyllable – emphasizes its jocularity.

---

3   This image of Mistral is enhanced by a tragic incident which occurred in her personal life. While a young woman living in Monterde, Chile, Mistral fell in love with a young office worker, Romelio Ureta; although they were in love, they did not marry, and, tragically, for reasons which have never been satisfactorily explained, Ureta took his own life in 1909. A legend thereby grew that much of the poetry Mistral was subsequently to write was inspired by the abrupt (and undeserved) loss of Ureta's love and of the children that she would have borne him had they married.

## Narrative Poetry

The most significant narrative poem of the latter half of the nineteenth century was *Martín Fierro* (Part I, 1872; Part II, 1879) by José Hernández (1834–1886). This grand poem, seen by some as the epic of the *gauchos*, strives to represent the speech, life-style and world-view of the *gauchos* who were soon to be brushed aside by the new urban-based Argentina which mushroomed in the last two decades of the nineteenth century. Unlike many of the works considered so far in this chapter, *Martín Fierro* was an extremely popular work, so popular in fact that Hernández was obliged to write a second installment of the poem, *La vuelta de Martín Fierro* (1879), because of public demand: 'Entrego a la benevolencia pública, con el título de *La vuelta de Martín Fierro*, la segunda parte de una obra que ha tenido una acogida tan generosa que en seis años se han repetido once ediciones con un total de cuarenta y ocho mil ejemplares' (qtd. in Rama, *Crítica* 74). A far cry, indeed, from the early days of the century when Bello berated a colleague for sending 750 copies of his book to Buenos Aires, thinking that 20 would have been sufficient. Hernández had some first-hand experience of the *gaucho* way of life, although he was not one himself; as a young man he was sent to the southern frontier and participated in the warfare which the *gauchos* were waging on the Indians. *Martín Fierro* is perhaps best read as a counter-response to Sarmiento's *Facundo* (see pp. 70–71) in which the odds are firmly stacked against the *gaucho* way of life. Hernández was a supporter of the Federalists and, when they were defeated in 1872, was forced to flee to Brazil. His text is thus to be seen not only in terms of a literary creation but also as a political statement which, through the *gauchos*, offers justification for the rough-and-tumble of the Federalist way of life.

In *Martín Fierro* Hernández presents the *gauchos* as a misunderstood, misrepresented group of individuals forced into recruitment to fight a war against the Indians in which they had no special advantage to gain. Martín Fierro's story is presented as a typical life history; wrenched from the domestic bliss of his home life on the *pampas* he is sent to the frontier to fight against savage Indians, for which he receives no monetary recompense, suffers hunger, inclement weather and lives in perpetual fear of death. To cap it all, when he finally decides to desert and return home, he finds his wife and children have disappeared; Martín's life from this point onwards becomes a monotonous ritual of drinking, tavern fights, murder and perpetual fleeing from the law. In Cantos X–XII we hear the life story of one Cruz which bears a striking resemblance to Martín's. The poem is written throughout in six-line octosyllabic stanzas and in such a way as to echo the verbal jousting of the *gaucho*. Because of the violence of the *gauchos'* actions (the tavern scene when Martín crudely insults a black woman and then stabs her husband to death outside is particularly notable; Part I, Canto VII), they are presented as social outlaws. Martín's repentant feelings after his wrongdoings, however, and his grief at finding his family scattered (Part I, Canto IX) give every appearance of sincerity. The destruction of his family home led to a restless life, a fact he often laments: 'Soy un gaucho desgraciado,/ no tengo dónde ampararme,/ ni un palo donde rascarme' (Part I, Canto IX, lines 285–90; Flores 240). The mixture here of sorrow and loneliness coupled with defiance of social convention is at the heart of the *gauchos'* troubled world-vision. In *Martín Fierro* Hernández expresses the cultural dilemma of the *gaucho* with a freshness of vision which countless imitations have never been able to surpass.

## Novel

According to the teleological reading of the nineteenth-century novel already sketched in Chapter 3, the Spanish-American novel comes of age in *El Periquillo Sarniento* after a succession of early premonitory drafts stretching back to the personal-experience chronicles of writers such as Núñez Cabeza de Vaca's *Naufragios* (1542) and with an important transition phase expressed in texts such as Carlos Sigüenza y Góngora's *Infortunios de Alonso Ramírez* (1690). But while a teleological reading has its advantages, we should avoid seeing the text which initiates the Spanish-American novel as solely produced by antecedent classics and see it also in the context of popular narrative discourse. As we have seen, the newspaper press in Spanish America burgeoned at the turn of the nineteenth century and with this came, as the century progressed, the *folletines.* The apogee of the *folletín* occurred roughly in the period 1880–1910 and, all over Spanish America, though most clearly in Buenos Aires, its growth coincided with the expansion of a literate urban proletariat. As has been pointed out, it 'served as a mediation between literature, consumed only by a small educated elite, and the masses'; its *criollista* ideology served a public 'in transition between the country and the city or who had recently entered Argentina as immigrants' (Rowe & Schelling 98). Print runs were huge compared to those normal for works of literature of the same period; while one thousand copies was usual for what we normally call a work of literature, the *folletín* would be published in tens of thousands of copies (a typical example being Gutiérrez's *folletín, Juan Moreira* which was published in serial form in the newspaper *La Patria Argentina* and subsequently published in book form under the imprint of the same newspaper (Rowe & Schelling 34).[4] The Mexican essayist, Ignacio Altamirano, wrote during this period of the novel's ability to reach the masses and how it was becoming an instructional tool (qtd. in Rama, *Crítica* 77).[5] Some works were

---

4   The first theatrical version of *Juan Moreira* occurred in the Politeama Theater in Buenos Aires in 1884 (Dauster 29); for further discussion, see the Theatre section.

5   Also interesting in this context is the fact that Altamirano identifies the new readers of the novel as women: 'el bello sexo, que es el que más lee y al que debe dirigirse con

re-formatted as *folletines*, such as Sarmiento's *Facundo*, Echeverría's *Dogma socialista*, Bartolomé Mitre's *Soledad*, Vicente Fidel López's *La novia del hereje*, and Alberto Blest Gana's *Martín Rivas*. There were a number of *folletín* writers in the nineteenth century among whom should be mentioned the Mexicans Justo Sierra, Manuel Payno, and Vicente Riva Palacio; the Colombians Eladio Vergara y Vergara, Bernardino Torres Torrente, and Mercedes Gómez Victoria; the Chileans Martín Palma, José Antonio Torres, and Daniel Barros Grez (for a discussion of the latter's theatre see below); and the Argentinian Eduardo Gutiérrez (Carilla, II, 106–108). The most representative and influential of these authors was Eduardo Gutiérrez (1851–1899), and especially his *Juan Moreira* (1879).

   Set in the appropiately named Matanzas, Argentina, *Juan Moreira*, published in the 'Dramas policiales' series, has all the ingredients of the *folletín* genre. The eponymous hero is presented as an honest, hard-working *gaucho* driven to crime by the corruption of the society in which he lives, epitomized by Francisco, the local judge, who covets and eventually steals from him his beautiful wife, Vicenta. In this way sympathy is engineered for Moreira, and it occurs even at those potentially most alienating points in the narrative when Moreira hacks his adversaries to pieces. Invariably, Moreira's action is justified as an example of honourable reprisal. The novel is structured chapter by chapter around the knife fights which are their climax and which normally show the same pattern: Moreira is threatened, he is persuaded to fight, he suffers a knife wound, and then quickly polishes off his assailant, a scene which the spectators watch with a mixture of horror and admiration. Though Gutiérrez's is an embellished account, it is based on a real-life individual; thus, the narrator feels confident enough to state in chapter V: 'No hacemos novela, narramos los hechos . . .' (Gutiérrez 68). In order to emphasize its veracity there are references to contemporary newspaper reports of Moreira's deeds, with which at one point the *folletín* takes issue (XIV; Gutiérrez 178–80), and a letter addressed to the author dated 20 March 1880, from one Julio Llanos, describing other of Moreira's marvellous feats (Gutiérrez 222–23). The main aim of this *folletín* is to give a positive portrayal of the *gaucho*'s way of life, his sense of honour as evidenced during the knife fight, and to emphasise that the responsibility for the waywardness of his life path lies ultimately with the society which produced him. It is written for an urban audience which was no doubt fascinated in the abstract by life on the wild side but would have found it repugnant if it interrupted everyday life in Buenos Aires in a concrete sense. Following in the *folletín* tradition, *Juan Moreira* specialises in melodrama, a good example of this being when Vicenta and Juan meet, one stormy winter night, many years

especialidad, porque es su género' (qtd. in Rama, *Crítica* 77). This is in line with Ian Watt's discoveries about the readership of the English novel in the nineteenth century.

after Vicenta had given him up for dead (X; Gutiérrez 136–38); it also consciously alludes to the Romantic literary tradition of the hero pursued by malignant fortune; in chapter XVI, for example, Moreira is described as 'uno de estos seres llenos de hermosas cualidades, con un espíritu noble e inquebrantable y dotados de un carácter hidalgo, lanzados al camino del crimen y empujados a una muerte horrible, por la maldad de uno de esos tenientes alcaldes de campaña a quienes desgraciadamente está librado el honor y la vida del humilde y noble gaucho porteño' (Gutiérrez 211). The reader's sympathies could not be more overtly directed. Moreira is finally killed by a posse from Buenos Aires although it is clear, given the pointers throughout the novel, that he accepts death of his own volition. In doing so, Juan Moreira in effect lays to rest the myth of the *gaucho* in the national psyche, thereby allowing Argentina more elbow room to build the skyscrapers which adorn Buenos Aires's skyline today.

*Cecilia Valdés o la Loma del Angel: novela de costumbres cubanas* (1882), by the Cuban novelist Cirilo Villaverde (1812–1894), was published while the author was in exile in New York. The novel opens with a portrayal of the childhood and adolescence of Cecilia Valdés, a beautiful mulatto woman who is a celebrated dancing singer in the bars of Havana at the beginning of the nineteenth century. Her origins are a mystery (specifically nobody knows who her father was) but, gradually, the reader is able to piece together the story. Many years before, a rich landowner in Havana, Don Cándido Gamboa, had had an illegitimate child and arranged for that child to be looked after via the services of his doctor friend. Gamboa's legitimate son, Leonardo, from his wife Doña Rosa, falls in love with Cecilia, and despite his father's admonitions, determines to marry her. This eventually leads to tragedy when a musician who plays in the same bar as Cecilia, José Dolores Pimienta, out of spite since he is in love with Cecilia, kills Leonardo during the wedding ceremony. The novel's sub-title ('novela de costumbres cubanas') indicates its *costumbrista* pedigree, but it is best to see the novel not as a late example of the *costumbrista* style in the Caribbean, but rather as an early example of the confluence of various discourses, such as Romanticism, *costumbrismo* and Realism. The first part of the novel was published in 1839, and the second, third and fourth parts, though written in the 1870s, follow the earlier formula – so much so that they constitute a re-writing of a pre-established formula rather than a venture into pastures new. *Cecilia Valdés* has Romantic elements such as the focus on socially forbidden love (Cecilia and Leonard, in effect, commit incest since they are half-brother and sister), *costumbrista* elements such as the description of the clothes worn, and the use of these clothes as a pointer to social class (Part I, chap. V), and Realist elements such as the stress upon the *empiric* nature of the events described (the novel is twice described as a 'verídica historia'; Part I, chap. X; Part II, chap. I).

The novel is very blunt about race, and characters are consistently typified according to their racial origin. Cecilia becomes a Caucasian-African Venus (Part I, chap. III), blacks are routinely described as savages (Part II, chap. II), Don Cándido refers to Negroes as 'sacks of coal' (Part II, chap. VI), blacks are described by one character as born for slavery (Part III, chap. III). Oppression of the African races is so intense that suicide seems an almost inevitable result; in one particularly grotesque episode we learn of how a black slave killed himself by swallowing his own tongue, a vivid metaphorical image of political unvoicing (Part III, chap. VII); in the same chapter slaves' bodies are found hanging from trees, ripped apart by passing vultures. As if to confirm that blackness is a projection of social class, the narrator at one point refers to how money corrects the impurity of blood and even the lack of virtue (Part I, chap. X). As with *Sab*, it is clear that there is a discontinuity between the author's self-avowed antislavery stance and the ideology that the events and imagery of *Cecilia Valdés* betoken. As Richard Jackson argues, in this novel, 'Villaverde describes excessively the ethnic differences in people and the various stratifications and divisions of Cuban society. But his accepting them as a *fait accompli* suggests that his antislavery argument is built on a false premise, or at least one that does not attempt to contradict the hierarchy of color' (*Black Image* 30).

The most striking feature of *Cecilia Valdés* is its use of mystery. Quite consistently, the narrator introduces a character, describes his/her actions, and only later reveals his/her identity. Thus, Cecilia is introduced on two separate occasions, as a young eleven- or twelve-year-old girl in Part I, chap. II, and as a cabaret singer in Part I, chap. V, and her identity is only revealed subsequently. The opening chapter of the novel describes the visit by a rich man to a shady part of town in Havana, but it is only later that we realize that this was Don Cándido visiting the mother who bore his illegitimate child. Likewise, we are not told who the Negro is who enters the ball and wishes to dance with Cecilia and then causes a scene when she refuses to do so; it is only later on that we realize it was Dionisio, María la Regla's long-lost husband. In this sense we can talk about the novel as echoing, in terms of its style of presentation, the thematic core of the novel, namely, the unspeakability and unknowability of incest within the family unit. Incest is, indeed, the ghost in the family wardrobe which finally emerges at the end of the novel. What is intriguing about this is that the sexual and the political plots are shown to interlope in the novel. For, just as the lower classes at first collude in keeping the family secret – the sexual crime – which, however, finally emerges, so the political crime of slavery, in which the lower classes collude, is finally revealed in all its horror in the closing stages of the novel at La Tinaja. José Dolores Pimienta's act of murder, which concludes the novel, can, thus, be seen as at once an act of sexual vengeance, but also an action with political resonance, since it is also a lower-class individual killing a member of the upper classes. Leonardo's family, it should be pointed out, are to be understood as typifying the *criollo* and patrician class; they exploit the

Negroes on La Tinaja, yet they feel aggrieved by the presence of the Spanish; at least this is what emerges from Leonardo's nationalistic discomfiture when he discovers that his sister, Adela, is being courted by a Spanish soldier.

One of the most significant novels published at the end of the nineteenth century was *Aves sin nido* (1899) by Clorinda Matto de Turner (1852–1909). This novel describes, with a Realism that verges on Naturalism, the plight of the Indians in a town called Killac (meaning in Quechua the genitive 'of the moon' [Quillac] and based on Tinta, the Andean town where the author spent much of her life after marriage) who are exploited by an unholy trinity of landowners, priests and lawyers. *Aves sin nido* may be described as a Naturalist novel in the sense that it emphasises a purely materialist view of human actions and the motives that underlie them. In particular, Matto de Turner's novel focusses on the wrongful killing of Marcela and Juan Yupanqui; Marcela and Juan ask for relief from the debt they owe jointly to the priest (Pascual Vargas) and the governor (Sebastián), at which point they are judged to be seditious and subsequently murdered. Between the Indians, represented by the Yupanquis in Part I of the novel and the Chumpis in Part II, and the evil elite, are Lucía and Fernando, a happily-married *criollo* couple. The latter attempt to mediate between the two political camps, but eventually give up and move back to Lima. Luis Alberto Sánchez has argued that *Aves sin nido* makes a break with previous idealised descriptions of Indian life since the Indians are no longer used for decoration but are studied as exploited human beings (Sánchez 35). The reader's sympathy is directed towards Lucía and Fernando, who symbolise a new emerging class in Peru in the second half of the nineteenth century, that is, the entrepreneurial middle class which was urban and Eurocentric in taste. (The economic boom of the second half of the nineteenth century in Peru, we may recall, was based on the industrial use of 'guano' found off the coastline of Peru and transformed into artificial fertiliser for export to Europe.) The other main characters in the story, Don Sebastián the governor, the priest Pascual Vargas, the colonel Paredes, and the lawyer, are to a man wedded to the ethos of the *ancien régime* of the landowning oligarchy. Despite the apparent pessimism of *Aves sin nido* (the new middle classes represented by Lucía and Fernando are defeated by the old oligarchy), there is another level in which Lucía and Fernando win out in the end. Manuel, the son of Sebastián and Doña Petronila (at least we think so until the end of the novel), in effect turns against his parents by seeking advice from his father's political enemy, Fernando; this advice has to do not only with a life-decision such as going to university, but also with future investments in the stock market. To make this distancing even more striking the novel also presents Manuel falling in love with one of the Yupanqui daughters, Margarita, who was taken in by Lucía after her parents, Juan and Marcela, were brutally murdered (hence the title 'aves sin nido' which refers to the two daughters).

There are two other significant points about the novel which ought to be mentioned and these are the incest theme and its feminist ideology. Incest is, of course, a very common theme in Romantic literature ranging from Lord Byron's poetry to Jorge Isaacs's *María*, and it has in *Aves sin nido* the same significance, namely, the cult of socially forbidden love as a metaphor of the primacy of individual desire. In Matto de Turner's novel, the theme of incest is revealed in the last paragraph of the novel when Margarita and Manuel discover that their father is one and the same person, Bishop Claro y Miranda, mentioned (with what irony) in the opening section of the novel as the angular stone of the Killac community. This revelation has all the high drama of a Romantic *folletín*. The feminist ideology is evident in this novel to the degree in which certain motifs common in the work of Matto de Turner's male contemporaries are given a new feminocentric focus. Incest plays its role here since it alludes not only to the cult of individualism in Romantic literature, but also has a feminist edge in that it specifically underlines the brutality of men against women: the priest Vargas, for example, is just as lascivious as Bishop Claro, co-habits with a woman despite his vows, and dies tormented by starkly sexual visions. Also tending to underline the feminist import of the novel is the fact that all of the positive human beings in the narrative are female; Marcela initiates the action, Lucía acts as the mediator, and even Margarita is more self-possessed than her beau, Manuel. *Aves sin nido* has been criticised for being badly structured and badly written, but this is not true; it is a subtle, complex novel which repays further attention and which hollows out the patriarchalism of Realism from within to hint at a world of feminine social harmony in which sacrifice is unnecessary and in which social sharing can take place.

## Prose

The Peruvian Ricardo Palma (1833–1919) is famous for his *Tradiciones peruanas*, which rank among the wittiest period pieces of the nineteenth century. The *tradiciones* were published by Palma in eleven series, without any particular chronological order from 1872 until 1915. They border on the short story and are not quite *cuadros de costumbres* understood in a strictly generic sense, and indeed succeed in creating a genre all of their own; as one critic suggests, '[l]a tradición es un género típicamente americano, un producto del romanticismo americano' (Carilla, II, 91). Normally the *tradición* is a short story based on an historical event – which is normally rooted in the colonial era – and told in a witty manner. Many of the *tradiciones* begin with a reference to a saying which Palma claims to have heard said in Lima, such as 'esto es más caro que la camisa de Margarita Pareja', or 'esto vale tanto como el alacrán de fray Gómez', but, as soon becomes clear, this is simply a convenient pretext which introduces the story and whets the reader's appetite for what is to come. Thus in one tradición, 'Capa colorada, caballo blanco y caja turún-tun-tun', popular culture in the form of gossip is used as a source rather than the written word: 'Muchas, pero desgraciadamente ineficaces, dilegencias he hechos para obtener copia de la respuesta del monarca, y tengo que conformarme con repetir lo que corre en boca de todos los vecinos de Puno' (Palma, I, 120). Typically, the *tradición* is set in the era of the viceroyalty, and the references to the Viceroy of the time, and even the most important personage to appear in the story, are historically based. Once the historical stage is set, Palma then proceeds to create his plot, and various techniques are employed to contrive a sense of verisimilitude, namely, the allusion to historical individuals, the reference to written records which the author has (normally with great difficulty) consulted, and citation of common proverbs. Many of the *tradiciones* focus on the power struggles of the colonial period. 'Las orejas del alcalde', for example, in a style reminiscent of Bartolomé Arzáns, narrates the story of one Don Diego de Esquivel, a gentleman who lived in Potosí in the middle of the sixteenth century and who was so affronted by the indignity of his treatment at the hands of the mayor that he vowed to cut off the latter's ears exactly one year after he was publicly flogged; Don Diego kept his word (Palma, I, 26). As this suggests, the *tradiciones* portray a world in which the laws of custom, especially as far as honour is concerned, are inflexible. Some of the *tradiciones* begin and end with the proverb being cited. 'Carta canta' relates the very humorous story of two Indians who are taking ten melons to their owner in Lima; they decide to eat two of them and they attempt to keep this a secret by hiding the letter under a stone so that it cannot see them (Palma, I, 46). Needless to say, their ruse is unsuccessful, and the explanation given by Don Antonio as to how he knew that the Indians were lying is 'Canta carta'; the *tradición* goes full circle and concludes with a reference to the proverb that initiated the narrative.

## Theatre

As earlier on in the century, this period was one in which theatrical productivity was heavily influenced by European and, especially, Spanish models. The *género chico* was imported to Argentina from Spain in the second half of the nineteenth century (the first recorded performance occurred in Buenos Aires in 1878) and caught on extremely well. A local imitation of the genre, the *género chico criollo*, soon followed. Mini-plays such as *De paso por aquí* by Miguel Ocampo, *De paseo por Buenos Aires* by Justo López de Gómara (both of 1890), and *Chin-Chun-Chan* (1904) by José F. Elizondo played well with the Buenos Aires middle-class theatre-going public (Dauster, *Historia* 40). *Chin-Chun-Chan*, astonishingly, was perfomed over one thousand times (Dauster, *Historia* 45). One of the most popular theatrical works, however, was undoubtedly *Juan Moreira*, a pantomime version of Eduardo Gutiérrez's *folletín* of the same name (see discussion in the 'Novel' section of this chapter above). Created by José J. Podestá (1858–1936), it was first staged in Chivilcoy in April 1886 (Luzuriaga & Reeve 406). The theatrical version more or less follows the *folletín* version in its depiction of Juan Moreira's various escapades, and it is always careful to retain the audience's sympathy for the outlaw. The first scene sets the stage for what is to follow; Moreira asks in a court setting for the return of some money he paid to one Sardetti (Luzuriaga & Reeve 408–409), and, for his impudence, he is flogged. Moreira subsequently kills Sardetti for this treachery and, from this point onwards, becomes an outlaw. As in the *folletín*, and in this he recalls the prototypical Romantic hero, Moreira blames fate for his misfortune: 'Yo era feliz al lao de mi mujer y de mi hijo y jamás hice a un hombre ninguna maldad. Pero yo habré nacido con algún sino fatal porque la suerte se me dio güelta y de repente me vi perseguido al extremo de pelear pa defender mi cabeza' (Luzuriaga & Reeve 418). Following the *gaucho* version of his predetermined fate, also apparent in Hernández's *Martín Fierro* (see pp. 84–85), Juan Moreira loses his wife after others spread the rumour that he has died (Luzuriaga & Reeve 419–21). It is clear that this pantomine version of *Juan Moreira* left much up to the individual ingenuity of the director; the last scene, for example, offers few stage directions other than to say that Moreira is killed (Luzuriaga & Reeve 423).

Alongside those works more appropriately classified under popular culture were those dramas in which the central issues perturbing the *criollo* middle to upper classes of the time were expressed. One of the best works of this type is *Como en Santiago* (1875) by the Chilean dramatist, Daniel Barros Grez (1834–1904). It focusses, like Ascensio Segura's *Ña Catita* of the previous decade (discussed in Chapter 3), on the conflict involved in the choice of a marriage partner within the family unit. A contrast is drawn up from the very beginning of the play between Dorotea, the priggish, self-important daughter of Don Victoriano and Doña Ruperta, and Victoriano's adopted niece, Inés, who is in love with Dorotea's betrothed, Silverio. Dorotea, aided by her mother, Ruperta, callously drops Silverio once a better candidate appears – a member of parliament, Don Faustino – and much of the drama, from that point onwards, focusses on the difference between Dorotea's materialistic, capitalist and power-based view of love and her cousin's Romantic 'true' love (she loves Silverio for who he is, not for what he can buy her). The plot is rather skimpy – it revolves around a false legal document created by Manuel, Silverio's father, in order to demonstrate that Faustino is only interested in money, and, as soon as he 'discovers' that marriage to Dorotea will not bring him the expected reward (a handsome dowry), he abandons her. There is also a capital versus provinces theme in the play which surfaces in Faustino's exclamation which concludes the play: '¡Pícaros provincianos, me quitaron un negocio de las manos!' (Luzuriaga & Reeve 405).

Arguably the best play of this period is *Barranca abajo* (1905) by Florencio

Sánchez (1875–1910); it is a bleak play about an old man, Zoilo, who loses his money and, as a result, is driven to suicide (at least in the second and final version of the play). The play may have some bearing on the author's life since Florencio Sánchez was known to prefer poverty rather than sell his talents (Dauster, *Historia* 33). A remarkable feature of *Barranca abajo* is the oblique way in which its subject matter is introduced; the tragedy of poverty is presented as experienced above all by the women of the family, Zoilo's wife (Misia Dolores), who is simply bewildered by the situation, his daughters Robusta and Prudiencia, who are desperate to marry and discover pastures new, and his sister, Rudelinda, whose inheritance he cynically squanders. The opening scene of the play, for example, simply shows the women of the family squabbling over domestic chores, and it is only gradually that the full extent of their financial ruin emerges. A hint appears in Act I, Scene vi; Rudelinda asks Zoilo if he did the errands she asked of him, and he is evasive about the money she gave him (Florencio Sánchez 117–18). She presses him later on, and he finally admits her inheritance no longer exists, in Act I, Scene xiv (Florencio Sánchez 126–27). The drama of the play, thus, occurs off-stage, as it were; the events we see only refer obliquely to that reality, as if the truth were too painful to talk about. Even the discussion between Zoilo, Butiérrez, and the former's creditor, Juan Luis (Act I, Scenes xvii–xxi) proceeds in an angular fashion, rather like the conversations in Chekhov's *The Cherry Garden*. Butiérrez's thrice-repeated refrain 'Qué embromar con las cosas', reminiscent of Misia Dolores's interjections to the Virgin Mary, seems almost a deliberate ploy to avoid the truth (Act I, Scenes xvii–xxi). As the play unfolds, the women get ready to abandon a sinking ship, which finally leads to Zoilo's suicide. In the first version of the play, the ending was more open in the sense that the possibility was left open that Zoilo took Anicito's advice and did not commit suicide. In the revised version, however, which Florencio Sánchez wrote as a result of the reviews of the opening night's performance, the ending was disambiguated. Despite Anicit's remonstrations, Zoilo puts his neck in the noose, with the words: 'Se deshace más fácilmente el nido de un hombre que el nido de un pájaro' (Florencio Sánchez 175).

The importance of *Barranca abajo* lies in its modern, capitalist ethos. The tragedy no longer lies in the malevolence of the gods, but arises as a result of poverty and the destruction of the bourgeois home, as the last lines of the play quoted above suggest. The significance of Florencio Sánchez's play rests on this. While it is clearly a product of its era in terms of the techniques it employs – namely, the Realism of the characters' speech, the Naturalism which surrounds the daughters' dilemma (in the sense of their situation being created by deterministic invariables) – the essence of the play is grasped when we compare it to the typical play of the Romantic era. For whereas there the hero and/or heroine would typically die as a result of the pangs of unrequited love, here it is poverty, and particularly the loss of the family fortune, which triggers the tragedy. In that sense it is a very apt voicing of the society in which it was created; the Southern Cone at the end of the nineteenth century and the beginning of the twentieth was caught up in an almost frenzied social programme of modernisation and urbanisation, which was hastened by the large-scale immigration of Europeans which characterised especially cities such as Montevideo and Buenos Aires. It is legitimate, thus, to interpret *Barranca abajo* as bidding farewell to the old, pre-capitalist way of life (the gradual demise of their lifestyle was inevitable), while simultaneously lamenting the demise of the same.

## *Essay*

By far the most significant essay of this period was Enrique Rodó's *Ariel* (1900), the 'founding essay in the modern Latin American essayistic tradition' in the words of one critic (González Echeverría 16), which proposed a character from Shakespeare's *The Tempest* as a model of Latin-American culture in contradistinction to the utilitarian and spiritless culture of North America. It is important to recall that this text was written at the end of a decade in which the United States had been flexing its military muscles in Central America and the Caribbean; the United States's military superiority was shown when Spain's navy was blown out of the water in a matter of days in the summer of 1898, causing Puerto Rico, Cuba and the Phillipines to be annexed to the United States. Shakespeare's Ariel is, in fact, only a front for the image of Graeco-Roman civilization which Rodó idealises in almost maudlin fashion, in a manner which is parallel to the poetry of the *modernistas*. In effect, this was the swan song of a culture which Western civilisation had emulated for nearly four hundred years since the Renaissance, admittedly in a book-based sense. In Rodó's work, Greece and Rome function as a synecdoche of a pre-Edenic cultural plenitude subsequently destroyed by the Fall of the Industrial Revolution, mechanism and materialism. A series of image associations is set up in *Ariel* according to which Ariel stands for the future, youth, energy, the spirit, nature, the inner life, classical 'otium', the imagination, literature, nobility, and contemplative life, specifically 'pensar, soñar, admirar' (Rodó 40). As might be guessed from the above, when Rodó comes to discuss the cultural alternative – the United States – all of the positive adjectives have been used up; in quick succession, in the second part of the essay, Rodó rejects the work ethic, utilitarianism, Puritanism and the cult of mediocrity which he sees as characteristic of North-American culture. The English too are to blame: 'Si ha podido decirse del utilitarismo, que es el verbo del espíritu inglés, los Estados Unidos pueden ser considerados la encarnación del verbo utilitario' (Rodó 69). The essay concludes with a call to the youth of Spanish America to throw off the yoke of 'nordomanía' (Rodó 70), since it hints at the possibility of 'una América *deslatinizada* por propia voluntad' (Rodó 70), an idea which causes him to shudder, in order to embrace their Latin heritage (Rodó 97). In the final pages of the book Rodó returns to the image of Ariel, described as 'la razón y el sentimiento superior' and 'este sublime instinto de perfectibilidad' (Rodó 101); the very last sentence ends with an evocation of Ariel as straddling, like some mythical Colossus, the mountain ranges of South America (Rodó 103). Rodó, like his contemporaries in Spain such as Angel Ganivet and Miguel de Unamuno, was loathe to focus on mundane matters such as his nation's economy or its industrial base; instead he pondered his vision of the future by focussing on ideas above all else. While Rodó may seem dated to the modern reader, his work is important as a turn-of-the-century statement of distrust towards North-American culture and, by implication, the symptom of an urgent re-evaluation of Latin-American culture. Rodó's view of culture is aristocratic and, at times, rabidly anti-democratic (Rodó 54–55). His sense of protectionism towards high culture is reinforced by the authors he quotes most frequently – Compte, Taine, Renan, and Carlyle – whose broad sweep of the materialism of modern urban life lends itself to a negative portrayal of that reality. His cultural elitism reveals itself equally when he re-writes Alberdi's famous dictum 'gobernar es poblar' to read: 'Gobernar es poblar, asimilando y en primer término: educando y seleccionando, después' (Rodó 56). Quality is more important, he goes on to say, than numbers. Rodó's use of Ariel as a symbol of all that Latin America should strive for perfectly evokes the Eurocentric decade in which it was written. Like the *modernistas*, Rodó idealised Graeco-Latin antiquity and its aristocratic aura; the importance of *Ariel* is confirmed when we consider that one of the major essayists of the second half of the twentieth century, Fernández Retamar, saw fit to break Rodó's Colossus into pieces, promoting instead the image of Ariel's oppositional double in Shakespeare's play, Caliban (see Chapter 6).

## The Multi-genre Writer

Typical of his century, José Martí (1853–1895) was not a writer with only one occupation; he combined the various fields of political activity, essay writing and poetic composition. Though both his parents were Spanish, he soon became identified with the Cuban independence movement; from 1892 he took over leadership of the Partido Revolucionario Cubano, and, in 1895 he was killed in action by Spanish soldiers while attempting to launch a pro-independence raid on Cuba from the United States. Martí's poetry is striking in its ability to bring the political and the personal to bear in one poem. Some of his poems, such as 'Yo soy un hombre sincero' and 'Quiero a la sombra de una ala', the celebrated poem about the Guatemalan girl who fell in love with him and died broken-hearted when he returned to Guatemala, now married, have become popular classics, put to music on innumerable occasions. But the collection of poems to which he owes his fame as a poet, *Versos sencillos* (1891), contains some poems which are intellectually complex. In some ways, Martí's poetry is closer to Andrés Bello's than it is to Rubén Darío's. He is at great pains, for example, to underline the ways in which his poetry differs from that of the *modernistas*. In 'Mi poesía' Martí, for example, differentiates himself from the *modernistas*: 'No la [la poesía] pinto de gualda y amaranto/ como aquesos poetas' (Martí, *Versos* 128). The preferred object of comparison for his poetry is nature: 'la vierto al mundo/ A que cree y fecunde, y ruede y crezca/ Libre cual las semillas por el viento' (Martí, *Versos* 128). Nature, as a number of other poems suggest, is, indeed, the central metaphor of *Versos sencillos*, and is used to signify all that is good and positive about human existence. Martí's attention to the civic sphere makes his poetry redolent, as mentioned above, of Bello's, but there is one crucial difference. While Bello was writing poetry in the early decades of the nineteenth century which essentially spoke on behalf of the new political regime which had recently won its independence from Spain, Martí was forced to evoke a dream that was not then a political reality. His ideological stance towards the state is, thus, much more aggressive, as 'Banquete de tiranos' clearly suggests. Martí was keenly aware of his new role as a writer on the side of the underdog. In the insightful poem, 'Hierro', Martí begins by stating that poetry is something to be written after his daily bread has been earned: 'Ganado tengo el pan: hágase el verso' (Martí, *Versos* 65). This will obviate the need to find a Maecenas, an idea he greets with bitter scorn: '¡póstrate, calle, cede, lame/ manos de potentado, ensalza, excusa/ defectos, tenlos . . .' (Martí, *Versos* 65). If the sycophant decides to do this, he will find his 'bare poorman's plate' turned into a 'plate of fine gold' but, as Martí goes on to point out, that gold is 'pawned' ('empañado'); here the suggestion is that the colonial power is paying for its cultural capital with money it does not own, but has 'borrowed' from the colonised people. Much better than gold, Martí suggests, is iron, since that metal can produce the weapons which are needed to overcome political slavery ('las armas son de hierro!' Martí, *Versos* 66). Martí thereby turns the value image system of the poetaster upside down, and in its place proposes a poetry which uncovers injustice and fights for liberty.

The overriding theme of Martí's essays, which comes as no surprise after reading his poetry, is the Spanish-American independence movement; his basic view, for which he suffered imprisonment, exile and death, is that Cuba should have followed the example of the rest of the Sub-Continent in cutting its political ties with Spain. The last stanza of the poem of independence, to use his own analogy, still needed to be written (Martí, *Prosas* 62). Martí's most influential essay on this topic was 'Nuestra América', published in the Mexican journal, *El Partido Liberal,* on 30 January 1891. The main idea advanced in this essay is that Latin America would be better off in future adopting its own system of government, education and philosophy, one which would grow out of its own culture rather than being simply adopted from Europe or the United States. For too long, he argued, the Latin-American people had simply been a heterogeneous mix of other cultures: 'Eramos unas máscaras, con los calzones de Inglaterra, el chaleco parisiense, el chaquetón de Norteamérica y la montera de España' (Martí, *Prosa escogida* 152). Echoing Sarmiento's dualistic distinction between the natural and the cultural, which Martí here projects using the metaphor of clothes, the Cuban writer reverses the privileged element in the analogy; it is now America, rather than Europe, which is foregrounded as important: 'La historia de América, de los incas a acá, ha de enseñarse de dedillo, aunque no se enseñe la de los arcontes de Grecia. Nuestra Grecia es preferible a la Grecia que no es nuestra' (Martí, *Prosa escogida* 149). Only once they have taken off their Yankee or French spectacles ('antiparras yanquis o francesas'; Martí, *Prosa escogida* 149) will the youth of South America truly be able to create an independent political system. As the above quotation makes quite clear, the future identity of Latin America must rely, in Martí's view, to a great degree on taking account of the Indian and Negro elements. As his essay concludes, the seed of the new America will spring from the nature god of the pre-Columbian Indians of the Antilles.

The afterlife of Martí has been an extremely interesting one in cultural-political terms, since he has been claimed as an icon by both revolutionary Cubans as well as Cubans in exile. Fidel Castro claimed that Martí was the 'intellectual author' of the attack he carried out, on 26 July 1953, on the Moncada barracks, and which was planned to coincide with the hundredth anniversary of Martí's birth (Judson 236). For their part, Cubans living in exile in the United States also claim cultural ownership over Martí. In the early 1980s, for example, a broadcasting station, Radio Antorcha Martiana, operated by the Movimiento Insurreccional Martiana, began to broadcast anti-Castro political messages from Miami which reached the whole Caribbean; as their name suggested they sought to reclaim the cultural capital of Martí's work for their own use. This was followed by the founding of Radio Martí, the official United States government propaganda service to Cuba, which began transmitting anti-revolutionary messages to Cuba in 1985 (Soley & Nichols 188–89). The afterlife of Martí's work is a good litmus test of the value of literature as a cultural capital which is employed for political purposes.

# Chapter 5

# TWENTIETH-CENTURY LITERATURE: PART I

We have already noted in previous chapters the shifts in emphasis in the publication industry which occurred at the beginning and end of the colonial era in Spanish America; from a state industry strictly controlled by regal or viceregal patronage it became an enterprise largely dominated by pro-independence factions. Another shift of emphasis is evident at the beginning of the twentieth century; the book industry now becomes part of a new print capitalism. The axiom of new events calling for new news is certainly relevant to the turbulent years of the Mexican Revolution; hundreds of new newspaper titles were generated throughout Mexico during the period 1910–1917. This print explosion of the dailies all over Latin America – Mexico was not the exception – was accompanied in the literary field by new avant-garde journals based on European models which were exploring the language of colours, the calligram, and the visual image. Certainly, many more specifically literary journals were published; in Argentina, for example, Lafleur lists 64 literary reviews for the period 1893–1914 compared to 188 for the period 1915–1939 (Lafleur 49–57, 156–75). One new feature of the literary world in the first few decades of the twentieth century was the growth, alongside the literary reviews, of inexpensive and accessible editions of works by contemporary authors. An example in Buenos Aires in the first decade of the century was the series 'Ediciones mínimas', which came out monthly, edited by Ernesto Morales and Leopoldo Durán, and which special-ised in short stories and novels. Given their low price, (10 centavos a copy), and higher than usual print runs, these series were highly successful, and led to spin-off series such as La novela sentimental (1917), La novela para todos (1918), La novela cordobesa (1919), La novela universitaria (1921), La novela femenina (1920), La novela porteña (1922), to name but a few (Lafleur 68). Another paradigm shift evident during this period was the gradual professionalisation of the literary profession and, with it, the creation of a new class of writer: the literary critic. The Argentine journal, *Nosotros*, during the 1920s began setting down markers describing the purview of its professional activity, and a boost was given to the institutionalisation of liter-ary criticism by the Instituto de Filología in Buenos Aires, especially under the inspired leadership of Américo Castro in the 1920s and Amado Alonso in the 1930s and 1940s.

*Poetry: The Avant-garde*

The avant-garde in Spanish America was above all expressed in a cluster of poets flocking around a number of literary journals. Contacts between Spain and Spanish America intensified during the avant-garde period and Huidobro played a crucial role in introducing the avant-garde from France to Spain and thence to Spanish America; Borges, likewise, brought the energy of the new Spanish *ultraísta* movement back to Buenos Aires in 1921. The avant-garde had many diverse ramifications in Spanish America, ranging from the *ultraísta* group in Buenos Aires centring around the reviews *Prisma* (1921–1922) and *Proa* (1922–1923), both of which were founded by Borges (1899–1986), to the more politicized *estridentista* movement founded by Manuel Maples Arce (1898–1963) in Mexico City, of which the main reviews were *Actual: Hoja de vanguardia* and *Irradiador*. In all of the various journals that sprang up in the Americas as a result of this European influence (the *Revista de Avance* [1927–1930] in Cuba, *Contemporáneos* [1928–1931] in Mexico, and *Claridad* [1926–] in Argentina), one factor was constant: the narrative use of typography to open up the spatial depth of the printed word.

The key figure of the avant-garde movement in Spanish America is the Chilean poet Vicente Huidobro (1893–1948). In a poem, 'Arte poética', from *Espejo del agua* (1916), for example, Huidobro expounded his new poetic creed, which, given its reliance on the notion of creation, came to be known as 'creacionismo': 'Por qué cantáis la rosa, ¡oh, Poetas!/ Hacedla florecer en el poema' (Huidobro 78). Two features of the poetry Huidobro wrote during this period in the avant-garde style ought to be emphasised. Firstly, and largely as a result of his enthusiasm for Marinetti's call for a new type of art inspired by the city, by its machines, its technology and its speed, Huidobro chose to focus on an urban, cosmopolitan environment as a backdrop to his poems. The first poem of his best collection of avant-garde poems, *Poemas árticos* (1918), for example, 'Exprés', mentions six European cities in the first four lines, London, Madrid, Paris, Rome, Naples and Zurich (Huidobro 211). The final section of *Ecuatorial* (1918), likewise, for example, describes a breathtakingly fast train ride (Huidobro 250). The second feature of Huidobro's poetry which needs to be foregrounded is its use of typographical spacing. Often Huidobro will use the white space on the page as a means of bodying forth a sense of nihilistic anguish. In the poem 'Universo' (Huidobro 232), for example, Huidobro is able to use the device of word spacing in order to enhance the meaning of the poem (which revolves around a sense of ontological lostness).

## Poetry: From Avant-garde to Revolution

Unlike Huidobro who remained true to his avant-garde roots, a number of poets of this era started as poets of the Vanguard but ended up as revolutionaries. César Vallejo and Pablo Neruda are exemplary in this regard; indeed, by exploring the public dimension of their social role as a poet, these two writers showed themselves to be the inheritors in the twentieth century of a tradition of civic poetry in Latin America which stretched back, via Martí and Bello, to Ercilla in the sixteenth. César Vallejo (1892–1938), who was born in Santiago de Chuco, a tiny town in the Peruvian Andes, and ended his days in Paris, is undoubtedly one of the finest, if not the finest, of all Spanish America's poets. While he wrote essays, short stories, a novel and some plays, he is mainly remembered for his poetry. His work is best understood if split into its five main stages which are: 1915–1918 *modernismo*; 1919–1926 the avant-garde; 1927–1931 Marxism (Trotskyism gradually transformed into Stalinism); 1932–1935 political disillusionment; 1936–1938 Christian Marxism. Representative of the first phase is his collection of poems, *Los heraldos negros* (1918), which shows clear signs of Vallejo's literary apprenticeship in *modernismo*, but also hints at a new poetic voice, one which eschews the Graeco-Roman world of mythology in favour of a poetics of the quotidian, and uses Christian symbolism in incongruous, disorientating contexts, such as in 'El pan nuestro'. Some poems openly question God's role in the universe ('Los dados eternos'), some demonstrate the stirrings of an Amerindian consciousness ('Huaco'), and others hint at the growth of social concern for the have-nots of the world ('El pan nuestro'). Poems such as 'A mi hermano Miguel' show Vallejo's skill in the use of colloquial language and everyday situations, tied to his ability to conjure up the world of the child, that would become the hallmark of his poetry. Some of these concerns would continue in his later collection, *Trilce* (1922), published, not coincidentally it would seem, in the same year as Joyce's *Ulysses*, particularly in those poems dedicated to his immediate family. But there is also a palpable change in poetic diction and subject-matter. Some of the poems talk about the sexual act in a way that is remarkably explicit given the time they were published, while most of them demonstrate Vallejo's willingness to expand the resources of the Spanish language in order to create a new vision: neologism, provincialism, archaism, typographical innovation, letter spacing, calligrammatics, slang and legal language all find their way into his poetic armoury.

The work on which his reputation largely rests is his collection of *Poemas humanos*, written over a long period from 1927 until 1936 in Paris, which show evidence of Vallejo's growing political commitment over those years (he was a frequent visitor to the bookstore of *L'Humanité*, the communist newspaper), and which were published posthumously along with the *Poemas en prosa* and *España, aparta de mí este cáliz*, by Vallejo's widow in 1939, the year after Vallejo's death. About one half of the poems of *Poemas humanos* take the collective as their point of departure; some, such as 'Los mineros salieron de la mina', express enthusiasm for the collective ethos of communism, some express dismay at the exploitation and pain experienced by the proletariat ('Los desgraciados'), while others express disillusionment with politics and politicians ('Despedida recordando un adiós'). *España, aparta de mí este cáliz*, published in 1939 and written during the first two years of the Spanish Civil War (1936–1938) which Vallejo did not live to see end, expresses a political faith in the Republican cause through the motif of Christian resurrection, a rather unusual choice given the proletarian and often anti-clerical bias of the Republicans, and especially the communists who supported the Republican war effort. The most famous poem of this collection is 'Masa' which uses the biblical parallel of Lazarus's resurrection to express the triumph of solidarity between all nations (Vallejo 300).

Pablo Neruda (1904–1973), the Chilean poet who won the Nobel Prize in 1971, né Ricardo Nefaltí Reyes Basoalto, is along with Vallejo one of the best Spanish-American poets of the twentieth century. His early work, *Veinte poemas de amor y una canción desesperada* (1924) is Romantic, his first two collections of *Residencia en la tierra* (Part I, 1933; Part II, 1935) have striking similarities with surrealism, while the poetry from *España en el corazón* (1937) onwards in the main is politically committed. *Veinte poemas de amor*, his most popular if not his best collection of poems, is addressed to two women who are given symbolic pseudonyms (Marisol from Temuco and Marisombra from Santiago), and expresses a view of love which is organicist, penetrative and phallic. The beloved is typically pictured as a bountiful and receptive earth, as in 'Cuerpo de mujer' (Neruda, *Twenty* 8). The poems of the second phase are more demanding and more intellectually rewarding. The main *topoi* of *Residencia en la tierra* are sex, death, and the decay of the universe. Often in these poems the reader becomes involved in the hermeneutic process itself, as if reliving the poetic subject's desperate groping for the meaning of the world, because of the stop-start nature of the syntax and the imagery. In 'Arte poética', for example, the poet's awareness of a 'confused name' (Neruda, *Residencia II* 40) is specifically related to his vision of the liquid drives which animate the human as well as the animal and plant kingdoms; some poems specifically concentrate on thanatos ('Sólo la muerte') and eros ('Agua sexual'), while others concentrate on those elements of human life which repress those instincts, as in 'Ritual de mis piernas', where the accoutrements of civilisation (manufactured objects, and particularly shoes) cut the poetic subject off from direct contact with those terrestrial energies (Neruda, *Residencia II* 59).

The Spanish Civil War changed abruptly Neruda's preoccupation with the space of the personal. As a result of his first-hand experience of the atrocities of war (he was ambassador to Chile in Madrid at the time), he became a communist, and his work reflects this ideological upheaval. *España en el corazón*, which was written as a result and which is now included in *Tercera residencia* (1947), is a bitter attack on the Nationalists with their ecclesiastical and aristocratic allies; it has a section devoted to the three principal Nationalist generals, Sanjurjo, Mola and Franco (all of whom are treated to a vision of what it will be like when they go to hell), and it eulogises the Republican troops using organicist metaphors and hammering out in every stanza the natural, organic connection between them and the earth. *España en el corazón* is an angry, circumstantial poem in which Neruda honed his diatribic skills, skills which he would use to devastating effect in his monumental epic poem, *Canto general* (1950). This collection of poems relates in verse the history of the South-American peoples, from their genesis in the remote mists of time to present-day Chile. Like the Old Testament it exudes a fascination with the genealogical along with the joy of new creation. The poet becomes the scribe of the limitless, unnamed reservoir of experience of the past (Canto I, xii; Neruda, *Canto* 38–39). Neruda writes the historical epic of the South-American peoples not from a Eurocentric point of view but rather from a worm's-eye view, from the vantage point of the down-trodden Indians, the Negro slaves, the working masses, the communists. Neruda's is, thus, a defiantly oppositional version of Latin-American history. The political thematics of Neruda's work remained fairly constant in the poetry published after 1950 – his parting shot before he died was a short poetic diatribe entitled *Incitación al Nixoncidio y alabanza de la revolución chilena* (1973) in which he charged President Nixon with having conspired to bring about the downfall of Salvador Allende – although he did write some charming poems about the beauties of everyday life, particularly in his celebrated *Odas elementales* (1954).

One other major poet of this period is Nicolás Guillén (1902–1989), Cuba's national poet and one who, in the words of one critic, 'for many years has preached the synthesis or the realisation of the universal man in an anti-racist society where brotherhood rather than narrow racialism is sought' (Jackson, *Black Image* 125). Like Vallejo and Neruda, his work was marked by the wave of politicisation which swept through Latin America in the 1930s. His work may, roughly speaking, be divided into two periods, the pre-political era, including works such as *Motivos de son* (1930) and *Sóngoro cosongo* (1931), in which the *negrista* mode is the dominant, and those works which are politicised in tone and subject matter, such as *West Indies Ltd.* (1934), *Cantos para soldados y sones para turistas* (1937), *España (Poemas en cuatro angustias y una esperanza)* (1937), based specifically on his experience of the Spanish Civil War, *El son entero* (1947) and *La paloma de vuelo popular* (1958). Though we may plot different phases of his work, there is a sense in which they flow together, in that the *negrista* ideology of the earlier works leads naturally into the anti-imperialist stage of the later works. The early work is concerned essentially with expressing the black experience of the everyday Cuban. 'Búcate plata', for example, from *Motivos de son*, focusses on the 'incorrect' speech of a young woman telling her lover she will leave him if he doesn't earn more money: 'búcate plata,/ búcate plata,/ porque me voy a correr' (Chang-Rodríguez, *Voces* 396). One of the most charming poems of the early work is 'Sensemayá (Canto para matar a una culebra)', from *Sóngoro cosongo*, based on an African chant designed to hypnotise the snake allowing the singer to kill it. The poem uses a refrain throughout ('¡Mayombé-bombé-mayombé!') which, through its chorus-like repetition of meaningless sounds (at least in Spanish), signals that the meaning of the poem centres around its use of musicality and rituality. Guillén's most powerful political poems are in *West Indies Ltd.* which homes in on the exploitation of Negroes in the sugar trade. Rather than overtly copy the language of the blacks and express sympathy linguistically (as was the case, for example, in the early works), now Guillén expresses solidarity in terms of the enunciation of political content. Guillén's work is varied. At its best it reveals a face of the Caribbean involving racism, and the ostracisation of the black Cuban from civil society, which many would have preferred not to see. In its honesty and integrity, Guillén achieves a voice of authenticity describing black experience which is unequalled in Spanish America.

The other main poet of the twentieth century, the Mexican Octavio Paz (1914–1998), is a figure whose work spans the chronological spectrum of this chapter and the next; he is also a noted essayist and his main essay, *El laberinto de la soledad* (1950) is discussed later on in this chapter. There are three main modes in Paz's poetry: surrealism, Buddhism, and visualism. During his early years, Paz was very much influenced by surrealism, particularly its French variety, and indeed, became a personal friend of André Breton. His poetry of this period is intensely visual, searches out intellectual contradictions, and seeks to resolve those contradictions within the space of the poem. Later on, in *Salamandra* (1958–61) and *Ladera este* (1962–68), Paz, as a result of his post as ambassador in India, turned for inspiration to many varieties of Eastern religion, especially Buddhism, on which he wrote a number of essays, such as *Conjunciones, disyunciones*, which help to lay out the intellectual aspirations of his poetry of the time. Many of the poems of this period turn from the disrespectful *boutade* to the otherworldly paradox of Zen. 'Custodia' from *Ladera este*, for example, demonstrates a characteristic trait of Paz's poetry, namely, the use of visual layout to underline the meaning of the poem:

El nombre
Sus  sombras
El hombre La hembra
El mazo  El gong
La i   La o
La torre  El aljibe
El índice  La hora
El hueso   La rosa
El rocío   La huesa
El venero  La llama
El tizón  La noche
El río  La ciudad
La quilla  El ancla
El hembro La hembra
El hombre
Su cuerpo de nombres
Tu nombre en mi nombre En tu nombre mi nombre
Uno frente al otro unto contra el otro uno en torno al otro
El uno en el otro
Sin nombres

Notice how the poem shows the two sexes as separate and then gradually brings them together, until, finally, the new fusion of the sexes leads to the creation of a new verbal reality, namely, the neologisms 'El hembro' and 'La hembra', which have taken phonemic parts of their opposite number to create a new word. In many ways, Paz's poetry is at its most successful when visually stimulating since it relies on the flash of inspiration for its meaning rather than a reflective reading. Paz employs the same principle of neologism in his poem 'Petrificada petrificante' in which words are fused together in a style redolent of James Joyce's; thus, the second line of the poem contains the word 'temezquible' which itself combines 'Mezquite' and 'temible'. Although there are different types of poem written by Octavio Paz, often they revolve around the creation of a new poetic reality which is able to fuse intellectual opposites together.[1]

---

[1] This section has necessarily had to sacrifice exhaustiveness in the interests of representativity; for an excellent selection of Mexican poetry of this period, see *Poesía en movimiento: México 1915–1966*, edited by Octavio Paz, *inter alia*.

## The Novel 1910–1930

The first two decades of the twentieth century were characterised in Latin America by a novel which amplified and extended the cult of Realism which defined the nineteenth-century novel, without fundamentally invalidating it. A landmark in the genre was *Los de abajo* (1915) by Mariano Azuela (1873–1952), a work dealing with the Mexican Revolution and based on first-hand experience (Azuela worked as a reporter covering the front line for most of the Revolution). Other novels which may fruitfully be grouped under this rubric are *La vorágine* (1924) by José Eustasio Rivera (1889–1928), *Don Segundo Sombra* (1926) by Ricardo Güiraldes (1886–1927) and *Doña Bárbara* (1929) by Rómulo Gallegos (1884–1969). All three of these novels, which are also known as 'novelas de la tierra' (see Shaw, *Doña Bárbara* 7), re-address an issue raised by Sarmiento some seventy years before in the context of Argentina's cultural spectrum: that of the struggle between civilisation and barbarism. For this reason, perhaps, the novels of this early period have a bilateral symmetry which seems crude when compared to the complex asymmetry of the Boom novels which followed.

The best novel of this group is *Doña Bárbara* which centres around the conflict between barbarism and civilisation. The plot is relatively straightforward. Santos Luzardo, a young man fresh out of university studies in Caracas, goes back to his family's ranch, Altamira, set deep in the outback of the Venezuelan plains. He soon becomes locked in conflict with a woman, Doña Bárbara, whose own ranch, El Miedo, has steadily over the years been encroaching on Santos Luzardo's family's territory. The family strife began many years before during the period immediately preceding the Spanish-American war of 1898, when José de los Santos divided the Altamira ranch up between his son, José, and his daughter, Panchita, who had married Sebastián Barquero. A lack of clarity in the title deed led to a dispute between José and Sebastián, which ended in the violent death of the latter at the hands of his brother-in-law. Later on José also killed Sebastián's eldest son, Félix, with a spear (Part I, chap. ii). The flaw of the action is thus set up in a way which is reminiscent of Aeschylus's *Oresteia* in that blood is spilled from generation to generation. When Santos Luzardo returns to Altamira, his first action is to pull the spear out of the wall, thus asserting his desire to break the cycle of violence and vengeance (Part I, chap. v). In order to fight against Doña Bárbara's lawlessness, and attempting to fix permanently the dividing line between the two properties, Santos Luzardo resorts to the law (what might be called the 'witchcraft' of Caracas). The conflict between Santos Luzardo and Doña Bárbara is not only a territorial dispute, but also becomes symbolic of a larger struggle between the forces of a traditional, rural way of life and a new modern way of life based on abiding by the law, education, and urban democracy. Doña Bárbara, raped at a tender age and seemingly doomed to a life absent of love, is described at the beginning of the novel as a 'devoradora de hombres' and the reader expects Santos Luzardo to fall for her. Just the opposite happens and Doña Bárbara, for the first time in her life, falls under the spell of a man. But Santos Luzardo does not feel any emotion for her in return; instead he falls in love with Doña Bárbara's illegitimate daughter, Marisela, whom she had conceived, many years before, with a descendant of the Barquero family, Lorenzo Barquero. Marisela's gradual growth into the ideal wife for Santos Luzardo contains the kernel of the message of the novel which advocates a growth in urban democracy through the active co-option of the forces of the 'llano'. Doña Bárbara is associated with the Indian and with the land, and the book may be interpreted, through the image of Marisela, as the expression of a city-based creation of the Venezuelan nation via the co-option of subaltern elements in the society of the time (such as the Indian, and the inhabitants of the plains).

*The Novel 1930–1960*

The novel of 1930–1960 was the result of the confluence of three competing artistic pressures which were: (i) the continuing influence of Realism, (ii) the emergence of a new type of novel with a social message, the *indigenista* novel, and (iii) the emergence of a structurally sophisticated novel form which hints at the Boom novel to come. In the first group should be included novels such as *Al filo del agua* (1947) by Agustín Yáñez (1904–1980), for example, which treats the aftermath of the Mexican Revolution in a Realist manner. Similarly *El Señor Presidente* (1946) by Miguel Angel Asturias (1899–1974), is narrated in a straightforwardly Realist way, as if to suggest that the theme is too important to be overlaid with a Byzantine emplotment. (Yet one should not for that reason disparage its importance; *El Señor Presidente* is a classic of the period, and deservedly so. Written in two phases in December 1922 and in 1925–1932, the novel had a pragmatic aim, that of exposing the crimes of the Guatemalan dictator, Manuel Estrada Cabrera (1857–1924), the most durable of all the dictators of Central America, who ruled Guatemala from 1898 to 1920.)

Similar in some important ways to the Realist novel (mainly in terms of its third-person objective style and its social message) was the *indigenista* novel which reached its peak impact during this period in a number of Andean works. At least three examples deserve special mention: *Huasipungo* (1934) by the Ecuadorian Jorge Icaza (1906–1978), *El mundo es ancho y ajeno* (1940) by the Peruvian Ciro Alegría (1909–1967), and the masterpiece of the genre, *Los ríos profundos* (1958) by the Peruvian José María Arguedas (1911–1969).[2]

---

[2]  Important precursory works were *Aves sin nido* (1889) by Clorinda Matto de Turner (1829–1909), discussed above in Chapter 4, and *Raza de bronce* (1919) by Alcides Arguedas (1878–1946) (see Rodríguez-Luis 17–87). Other works of this period by José

Literary *indigenismo* is to be understood as a literary movement which asserts the need for the social recognition of the economic, political and cultural rights of the Indian population; unlike *indianismo*, which is utopian and unpoliticised since it offers an exoticised view of the Indian, *indigenismo* homes in on specific instances of oppression experienced by the local Indian community during the period the novel was published and in a particularised enviroment. Indeed, *indigenista* works are unlikely to be properly understood when removed from the particular historical circumstances which gave rise to the political dilemma which they describe.

*Los ríos profundos* tells the story of the growth into adulthood of a young fourteen-year-old boy, Ernesto, his experience in a boarding school run by priests, his participation in a riot in which some salt is stolen, and his subsequent punishment. Ernesto's native language is Quechua, he feels in tune with Incan culture, and yet his final experience in the Peru of his day is that of an outsider. In this sense, the novel functions not only as the story of a young boy's growth into adulthood, but also that of Incan culture which achieves consciousness. The narrator becomes the point of intersection between the power of the oppressors and the resistance of the oppressed – which is epitomised by the *cholas* who take control of the town and reclaim the salt which they argue has been taken from them (the salt operates here not only in an empiric sense as an intrinsic part of their everyday livelihood, but also simultaneously alludes to the essence of life itself). The struggle within the seminary between the young boys and their priests is a microcosm of the struggle in the town for political power, which is expressed in clear-cut economic, cultural and linguistic lines. One of the first of its kind to see the world of the Indians from the inside, as it were, *Los ríos profundos* is a bilingual novel, in which Quechua is frequently alluded to – in the expression 'le dije en quechua . . .' – or used in the text, typically in the form of citation of oral poetry, which is then translated into Spanish. This provides the impression that the novel itself is evolving an act of transculturation, re-creating the Incan universe, before the eyes of a Spanish-speaking audience. Through Ernesto's eyes, two institutions stand out as oppressive, the Church as symbolized by the Director, and the Army, as embodied by the soldiers who occupy Patibamba after the riot, and, here, Arguedas is clearly making a post-colonial point since the two forces which most clearly epitomized the Spanish conquest of the Incas were the Church and the Army. Yet, it would be a mistake to see Arguedas's novel as simply an indictment of oppression, since it is skilful at capturing the essence of the Incan culture, which is

María Arguedas can also be grouped under the rubric of *indigenismo* such as the short stories in *Agua* (1935), and the novels *Yawar fiesta* (1940), and *Todas las sangres* (1964). There were examples of the *indigenista* novel in Mexico, such as *El indio* (1935) by Gregorio López y Fuentes, and *El resplandor* (1937) by Mauricio Magdaleno (Rodríguez-Luis 252), but these are formula-driven rather than creative works of art.

mainly engineered through the evocation of popular songs interspersed throughout the narrative; perhaps most emblematic is the 'huayno' which describes the way in which Doña Felipa, the ringleader of the *cholas*, outmastered her masters, and which, as a result of being sung, causes its singer to be arrested (Arguedas 195–201). *Los ríos profundos* marked a new departure in the evolution of the Spanish-American novel, evoking with a freshness unequalled since its publication, the world of the Incas as it comes into contact with the world of the Spanish, as mediated through the mind of an astute, fourteen-year-old boy.

Apart from those novels which were characterised by some (perhaps unfairly) in terms of a 'realismo trasnochado', and the *indigenista* novels, there were others which experimented with the structure of the novel. This was due, in large measure, to the impact in Latin-American literary circles of the experimental work of European writers such as Proust, Camus, Woolf, and Joyce, and North-American authors such as Steinbeck and Faulkner, and particularly the latters' use of the stream-of-consciousness technique, free association, and the disruption of spatial and temporal parameters: in summation, internal logic rather than objective reality. *La última niebla* (1934) and *La amortajada* (1938), for example, by María Luisa Bombal (1910–1980) are typical in this respect in that they demonstrate a readiness to experiment with the boundaries of what the novel can do. The latter novel, for example, in the manner of Zola's *La Terre*, recreates the thoughts of a woman as she lies in her coffin as if witnessing her relatives during the funeral wake (for further discussion of *La amortajada*, see Hart, *White* 37–45). *El túnel* (1948) by Ernesto Sábato (b.1911), likewise, tends to focus on the paranormal and is an elegantly written novel about the growth of obsession and madness in the life of a young man. Related to the vogue of greater experimentalism was the search among the writers of this generation for what might be called cultural roots. In the work of Miguel Angel Asturias and Alejo Carpentier, for example, the fragmented legacy of 'other' cultures – the Amerindian in the first and the African in the second – provides an image of a past of immanent meaning to which the alienated individual of the modern world feels drawn.

In Asturias's *Hombres de maíz* (1949), considered by some as the matrix text of magical realism, the fantastic and the originary are merged to create a world which is 'semisueño y semirrealidad' (Asturias 303). The novel homes in on a group of native Maya tribesmen led by Gaspar Ilóm who struggle in vain to protect their ancestral home in the highlands of Guatemala against the encroachment of the emerging capitalist, state-directed economy. The conflict is portrayed via frequent shifts between the discourse of the everyday (the whites burning down the Indians' trees for material profit) and the Jungian voices of the Indians; these latter voices do not belong to individuals but articulate a genetically inscribed memory. As one character says: 'Cuando uno cuenta lo que no se cuenta, dice uno, yo lo inventé, es mío. Pero lo que uno efectivamente está haciendo es recordar; vos recordaste en tu borrachera lo que la memoria de tus antepasados dejó en tu sangre' (Asturias 241). The governing principle of Asturias's novel is finally shown to be not the narrative action but the Amerindian worldview which weaves together the human, animal and vegetable kingdoms, making a man indistinguishable from maize, a postman merge with a coyote, and (echoing a Maya trope) a man's thoughts turn into flowers. Published four years after Asturias's *Hombres de maíz*, Carpentier's *Los pasos perdidos* (1953), likewise, epitomises the main thematic strands of the pre-Boom novel, namely: (i) the fusion of national and personal narratives, (ii) the search for lost cultural origins (called in the novel 'ciertos modos de vivir que el hombre había perdido para siempre'; Carpentier 38), and (iii) the incorporation of myth. *Los pasos perdidos* tells the story of an individual bored with the Western paradigm of knowledge, who goes on a research trip to the Amazon to find himself; the journey becomes 'una suerte de retroceso del tiempo a los años de mi infancia' (Carpentier 79), and eventually leads to a passionate love affair with an earth mother type, Rosario, whom he loses tragically soon after finding her. The protagonist not only loses Rosario but also the musical work he composed while in the jungle entitled *Trueno* – which manages to combine the sounds of nature with human music – and which fulfils the function of origin in the novel, now displaced. Some features of Carpentier's work were prescient about the direction the Spanish-American novel would take; his understanding of the coterminacy of the sexual and the ontological search would reappear later in Cortázar's fiction, and his sense of the interlocking nature of the fantastic and the real (which he dubbed 'lo real maravilloso') would find an echo in García Márquez's subsequent fiction.

  *Pedro Páramo* (1955) by Juan Rulfo (1916–1986) is the best example of the pre-Boom experimental novel. Set in a Mexican village, Comala, expanded to universalist proportions, the novel opens with the narrator searching for his father, Pedro Páramo. It gradually emerges that all the inhabitants of the village are dead, as is the narrator. Through the flashbacks which intersperse the narrative, we learn of the drama that reduced the inhabitants of Comala to their purgatorial predicament; it was the will of one man, Pedro Páramo, who acts in various roles as the *cacique* of the village and thereby claims rights over the villagers which are normally reserved for God. The flashbacks also give insight into Pedro Páramo's own desperate love; though he is the goal of others' search, he also is searching; the sense of an attainable origin is thus collapsed to produce a dizzying series of self-eliding substitute objects of desire. Rulfo's novel typifies a number of features of the pre-Boom novel; like *Los pasos perdidos* it emphasizes the fusion of personal and national destinies (the narrator is at once an individual and an archetype of the search for Mexican identity), the importance of the search (even if frustrated, as here), and the obsessive allusion to mythic texts. Thus, the narrator's quest echoes those quest-narratives of Greek mythology, such as Oedipus and Ulysses, although it is a truncated version in the sense that even the object of the quest is a shadowy figure, who disappears, true to the literal meaning of his name (Pedro is related to stone ['piedra'], while Páramo means 'wasteland'), into a pile of stones at the end of the novel. Perhaps most intriguing about Rulfo's novel is its ability to give a vision of an ultraterrene existence in a matter-of-fact way, an important characteristic of the magical-realist novel. In historico-political terms, *Pedro Páramo* expresses the *angst* of a rootless Mexican populace, displaced by the upheavals of the Revolution (1911–1917), and for whom the old certainties of previously-cherished ideologies – the landowning elite, the Church – have disappeared for ever, leaving for a number of years a political vacuum. These political uncertainties find expression in the elision of the difference between life and death, illusion and reality, and the distinctiveness of family roles (the narrator acts as brother, husband, and son in quick succession to people he does not know) and gender. Political and historical uncertainty is thereby translated onto an ontological level.


*Short Story*

The Spanish-American short story came into its own during this period. One of the best *cuentistas* writing in the early decades of the century was Horacio Quiroga (1878–1937); his main short story collections are *Cuentos de amor, de locura y de muerte* (1917), *Cuentos de la selva para niños* (1918), *El salvaje* (1919), and *Anaconda* (1921). The main theme of Quiroga's short stories is the struggle between man and his environment, in which, despite the dogged and sometimes heroic efforts of the (normally male) protagonist, he loses the battle and dies. In the typical short story by Quiroga, description is kept to a bare minimum and only used when it echoes the thrust of the main events. Exploration of the inner psychology of the individual is kept to a bare minimum, which tends to reinforce Quiroga's essentially mechanistic and materialist view of humankind. 'El hombre muerto' is typical in this respect in that it has the stock ingredients of a bitter struggle of man against death told in stark, unencumbered prose. By the second paragraph of the story, the protagonist, simply called 'el hombre' as if to emphasize the generic nature of his plight, is already dead; he falls on his machete knife and kills himself (Quiroga 160). 'A la deriva' is similar. Again, the protagonist is nameless and, by the very first sentence of the story, he is doomed; he has trodden on a snake which bites him (Quiroga 156). He then kills the snake, drinks some whisky, and then sets off on a boat journey along the Paraná river to seek medical help. As the title of the story already forewarns us, he is going nowhere. What is perhaps most interesting about Quiroga's short stories is their combination of the close attention to the here and now, described often with a scientific objectivity, with a hint of the supernatural, a device which Quiroga may well have learned from his master, Edgar Allan

Poe, but which he transforms to produce a narrative unmatched in its use of suspense.

Another significant short-story writer of this period is the Mexican Juan José Arreola (b.1918). His significance lies as much as in the tutelage he provided for an up-and-coming generation of Mexican writers as in his own literary output. In the 1950s he founded a book series, Los Presentes, which aimed to publish new Mexican writers, and with Juan Rulfo, under the auspices of the Centro Mexicano de Escritores in Mexico City, he taught a generation of writers how to write, including Homero Aridjis, Inés Arredondo, Emilio Carballido, Rosario Castellanos, Alí Chumacero, Fernando del Paso, Salvador Elizondo, Carlos Fuentes, Luisa Josefina Hernández, Jorge Ibargüengoitia, José Agustín, Vicente Leñero, Carlos Monsiváis, and Gustavo Sainz. Intriguingly, Arreola's literary output, compared to that of some of the writers he coached, is small. What is more, some of his short stories are small even by the standards of the genre (barely a page long). His most anthologised story, 'El guardagujas', is exemplary. It opens with an unnamed 'forastero' who arrives at a railway station waiting for a train to take him to a place called T.; he engages in a conversation with a little old man (who is later revealed to be the switchman of the title), who advises him to forget about catching a train, but instead to look for lodging in the inn. The traveller is then regaled with a Kafkaesque description of how trains are very irregular, how they often do not go where they are meant to, and how the derailment of one train led to the foundation of a village. Finally, a whistle is heard in the distance and the train arrives. In this short story, Arreola manages to convert an everyday situation, such as waiting for a train, into an allegory of the Mexican nation (bureaucracy gone wild) as well as an existentialist tale of metaphysical aimlessness (the train, like life, leads nowhere).

One of the most distinctive short-story writers of this period is Juan Rulfo, whose novel *Pedro Páramo* has been discussed above (see pp. 109–10). Like Arreola, Rulfo was not a prolific writer. The seventeen short stories collected in *El llano en llamas* (1953) focus on themes which would also be present in his novel published two years later, such as existential lostness, the mythical search for ontological meaning, the inhospitability of climate (many of the stories take place against the backdrop of an arid, hot Mexican plain), an overpowering sense of guilt and a frustrated desire for redemption. There are, however, some leitmotifs which have a distinctive resonance in the short stories. Underlying the narrative of the typical short story is a murder in the past which erupts into the present, but which is remembered only fragmentarily or not at all by the perpetrator of the deed, who is often the narrator of the story itself, a technique which raises the device of the unreliable narrator to a new level. The narrator of 'El hombre', for example, does not recall committing the act of murder, but all the internal evidence points that way (Rulfo 22–28). The two best stories in *El llano en llamas* are 'Nos han dado la tierra' and 'Es que somos muy pobres'. The first story focusses on the story of four travellers, Melitón, Esteban, Faustino, and the narrator, who are walking to the arable land promised to them by the government authorities. The land is no more than a desert (Rulfo 4). The description of the journey, which comes to take on the ironically mythical proportions of a pilgrimage to the promised land, is interrupted by the memory of the conversation they had with a delegate who tells them not to be alarmed by having so much land (Rulfo 5), and, when they complain about its quality, tells them to put their complaint in writing, though he knows full well they cannot write ('Eso manifiéstalo por escrito', Rulfo 5). 'Es que somos muy pobres' is a tragic tale of a young girl, Tacha, whose cow, her only hope of a dowry, has been swept away by a river which has burst its banks, and is therefore in effect condemned to a life of prostitution like her two older sisters. The last paragraph of the story, in describing Tacha's tears, manages to give an eerie sense of identity of inner and outer worlds, since her tears are like the swell of the river (Rulfo 17). Tacha's moral downfall is shown to be as inevitable as the growth of her breasts. The short stories collected in *El llano en llamas* have a dramatic intensity which is redolent of Aeschylus in that they focus on the eternal cycle of murder and vengeance. But perhaps most impressive about these stories is their laconic style. Description and dialogue are kept to a bare minimum, the external world is described at the expense of the portrayal of psychological reality, and the stories have a swiftness of pace which is well suited to the structure of the short story.

The master of the short story of this period was Jorge Luis Borges (1899–1986); the first edition of his *Ficciones* was published in 1944, and the complete second edition in 1956. The main idea of this collection of short stories is, as the title suggests, fiction; here fiction is to be understood in the wider sense of the word to encompass cultural constructs such as society, mythology, metaphysics, religion. A recurring theme of *Ficciones* is the way in which mankind constructs fictions which envelop the individual like a labyrinth and in which he gets lost. The guiding archetype of the *Ficciones* is the futility of all human endeavour, especially when expressed as an intellectual desire for truth, coupled with an impish delight in intellectual conundrums. The reader is required to become the detective of the story and piece together the clues which, as he discovers on re-reading, never quite add up. The most important Borgesian metaphor, one which synthesises all the others, is the book; the indecipherable book, for example, a common enough stage prop in Borges's short stories, stands for the unknowable universe, the forever out-of-reach objective of the quest-narrative of human existence. In 'Tlön, Uqbar, Orbis Tertius', for example, Borges goes to great lengths in providing a believable narrative which substantiates the account of an imaginary universe (described at the end of one version of *The Anglo-American Cyclopaedia* published in 1917, and confirmed by a book received in the mail in 1937 by a certain Englishman, Herbert Ashe, living in Argentina). Much of the text is taken up with a description of the laws of the planet Tlön, whose religion and metaphysics are idealist, whose languages have verbs but no nouns, and whose inhabitants reject as contrary to common sense the notions of causal effect and temporal succession. The story concludes with a post-script which describes the irruption of this ideal universe into the everyday universe inhabitated by the narrator (Tlön alphabetical characters appear on a compass and a cone of shining metal too heavy to be of this world) (Borges 35). Borges's *Ficciones*, as we can see, tend to undermine the hierarchy of different types of knowledge by suggesting that, because they are verbal, they are therefore also imaginary and fictitious. As the philosophers of Tlön argue, in a sentence that is typical of the world-view of the *Ficciones* as a whole, 'la metafísica es una rama de la literatura fantástica' (Borges 24). Borges's short stories are concerned with mapping the quintessence of fictionality and dem-onstrating that the fictions in which man finds himself trapped are not exter-nally created labyrinths but natural outgrowths of the human mind; 'to think is to abstract is to distort' could almost be a motto of these intriguing brain teasers. Borges's influence on his own and the succeeding generation of Spanish American writers was immense; the Boom writers, in particular García Márquez, Carlos Fuentes, and Cortázar, all stressed the importance of his work. Although he would have been loathe to admit it, Borges's work gained ground immensely during the 1960s when Latin-American writers suddenly became all the rage in Europe and the United States. Given the early translation of his work into English and French, he also soon achieved an international readership and, indeed, was one of the first Latin American writers to do so.

## Theatre

The difficulty in writing about the major dramatic works of the first half of the twentieth century is that there is little consensus about the canon. Three retrospective anthologies published in the early 1970s, for example, promote different writers as representatives of Latin-American drama.[3] This period saw a number of independent theatrical groups spring up, such as the Teatro Experimental de la Universidad de Chile in 1941, and the Teatro Galpón

---

3   An anthology of *El teatro actual latinoamericano* (1972), edited by Carlos Solór-zano, contains works by Carlos Gorostiza, Guillermo Francovich, Enrique Buenaventura, Daniel Gallegos, Antón Arrefat, Isidora Aguirre, and Demetrio Aguilera Malta. The works chosen in *Los clásicos del teatro hispanoamericano* (1975), edited by Luzuriaga and Reeve, to represent the same period, are by Armando Moock, Samuel Eichelbaum, Xavier Villarrutia, Rodolfo Usigli, and Celestino Gorostiza. The works chosen in *The Modern Stage in Latin America: Six Plays* (1972), edited by George Woodyard, are by René Mar-qués, Alfredo Dias Gomes, Osvaldo Dragún, Jorge Díaz, José Triana, and Emilio Carbal-lido. Since not one dramatist appears twice in any of these three anthologies, this suggests a lack of agreement about which the major works are.

(1949) in Uruguay under the direction of Atahualpa del Cioppo; in 1957 the First Festival de Teatro Libre was held in Buenos Aires. Given the great diversity of dramatic works during this period, I will focus on two geographic areas, the Southern Cone together with Mexico and the Caribbean; as we shall see, the former is concerned with the tensions within the bourgeois institution of the family, while the latter is preoccupied with the elusiveness of (national) identity.[4]

A number of the plays of this period from the Southern Cone centre almost obsessively on sexual relationships. *La serpiente* (1920) by the Chilean dramatist Armando Moock (1894–1942), for instance, focusses on the satanic attraction that women exert on men; its main thesis is that women ruin the artist's creative gift, and thus it is just in the nick of time that Pedro escapes the temptation of Luciana, the 'serpent'. Even in plays which ostensibly have other thematic purposes, this obsession emerges. *Un guapo del 900* (1940) by the Argentine writer Samuel Eichelbaum (1894–1969), for example, appears at first glance to be a play about the struggle for political power, since it tells the story of one Ecuménico who kills Clemente Ordóñez, the political rival to his own boss, Don Alejo. However, as the play unravels, it becomes transparently clear that the reason Ecuménico killed Ordóñez was because the latter had been having an affair with Don Alejo's wife. Anger about adultery, or the flouting of the institution of marriage, rather than the struggle for power, is shown to be the real reason for Ecuménico's rage. As he says at one point, he would have been unable to respect a man as his leader if he were known to be a cuckold (Luzuriaga & Reeve 652). *El pacto de Cristina* (1945) by Conrado Nalé Roxlo (1898–1971), on the surface, is a reworking of Goethe's *Faust*; here it is a woman, Cristina, who sells her future son, rather than her soul, to the devil, in order to obtain by supernatural means a man's love. Though set in the Middle Ages, and appropriately couched in the language of romantic love, this play focusses on the problems inherent in sexual love, and, in effect, criminalises female sexual desire. Realising she has gone too far, Cristina commits suicide on her wedding night.

Plays written in Mexico and the Caribbean focus typically on the elusiveness of personal and national identity. Some plays raise this theme in the context of metaphysical unknowing. *Parece mentira* (1934) by the Mexican Xavier Villarrutia (1903–1950), for example, is a Kafkaesque play in which a man visits a lawyer's office after receiving an anonymous note which suggests that he must do so in order to discover his wife's secret life, and then sees three identical women who walk across the stage and then disappear

---

4 This section deals in the main with plays understood in the conventional sense of the term. It could be argued, however, that Spanish America's most successful theatrical genre is 'teatro breve' which, for reasons of space, it has not been possible to treat here; for an excellent anthology including work by the masters of this genre (Dragún, Solórzano and Garro), see *Teatro breve hispanoamericano*, ed. Carlos Solórzano.

mysteriously. As in the Theatre of the Absurd, an enigmatic situation is presented to the audience, but the spectators are no wiser about the 'meaning' of the events they have witnessed when the curtain falls than when it rose. Other plays of this period address the issue of national identity more directly. *El color de nuestra piel* (1952) by the Mexican Celestino Gorostiza (1904–1967), for instance, treats the clash of ideologies within a family unit, as encapsulated, on the one hand, by the racist and pro-American father, Don Ricardo, who favours his 'white' son, Héctor, and the mother, Beatriz, who is identified with Mexican *mestizo* identity. The father's option is shown ultimately to be erroneous for Mexico, since his favourite son is eventually revealed to be the culprit behind the scandal at the family-owned laboratory; he was passing off old stock as new, and pocketing the proceeds.

The single most important drama of this period was *El gesticulador* (1937) by the Mexican Rodolfo Usigli (1905–1980). This play tells the story of a disillusioned university professor, César Rubio, who has moved from Mexico City to a provincial town in North Mexico and who, quite by chance, meets a Harvard professor, Oliver Bolton, whom he leads to believe, by virtue of spurious documentation, that he is a long-lost hero of the Mexican Revolution. As a result of this deception César is persuaded to stand in the elections for governor in his home state. Thus his political career begins, until it is brought abruptly to a halt when he is murdered by a political opponent, Navarro. The reason why César decides to live the lie emerges in the *agnorisis* scene between César and Navarro in Act III when Navarro accuses him of being an imposter, to which César replies that Mexico is a country of imposters: '¿Quién es cada uno en México? Dondequiera encuentras impostores, impersonadores, simuladores' (Usigli 254). At which point perhaps the most intriguing insight of the play emerges, namely, not only that people are imposters but that they allow others to retain their façades since it is in their own interest to do so. Thus César uses his knowledge that Navarro killed César Rubio, the revolutionary, in order to blackmail Navarro into silence (Usigli 256–58). César believes that this lying contract, by which we are given to understand society functions, justifies his new identity (Usigli 260). Even after César is murdered by Navarro (although the latter does not of course admit to the deed in public), the social contract of deception is perpetuated in the relationship between Navarro and César's son, Miguel. For Miguel to point the finger at Navarro inevitably means exposing his father as an imposter and thereby endangering his mother's state pension. *El gesticulador*, thus, presents a grotesque version of deception in political office, which is maintained through the collusion and self-interest of others. Miguel, at the conclusion of the play, is left with this troubling knowledge (Usigli 273). Usigli's play is technically innovative, particularly in its use of dramatic tension in the gradual unfolding of the truth, and of suspense, in the gap between the characters' and the audience's knowledge of events. Particularly skilful are the *agnorisis* scenes, such as between Bolton and César (Act I) and

Navarro and César (Act III) in which the audience is kept in the dark about César's motives until the last moment.

*La muerte no entrará en palacio* (1957) by the Puerto Rican dramatist René Marqués (1919–1979), like *El gesticulador*, focusses on the issue of an elusive national identity. It is a political drama in the sense that it alludes to the transition from colony to protectorate which occurred in Puerto Rico in 1952 when the island was given commonwealth status with the United States, a unique, hitherto unknown, political status. The ideology of the play clearly regrets this position and, indeed, presents this event as if it never took place; Don José, Governor of the Isla (as it is elliptically referred to throughout the play), is shot by his daughter, Casandra, before he can sign the agreement with the United States ambassador. The ideal which the play supports is that embodied by Don Rodrigo, who fought for Puerto Rico's independence at Don José's side during their youth, for which he was imprisoned, unlike Don José, who turned his back on his rebellious past in order to pursue a political career. Rodrigo never makes an appearance on stage but his presence is assured through his son, Alberto, who works as a military aide in the Governor's palace but in whom Rodrigo's ideals burn brightly. Alberto could be seen as the main tragic figure in the play (*La muerte no entrará en palacio* was called a tragedy by its author), although the manner of his death (accidentally shot by his bethrothed, Casandra) is melodramatic rather than tragic; however, Casandra could be seen as a tragic figure since her political idealism obliges her to kill her political enemy, who happens to be her father, Don José.

## The Essay

José Carlos Mariátegui (1894–1930) is one of the most significant essay writers of twentieth-century Latin America. Like many Latin American intellectuals of his generation, he travelled to Europe (1919–1923), spending most of his time in Italy, an experience which led him to embrace communism. On his return to Lima in 1923, Mariátegui became politically involved in his country's affairs, soon becoming a prominent spokesman of the Left. In 1928 his *Siete ensayos de interpretación de la realidad peruana* was published, on which his fame largely rests; he died of ill health at the tragically young age of thirty-six. Each of the seven essays has a specific theme (economic development, the Indian problem, the land problem, public education, religion, regionalism versus centralism, and literature), but one main idea threads its way through all of these essays and that is the coincidence between communism and the Incan system of government. As one would expect from a Marxist thinker, Mariátegui rejects the ideology of conquest and colonisation, and is caustic in his assessment of the continued existence of this mindset in post-independence Peru. He argues forcefully for seeing the problem of the Indian in economic rather than racial or moral terms (Mariátegui 20–30). He shows that the lot of the Indian sub-class grew even worse in the Republic despite the rhetoric of liberation typical of the independence movement (Mariátegui 31–67). He compares the colonial system instituted by the Spanish with that instituted in North America, and the former comes off worse in his estimation; he goes on to argue that the religion of the Incas was socio-political rather than theological and this was why it disappeared when confronted by Catholicism (Mariátegui 105–10). Lastly, Mariátegui's essays on various Peruvian literary figures, ranging from Ricardo Palma to César Vallejo, are sensitive to racial, ethnic and historical variables in the literary works they treat. The most contentious and potentially intriguing element in Mariátegui's thesis was his view of the similarities existing between twentieth-century communism and pre-Columbian societies. While the truth value of Mariátegui's thesis with regard to this idea may be limited, it was clearly an important statement of his desire to ground the need for communism in twentieth-century Latin America in a prelapsarian space associated with the period before the Fall initiated by the conquest.

The political affiliation of *Radiografía de la pampa* (1933) by Ezequiel Martínez Estrada (1895–1964) could not be more different from Mariátegui's *Siete ensayos*. The aims of the two writers are similar – both set out to give a broad picture of the culture of their compatriots – but the results are diametrically opposed. Martínez Estrada's *Radiografía de la pampa*, unlike Mariátegui's work, pursues an anti-Indian thesis to its radical (and execrable) conclusion. Following the lead of Sarmiento's *Facundo* of the previous century, Martínez Estrada attempts to map out the contours of the soul of Argentina, drawing much inspiration for this from the vast terrain of the pampa around Buenos Aires. *Radiografía de la pampa* has six parts, the first of which is broadly historical, while the subsequent parts address themes such as 'Solitude', 'Primitive Forces', 'Buenos Aires', 'Fear', and 'Pseudo-Structures', and attempt to re-create the distinctiveness of the life-experience of the so-called 'homo pampaeus' (Martínez Estrada 146). The main focus of the work is man's endless struggle against adversity which is incarnated in a number of forms, such as nature, loneliness, the fear of the unknown, the Indian, and the void; sometimes these motifs are rolled indiscriminately into one to symbolize the enemy of (Caucasian) man.

One essay of this period whose significance would only be grasped later was *Contrapunto cubano del tabaco y el azúcar* (1940) by the Cuban essayist and sociologist, Fernando Ortiz (1881–1969). In this essay Ortiz uses two Cuban products, tobacco and sugar, as a means of investigating the complex process whereby cultures intermingle and produce a new cultural reality. The study begins with a description of the physical appearance of the two plants which produce tobacco and sugar, their origins and cultural associations. Much is made in the opening section of the difference between the two, expressed in terms of gender: 'Si tabaco es varón, azucar es hembra' (Ortiz

20). Ortiz goes on to discuss the manufacturing process by which the refined products are made, its social implications, and its relationship with slavery and the growth of capital-based industrialisation in the nineteenth century. In order better to understand the complex historical process whereby products invade other cultures, Ortiz introduces the term 'transculturación', a neologism which he sees as more appropriate than its competitor term 'aculturation' (Ortiz 137). Transculturation is based on the insight that 'en todo abrazo de culturas sucede lo que en la cópula genética de los individuos: la criatura siempre es distinta de cada uno de los dos' (Ortiz 142). Ortiz subsequently conducts a fascinating and well-researched narrative of the use of tobacco and sugar and their transculturation when they traverse the Atlantic Ocean on their way to European society, as gleaned from an abundance of printed sources, which range from contemporary scientific studies (including medical reports positing a link between cigarette smoking and cancer) to the work of early chroniclers such as Fray Mendieta, Fernández de Oviedo, and Díaz del Castillo.

Undoubtedly the most influential – and, in some, particulary feminist, quarters, most reviled – essay written during this period was Octavio Paz's *El laberinto de la soledad* (1950). Paz begins this essay with a discussion of the *pachucos* of Mexican descent who live in Los Angeles. The second chapter, 'Máscaras mexicanas', potentially the most interesting, discusses the role played by social masks in modern-day Mexico. Chapter 3 examines the way in which festivals and social celebrations, such as the 'Día de Muertos', bring an element of participation into a daily routine dominated by existential loneliness. In chapter 4 Paz introduces one of the most contentious theses of his essay, that is, the origin of Mexican identity. Mexicans, he argues, are the children of La Malinche and Cortés, and, following the gender-specific lines already traced in chapter 2, he identifies Malinche as passive, raped ('chingada') and therefore 'open' (*Laberinto* 78). It is clear that Paz is conflating the Oedipal scene of the jealous son, taken from Freud's analysis of the development of the human personality, with the historical scene of the martial conquest by Spain of Mesoamerica, and thus interpreting one in terms of the other. Cortés's love-making with La Malinche, in effect, becomes the primal scene of Mexico's birth. Paz's choice of Cortés and La Malinche is highly symbolic, since they do not loom large in popular mythology. Though it might be criticised for 'racialising' the history of Mexico (namely, by seeing the creation of *mestizo* culture in post-Edenic terms as a fall from grace caused by the rape of one race by another), *El laberinto de la soledad* is an imaginative and insightful essay on the symbolism of Mexican nationhood.[5]

---

[5] The popularity of this work is suggested by sales. From the second edition which came out in 1959 until 1984 there were thirteen reprints. In 1984 alone 50,000 copies of the book were printed in the Colección Popular series for the Fondo de Cultura Económica publishing house.

## The Multi-genre Writer

One of the most significant multi-genre writers of this era was the Mexican Rosario Castellanos (1925–1974). University professor, ambassador, translator, essayist, short-story writer, novelist, dramatist and poet, Castellanos is now seen as a major literary figure of her time. Castellanos's poetry is conversational and focusses on cultural and gender oppression from a subjective angle. One of her most famous poems is 'Meditación en el umbral' which expresses disappointment at the roles traditionally allotted to women, which range from the literary stereotype (Tolstoy's Ana, Flaubert's Madame Bovary) to the literary writer (Santa Teresa, Sor Juana, and Emily Dickinson), and leaves the reader at the threshold of 'another way of being' (*Meditation* 48). Some of Castellanos's best poems contemplate the dilemma at the intersection of gender and race. In 'Malinche', for example, Castellanos re-writes the narrative of La Malinche's life, diverging from the standard view of her as Cortés's interpreter-concubine who betrayed her native land for personal gain, as given by historians such as Díaz del Castillo (see 78–79), and, indeed, Paz (see above), and instead focusses on her sorrow at being rejected by her mother. Castellanos thereby in effect writes 'herstory' rather than history.

Castellanos's novel *Oficio de tinieblas* (1962) is set in a town called Ciudad Real – the connotations of royalty are not coincidental – and focusses on the tragic conflict between the Indians and the *ladinos* (called *caxclanes* by the Indians) in that community. Much of the novel is concerned with tracing the gradual intensification of the conflict between the *caxlanes* and the Indians. The true depths of the horror of the social conflict are revealed on Good Friday when the Indian community sacrifice a young male child, Domingo, as a means of appropriating the cultural-religious dominance of the *ladinos*. Overall, the novel provides a pessimistic vision of the relationship between Indians and non-Indians in modern-day Mexico. The Indian population's re-appropriation of the symbolism of Christianity is, after all, grotesque in the extreme.

Castellanos's short stories follow a similar theme and are the genre in which she excels. *Album de familia* (1971) contains four stories which focus on the emotional traumas which underlie everyday life in middle-class Mexican society. The masterpiece of this collection of short stories is 'Lección de cocina' which concentrates on the split between the role expected of Mexican women and the identity they wish to create for themselves. The action takes place in the mind of a woman preparing a meal for her husband who will shortly be returning from work, and it enacts a type of self-discovery. As the meat which she is preparing slowly disappears, so does her acceptance of patriarchy. In this short story, Castellanos adopts a mock-ignorant stance in order to give more urgency to her critique of the patriarchal institution of marriage. Her novella, *Balún-Canán* (1957), seen by many as her masterpiece, is set in an imaginary town, Balún-Canán in Chiapas, and presents some of the societal conflicts sketched in *Oficio de tinieblas*, but through the eyes of a child. Social conflict is expressed almost exclusively within the space of the local school – the Indians want their children to be educated (which is not unreasonable since this had become state policy in Cárdenas's post-Revolution Mexico) while the local oligarch, César, resists this development – and the children whose education is being denied are about the same age as the narrator, César's daughter (she is seven years old when the narrative begins). The build-up of political tension between the two social groups is presented suspensefully in the novel, beginning with the murder of one of the farm-hands who supports his political master rather than his fellow workers, leading through a series of visits from inspectors from the capital who attempt to enforce the establishment of a school, and climaxing with the arson attack on César's property and livestock after he closes the local school down and forces the workers to go back to work. The novel concludes on a pessimistic note with the death of the narrator's younger brother and the banishment of the nanny who had predicted that a tragedy of this kind would occur because of the father's actions. The strength of this novel lies not only in its use of the child narrator but its ability to merge seamlessly the language of the supernatural world with that of concrete societal conflict. The novel has, strikingly, taken on greater significance since the outbreak of political violence in the Chiapas region since 1994; the warring parties are, indeed, none other than those described in Castellanos's novel.

Castellanos's play *El eterno femenino* (1975), published posthumously, describes itself as a farce. The butt of its humour are the manifold versions of Mexican womanhood which are imposed on Mexican women; the critique of this practice is burlesque and light-hearted rather than serious and moralising. The play re-creates a number of scenes from the past – whether they be 'universal' history, or Mexican history – and provides a new, anti-patriarchal slant on those events. The Adam and Eve scene, for example, shows Eve running intellectual rings around Adam and even the serpent (*Eterno* 74–85). The scene in which Charlotte and Maximilian are discussing their options in nineteenth-century Mexico also reveals the familiar pattern of the woman as the active, intelligent party and the man as the unresourceful, slow agent in the relationship (*Eterno* 120–27). Another scene – iconoclastically – shows Sor Juana reciting her love poems not to a man, but to another woman, Celia (*Eterno* 106). The play concludes on a metatheatrical note. A number of women sit around having listened to the play, and proceed to castigate its author mercilessly, accusing her of attacking the sacred values of family, religion and motherland (*Eterno* 181–94). The play thereby contains and, in effect, deflates by anticipation any conservative critique of its feminist message.

Chapter 6

# TWENTIETH-CENTURY LITERATURE: PART II

Alan Sinfield has described effectively the change which occurred in the literary field in the 1960s: 'Literature since the 1960s has . . . looked increasingly like a commodity (with, for instance, a top ten like pop records). Books may be conceived not by authors, but by publishers who commission a work they believe they can sell. . . . The idea of literary quality is used as a manifest marketing ploy – in literary prizes such as the Booker (with the final announcement live on television), in the promotion of book clubs, and in the selling of films and television serials through their derivation from a literary classic – and then the book though its connections with the screen version' (Sinfield 291). A similar type of commodification of literature began to emerge during this era in Latin America. As Fernández Retamar recalls of the early 1970s: 'Grants proliferated, colloquiums flourished, chairs to study and dissect us sprouted like toadstools after a rainstorm. There was even talk, in the most wretched stock-market taste, of the Boom of the Latin-American novel' (*Caliban Revisited* 48). These were new times in which Latin-American writers, in direct contradistinction to a previous era, could gain substantial royalties for their work, win highly lucrative literary prizes and be lionised by the world press. The Boom of Spanish-American literature – centreing on writers such as Gabriel García Márquez, Julio Cortázar, Carlos Fuentes, and Mario Vargas Llosa – signalled the definitive birth of Spanish-American literature, thrusting it to the centre of the world's literary stage (see, in particular, 'The Boom Novel' below).

## Poetry

The most significant poet of this period is Nicanor Parra (b.1914); born in Chillán, a small town two hundred miles to the south of Santiago, Chile, he graduated in 1938 in mathematics and physics at the University of Chile in Santiago. Rather surprisingly, though, he became famous not as a physicist but as a poet. There are three discernible stages in Parra's work which, excluding his juvenilia (1937–1950), are 'antipoesía' (1954–1967), poetry characterised by bitter social critique (1968–1976), and poetry with a prophetic style (1977 to present day). In the 1960s Parra created the 'antipoem' for which his work is famous, that is, the poem which rejects the artificial and high-flown language we normally associate with poetry and attempts to speak with a voice that is recognised by everybody and not just the elite. Thus, Parra rejects the conventions of poetry, seeing poems as mathematical theorems. 'Maximum content, minimum of words. . . . Economy of language, no metaphors, no literary tropes.' In 'La montaña rusa', from *Versos de salón* (1962), for example, Parra shows how Mount Olympus, where the poets traditionally went to drink inspiration in the spring of Castalia, has given way to the roller coaster. The thrill of Parra's poetry has more in common with the modern world; it is neither gentle nor soul-uplifting. It may even lead to a nose bleed (Parra 42). During the 1970s, Parra expanded his poetic repertoire to include the merciless exposure of social ills. Parra rejects both communism and capitalism as systems which are simply foisted on the common people. The United States is described as a place, 'Donde la libertad/ es una estatua'. Cuba does not fare much better; parodying Fidel Castro's words, he writes: 'Si fuera justo Fidel/ debiera creer en mí/ tal como yo creo en él:/ la historia me absolverá' (Parra 114). In his later poetry, Parra employs the Bible as ammunition for his social critique; in *Sermones y prédicas del Cristo de Elqui* (1977), for example, he takes on the persona of an itinerant preacher, Domingo Zárate Vega, he had seen preaching in his childhood in Chile during the 1920s. Zárate Vega, who left his job as a construction foreman in order to preach to the masses on street corners, was known popularly as El Cristo de Elqui because he made no secret of his belief that he was the re-incarnation of Christ. The Christ of Elqui in Parra's poetry, for example, starts off by giving his flock some advice of a 'practical nature', which includes 'get up early', 'don't wear tight shoes', and 'don't keep gas in your stomach'. In section XXIII he dares his audience to take communion without first making confession, use the Bible for toilet paper, and spit on the Chilean flag (Parra 124–40). Parra's poetry has not mellowed with age, as one might expect; his recent poetry is as iconoclastic as ever. He rejects rhetoric, lies, and the rich, and stands for antipoetry, truth and the underdog.

'[U]ndoubtedly one of the most important Spanish-American poets of the day' (Fernández Retamar, *Prologue* 103), the Nicaraguan Ernesto Cardenal (b.1925) is a poet whose work skilfully combines interest in the political, the religious and the quotidian. A priest and one-time Minister of Culture for the Sandinistas in Nicaragua, Cardenal's work is well-known both in Latin America and abroad and has an immediate relevance to the political situation of contemporary Latin America. This charismatic Nicarguan writer is at his best when he writes verse with a political-cum-religious resonance; exemplary are his poetic versions of the Psalms. The call for the enactment of God's justice in the here-and-now and for retribution on the enemies of Israel which resounds in the biblical Psalms is applied in these works to the context of modern-day Latin America, and specifically Nicaragua with its dictators and henchmen. His version of Psalm 11 opens: 'Libértanos tú/ porque no nos libertarán sus partidos . . .' (Cardenal 43). The favourite rhetorical trope in

Cardenal's repertoire, as will already be obvious, is that of recuperation, in the sense that classic texts are used in his work as a backdrop against which the silhouette of modern-day events is displayed. This can take the form of a simple one-line quotation, as in 'De pronto suena en la noche una sirena . . .', when Cardenal alludes to Bécquer's famous Rima which concludes with 'Es el amor que pasa' in order to draw attention to the contrast between Bécquer's love and Somoza's hate: 'De pronto suena en la noche una sirena/ de alarma, larga, larga . . ./ No es incendio ni muerte:/ Es Somoza que pasa' (Cardenal 11). Or this intertextuality can take the form of an extended re-writing of other texts. His poem, 'Coplas a la muerte de Merton', for example, dedicated to Thomas Merton begins with a re-writing of the famous lines of Jorge Manrique's 'Nuestras vidas son los ríos que van a la mar que es la muerte', which is transformed in order to imbue it with an otherwordly resonance: 'Nuestras vidas son los ríos/ que van a dar a la muerte/ que es la vida . . .' (Cardenal 132). Cardenal's most famous poem is 'Oración por Marilyn Monroe' in which he skilfully interweaves the language of Christianity, with its emphasis upon sin, redemption, and forgiveness, with that of Hollywood, with its espousal of physical beauty, money and pleasure. The poem has some striking contrasts; Cardenal imagines Monroe before God denuded of her make-up: 'ahora se presenta ante Ti sin ningún maquillaje/ sin su Agente de Prensa/ sin fotógrafos y sin firmar autógrafos/ sola como un astronauta frente a la noche espacial' (Cardenal 42). Mid-way through the poem, Cardenal asks God to forgive Monroe and, at its conclusion, in a scene reminiscent of a Hitchcock thriller, he imagines the Hollywood actress trying desperately to contact someone minutes before she would take her own life: 'Señor/ quienquiera que haya sido el que ella iba a llamar/ y no llamó (y tal vez no era nadie/ o era Alguien cuyo número no está en el Directorio de Los Angeles)/ contesta Tú el teléfono' (Cardenal 42–43). As this poem demonstrates, Cardenal is at his best when he combines the different languages of Christianity and popular culture, identifying coincidence where none was first divined.[1]

It was in the 1970s that there emerged a new sense of the distinctiveness of women's writing in Spanish America, particularly in the genre of poetry, and largely as a result of the international impact of Anglo-Saxon and, particularly, French feminism. The important question to be addressed in this section is the extent to which women's writing of the contemporary period enunciates a vision of reality which is recognisably distinct from that of their male counterparts. In an article, 'Is Women's Writing in Spanish America Gender-Specific?', I have argued that the difference between men's and

---

[1]  Other significant poets of this period whose work is not discussed here are Alvaro Mutis (b.1923), Carlos Germán Belli (b.1927), and Antonio Cisneros (b.1942). For an overview of poetry of this period which has some discussion of their work, see José Quiroga, 'Spanish American Poetry from 1922 to 1975', *Cambridge History*, vol. 2, 303–64.

women's writing only truly emerges after the 1960s (Hart, *Women's Writing*), and that is the argument pursued in what follows.

It is invidious to choose some figures over and above others, but the work of certain female poets does stand out, such as that of the Argentine poet, Alejandra Pizarnik (1936–1972) and that of the Salvadorean, Claribel Alegría (b.1924). Alejandra Pizarnik is one of the best female poets of the modern era. Her work is visionary, difficult and clearly shows the traces of the surrealistic authors she studied and imitated. Like the surrealists, Pizarnik's poems deal in apparently disconnected sets of images which operate in terms of emotional and visual impact; they deliberately lack a clear narrative. Often, Pizarnik's poems deal in liminality and imminence, portraying a psychical reality which typically is about to happen and which then retreats from the poem's field of vision (Cobo Borda 95). 'Ojos primitivos', for example, indicates that Pizarnik's aim was to retrieve the visionary freshness of a prelapsarian view of the world, which is at once 'el silencio del mero estar' and 'la bella alegría animal' (Crow 46). Yet, one of the most disarming insights of Pizarnik's verse is the connection it elicits between poetic creativity and death. As many of her later poems suggest, it is only through death – whether expressed as emotional death, self-death, or suicide – that her poetic voice is able to flourish. Her poem, 'Cantora nocturna', for instance, projects herself as already dead and singing (Crow 54). The colour blue appears here, as elsewhere in the later poetic works, to signify death, in contradistinction to the *modernistas* for whom blue stood for the ideal. One of Pizarnik's most haunting poems is 'El sueño de la muerte o el lugar de los cuerpos poéticos' from *Extracción de la piedra de locura*. This poem, which is written in prose and has strong parallels with Lautréamont's *Les Chants de Maldoror*, explores the link between poetic creation and death. Here, as in *La condesa sangrienta* (1971), Pizarnik alludes to the sadistic practices of the sixteenth-century Hungarian Countess Erzébet Báthory who was accused of the death by torture of over six hundred girls between the ages of twelve and eighteen; she indulged in a programme of seduction, torment and murder of her victims (Foster 97). In her poem Pizarnik alludes to this image and places her poetic creation against that backdrop, as if to suggest that her poetry feeds on that image of death (*Extracción* 61). Our final impression of Pizarnik's work is one of a haunting, melancholic and at times unnerving poetic voice orientated towards the unconscious and death.

Born in Nicaragua in 1924, Alegría grew up in El Salvador, moved to the United States in 1943 and has lived subsequently in Mexico, Chile, Uruguay and the Canary Isles. In 1978 her poetry won Cuba's prestigious Casa de las Américas prize. Alegría is renowned for the political bent of her work; an important theme of her poetry is the concept of revolution understood as much in a political as a natural sense (namely, the Izalco volcano which periodically erupts in modern times). Alegría's most significant poetic collection is *Flores del volcán* which is lyrical, politically committed and feminist. The style adopted throughout is prosaic, political and confrontational. In 'Flores del volcán', for example, Alegría compares the wanton killing of guerrillas in El Salvador during the Civil War of the 1980s with the blood sacrifices of the Mayas who dedicated youths' hearts to the God of Rain, Chac (*Flowers* 46). This ancient world, however, seems to have been destroyed beneath the modern monster of United States capitalism, which is able to turn Central American food commodities such as coffee into gold (*Flowers* 48). But, as the poem concludes, the modern calamities are due to Chac's desire for revenge (*Flores* 50).[2]

## The Boom Novel

The novels which are traditionally included in the generic title of the Boom novel are: *Rayuela* (1963) by Julio Cortázar (1914–1984), *La muerte de Artemio Cruz* (1962) and *Cambio de piel* (1967) by Carlos Fuentes (b.1928), *La ciudad y los perros* (1962) and *La casa verde* (1966) by Mario Vargas Llosa (b.1936), and *Cien años de soledad* (1967) by Gabriel García Márquez (b.1928). My intention here has not been to narrow the Boom down to only a few novels. Indeed, a significant number of novels were published during the 1960s which are not normally included in the generic title of the Boom novel, some of which include novels written by authors who had established their reputation in an earlier generation, such as Sábato's *Sobre héroes y tumbas*, and Carpentier's *El siglo de las luces*, both of 1962, and some of which include writers whose work was not caught up in the mass publicisation that writers such as Fuentes, Cortázar, García Márquez and Vargas Llosa enjoyed, such as *Los recuerdos del porvenir* (1963) by Elena Garro (1920–1998). However, for the purposes of clarity I shall be discussing in this section only those works which are unmistakably associated with the Boom novel.

José Donoso provides a clear description of the Boom in his *Historia personal del 'Boom'* (1972). In that work he describes how the Boom suddenly internationalised Latin-American novelists; the pre-Boom literary generation espoused a nationalist regionalist ethos (*Historia* 24–25). Donoso recalls how Jorge Edwards caused a scandal when he stated that he was more interested in foreign than Chilean literature (*Historia* 24). Linked to this internationalism was a new sense of Latin-American political identity produced by wide-

---

2 Other significant female poets whose work is not discussed here are Ulalume González de León (b.1932), Rita Geada (b.1937), Delia Domínguez (b.1934), Circe Maia (b.1932), Violeta Parra (1917–1967), María Mercedes Carranza (b.1945), Nancy Morejón (b.1944), Raquel Jodorowsky (b.1927), Olga Orozco (b.1920), and Carmen Ollé (b.1947). For some discussion of their work, see Mary Crow, and José Quiroga, 'Spanish American Poetry from 1922 to 1975', *Cambridge History*, vol. 2, 303–64.

spread support for the Cuban Revolution, expressed, as Donoso remembers, during a conference held at the Universidad de Concepción in Chile in 1962, which was attended by a number of prominent writers of the day (Pablo Neruda, José María Arguedas, Augusto Roa Bastos, Carlos Fuentes, Claribel Alegría, Alejo Carpentier) (*Historia* 34–36). The bubble of support for Cuba, however, burst in 1971 when the scandal of the Padilla affair broke the until then serried ranks of the Latin-American intelligentsia. Like other communists such as Jean-Paul Sartre and Hans Magnus Enzensberger, many of the Boom writers (and, in particular, Vargas Llosa) turned away from Cuba as a source of political inspiration.

An important indication of the difference between the pre-Boom and the Boom novel appears in their respective circulation figures. Donoso's *Veraneo* (1955), published in the pre-Boom era, came out in a print-run of 1,000, of which Donoso had himself to sell 900 (*Historia* 26–27). The Boom, however, changed all that, and literature became a lucrative industry. As is well known, the Boom novel was the result of a felicitous mix of a far-sighted editor, the Spaniard Carlos Barral, editor of Seix Barral of Barcelona, and a new type of writing from Latin America which caught his attention. Cortázar's *Rayuela*, for example, began with a print-run of 4,000 in 1963, shot to 10,000 for 1966 and 1967, and then rocketed to 26,000 and 25,000 for the years 1968 and 1969 respectively. The novel which fundamentally changed the paradigm was García Márquez's *Cien años de soledad* which sold more than 50,000 copies in the year of publication (1967), and from 1968 onwards has sold about 100,000 copies per year (Rama, *Crítica* 291–92). Perhaps inevitably, since the Boom novel threw a new generation of Latin-American writers into the international limelight in an unprecedented way, the movement had its detractors. Miguel Angel Asturias, for example, accused the Boom novels of being 'meros productos de la publicidad' (qtd. in Donoso, *Historia* 15). However one views the Boom novelists, they were the first generation of Spanish-American writers who were able to live from the labour of their pens; in effect, they brought Latin-American literature from the backwaters to the centre-stage of the literary world.

*La muerte de Artemio Cruz* (1962) by Carlos Fuentes, winner of the Príncipe de Asturias prize in 1994, is one of the first major Boom novels, and demonstrates the main characteristics of the genre. Its basic narrative concerns the life story of Artemio Cruz, born on 9 April 1889, an individual who fought in and survived the Mexican Revolution, got involved in the reconstruction programme afterwards (specifically attracting and overseeing United States investment), married Catalina, the daughter of Don Gamaliel Bernal, a wealthy landowner, and died on 10 April 1959, surrounded by friends and relatives. The novel is essentially the testimony of his life and is meant also to be representative of the history of Mexico. The most striking innovation of the novel is its use of tense and person. Whereas the Realist novel usually employs grammatical person in the following way (I-narrator present-tense; you-reader present-tense; (s)he-protagonist past-tense), *La muerte de Artemio Cruz* employs the following innovative format: I-Artemio Cruz present-tense; you-Artemio Cruz future-tense; he-Artemio Cruz past-tense. The novel is divided up between these three voices, the 'él' section taking up two thirds of the available space, with the 'yo' and the 'tú' segments taking up roughly one sixth each. Of the three sections the 'él' passages, given their use of dates and the third-person narrator, approximate more to the expectations of traditional Realism. The 'tú' section, though expressed in the future, gives the impression of being an omniscient conscience which knows Artemio Cruz's destiny and unpacks it before his, and indeed our, eyes. The 'yo' passages, according to the novel's logic narrated on the day of Artemio's death (10 April 1959), are very body-orientated and home in obsessively on corporeal sensation. As the above suggests, *La muerte de Artemio Cruz* is an experimentation in the intercrossings of tense and person and, by implication, time, space and identity. But it is also specifically a novel about the genesis of Mexican identity. In a section roughly mid-way through the novel, Paz's notion of Mexicans as 'hijos de la chingada' is taken up and exploited in a meandering, taboo-breaking passage: 'eres hijo de los hijos de la chingada; serás padre de más hijos de la chingada: nuestra palabra, detrás de cada rostro, de cada signo, de cada peperada: pinga de la chingada, verga de la chingada, culo de la chingada' (*Muerte* 145). In a gesture typical of the Boom novel, Fuentes casts fear of taboo to one side and, indeed, exploits the resonance of dirty words to reach a deeper level of understanding of existence (the quest pursued by the protagonists of his novels, though it breaks down taboo, is always mythical, always Jungian).

One of the foundational Boom novels was *La ciudad y los perros* (1963) by Mario Vargas Llosa, which tells the story of the murder of a fourth-year intern at the Leoncio Prado Military Academy in Lima because he had blown the whistle on his friends about cheating for a chemistry exam. The novel is based on Vargas Llosa's own experience at the Academy from 1950 to 1952, and is, at the most fundamental level, a record of his personal perception of the spiritual sterility and moral corruption produced by military life. Though not as formally innovative as some of the other Boom novels, *La ciudad y los perros* is superb in bringing to life the world of the adolescent trapped within the straightjacket of social institutions, and struggling to find and achieve an authentic identity. The world of the adolescents is shown to be a cruel and brutalising one: in the Leoncio Prado Military Academy, for example, the interns are treated barbarically by their military overseers and even worse by their peers. The important metaphor is, as the title suggests, animality and its juxtaposition with the apparently civilised world of the city outside. The structure of the novel is rather like Dickens's *Tale of Two Cities* in that it begins by showing two worlds as separate, and then gradually shows how they are interconnected. The animality of the cadets' behaviour – they are given nicknames such as Boa and Jaguar which they thoroughly deserve, and

the nickname for first-year cadets is 'los perros' – is underlined through juxtaposition with the dog, La Malpapeada, which is treated lovingly by its
owner, and therefore appears to be more 'human' than the humans. When
Ricardo Arana, nicknamed Esclavo, is found badly injured on the ground
during a military manoeuvre, at the conclusion of Part I of the novel, the line-
arity of the novel is thenceforth disrupted, as if to emphasise the temporal
centrality of that discovery; Part II opens with the novel delving into the past.
Though the world of the adolescents is cruel, that of the 'adult world' is even
more harsh, since it is governed by the laws of collusion and corruption. A
great deal of pressure is brought to bear on one of the officers, Gamboa, to
prevent him from officially transmitting a deposition in which he records his
suspicion that Arana was murdered (which, in the epilogue to the novel, is
shown to be true). For his temerity in fighting against the system he is banished to an out-of-the-way military post in the jungle. Alberto (clearly a projection of Vargas Llosa as a young man) blows the whistle on his fellow
cadets, but he too is forced to retract when the Head of the Academy threat-
ens to blackmail him (Alberto has been writing pornographic novels and the
Colonel has copies). The most intriguing feature of La ciudad y los perros is
the status that literature plays within the novel. Alberto, nicknamed 'el
poeta', emerges as the hero of the piece in that he is prepared, against all the
odds, to denounce the crime for which Arana suffered, and yet, when he does
so, his action is seen as reprehensible and novelistic. Thus, literature finally
reveals the truth about social institutions such as the military academy and
marriage (both as seen through Alberto's wise eyes) that society is determined not to reveal. Perhaps most interesting about La ciudad y los perros is
the fact that it so incensed the authorities of the Leoncio Prado Military
Academy that they attempted to discredit Vargas Llosa publicly by publishing details of his poor academic record while at the Academy, and by inciner-
ating one thousand copies of the book in the parade ground outside the
Academy shortly after the book was published, thereby, unwittingly, ensuring its fame for years to come.

   Rayuela (1963) by Julio Cortázar (1914–1984) is the most intellectually
sophisticated novel of the Boom, describing the search for ontological
meaning of Oliveira, a young Argentine man, in Paris and later in Buenos
Aires. The novel has three parts and is set respectively in Paris ('del lado de
allá'), Buenos Aires ('del lado de acá'), and concludes with a theory-of-the-
novel section in which a novelist, Morelli, theorises on the novel, rejects the
old Galdosian format and proposes a self-reflexive, open work of art ('de
otros lados'). Oliveira is involved in a search for transcendental meaning,
predicated on the rejection of Western notions about thought, including the
dual Kantian categories of time and space; the form and technique of the
novel echo the open-ended nature of his quest. Rayuela dismantles time in
the sense that there are at least two ways of reading the novel, one of which is
a linear reading beginning at chapter 1 and ending at chapter 56, the second

of which is the hopscotch version as described in the 'Tablero de dirección'. Space is deconstructed in the novel by virtue of the reader moving backwards and forwards in the hopscotch reading process, and also in the sense that the two main spaces of the novel, Paris and Buenos Aires, are shown to be inter-linked to such an extent that one can talk of a Paris in Buenos Aires and a Buenos Aires in Paris. Given this subversion of the spatio-temporal contin-uum, it is only natural that *Rayuela* should have three possible endings: (i) Oliveira goes mad, (ii) he commits suicide by throwing himself out of the window of the lunatic asylum, or (iii) he plans to go and see a film with his girlfriend, Gekrepten (Boldy 89). A more radical deconstructive move in the novel is its dismantling of language. This process is evident in a number of ways but all point to the fundamental desire to open language up to new expressive possibilities. Thus Cortázar employs a number of languages in the novel, namely (self-consciously Argentine) Spanish, French, Latin, Italian, French, German, English, and even *glíglico*, the nonsense language Olivei-ra's girlfriend, La Maga, uses to talk about sex (Cortázar 104–105). In Joycean fashion, Cortázar invents porte-manteau words by running them together ('corriócomounreguerodepólvora'), or splitting them up ('se-re-torcía-las-manos'), or misspelling them for comic effect (Cortázar 492, 379). This more demanding artistic form requires more active participation on the part of the reader, for whom Morelli invents the distinction of 'lector-có-mplice', in opposition to the reader (in a slight which feminists have never allowed him to forget) who is passive and inactive, called 'el lector-hembra' (Cortázar 453, 508).

   *La casa verde* (1966) by Vargas Llosa is a novel which has two basic nar-rative strands: one describes the events occurring in a brothel called La Casa Verde, which is based on an actual brothel of that name which had fascinated the author as a young man living in Piura, and the other is a *tranche de vie* of a number of individuals living in the Amazon, which was likewise based on the author's life experience (he visited the Upper Marañón region in 1958 with the Mexican anthropologist, Juan Comas) (Vargas Llosa, *La historia secreta*). But more important than the biographical sources of the novel is the artistry with which the various strands of the lives of the characters are woven together. Like *La ciudad y los perros*, *La casa verde* employs the Faulknerian technique of cutting unexpectedly from one scene to another and from one set of characters to another, and typically oscillates between the objective transcription of dialogue and the third-person description of events or places or objects. The main structure of the novel is provided not by the unity of the characters' lives – the disconnected narrative style works against that – but rather through the patterning of oppositions throughout the novel, which range from jungle (Santa María Nieves in Marañón) versus aridity (Piura), repression (La Misión) versus lust (La Casa Verde), barbarism (the lowlife *inconquistables*) versus civilisation (Padre García). On one level, these oppositions are reinforced as the novel progresses; thus, in the last chapter of the novel, Padre García and Lituma, one of the *inconquistables*, trade insults, as if to underline that the worlds for which they stand will never see eye to eye. But there is a deeper sense in which these apparently different worlds are connected, and Bonifacia, one of the main female characters, is crucial in this context. The fact that she moves from one world to the next – from the nunnery to the brothel – serves to underline how deception, corruption and exploitation are at the root of human life. There is, after all, hardly a character who does not become victim of his or her circumstances; Fuschía, the Japanese smuggler, contracts leprosy and is left to die in a leper colony, Padre García is victimised by the *inconquistables*, the *inconquistables* are oppressed by the law, and Don Anselmo, the owner of the Casa Verde, is ostracised by the town (the brothel is burnt down) when his wrongdoing is discovered (he seduced a blind girl and, when she died in childbirth, had her secretly buried). Rather than conferring a sense of ethical justification on the rewards meted out to his characters, Vargas Llosa presents a gripping vision of dog-eat-dog materialism in which the struggle to survive seemingly renders moral criteria irrelevant.

*Cambio de piel* (1967), by Carlos Fuentes, follows the Boom formula in that it is technically innovative and strives to weave together mythic and quotidian levels. Fuentes's novel takes its point of departure from the daily lives of four people, Elizabeth and Javier, Isabel and Franz, travelling from Mexico City to Veracruz; their lives are informed, we find out as the novel progresses, by the historical neuroses of the cultures to which they belong. A common technique, for example, is for the narrative to cut suddenly from the present of the novel (the 1960s) to Cortés's conquest of Amerindia or the concentration camps of World War II. One other important motif of the text is the primacy given to the sexual act, which is understood as an archetypal return to all sexual encounters: hence the slippage between cultures. The panculturalism of the narrative is echoed by the many languages used in the narrative: Spanish, French, English, German, Latin, Portuguese. The title 'cambio de piel' is a reference to the Aztec God, Xipe Totec, reputed to be able to change his skin and take on a different human form. The novel climaxes in the third chapter, which is set in the chambers beneath the Pyramid of Cholula. Given that we witness what appears to be Franz's body being carried out of the chambers, we might at first assume that the chapter is concerned with the details of and motives for a vengeful murder. But the chapter is more interested in the archetypal nature of human passion, the truth of creation (Fuentes, *Cambio* 479), and projects orgasm as one of the pointers to that truth. *Cambio de piel* is a complex novel, more complex than a few lines about it can suggest, and epitomises the mythicist, sexological and panculturalist side of the Boom novel. Its bewildering range of cultural and literary reference is suggested by the fact that it even has a reference to Cortázar's *Rayuela*, which is being used as a pillow (Fuentes, *Cambio* 431).

Gabriel García Márquez's novel, *Cien años de soledad* (1967), is now universally seen as a classic, 'the Latin American Don Quixote' as one critic called it; it established García Márquez's fame overnight (it sold 50,000 copies in two weeks in Buenos Aires alone soon after publication). It tells the story of the five generations of the Buendía family, beginning with the patriarchal figure, José Arcadio Buendía, and ending with the child, Aureliano, who is born with a pig's tail, in the mythical town of Macondo over a period of one hundred years (the number is meant to be reminiscent of the hundred year period in the fairy-tale world of *Sleeping Beauty*). The lives of the Buendía men are shown to be nothing more than a repetition of the lives of their forbears; their options seem to be either war (as happens most notably in the case of Colonel Aureliano Buendía who organised thirty-two armed uprisings, although he lost all of them; García Márquez 88), or alchemy/ science (epitomised by the study to which the Colonel as well as his nephew, José Arcadio Segundo, later retreat). Without exception they all suffer the temptation of incest which becomes fatal in the fourth generation when Aureliano has a child with his sister, Amaranta Ursula. On the contrary, the women who marry the Buendía men, of whom Ursula Iguarán is the most representative example, remain within the domestic sphere and are presented as more level-headed than the menfolk; they also live longer – Ursula sees four generations come and go. *Cien años de soledad* has twenty (unnumbered) chapters which, given the repeated references to how the characters will meet their death as well as the demise of Macondo, give the text a sense of foreboding reminiscent of the Maya Quiché *Popol Vuh*; the number system of the Mayas was, we may recall, duodecimal. Certainly the end of the novel in which Aureliano deciphers the destruction of Macondo and his own death is as final as the last sentence of the Maya Quiché text (García Márquez 334; see above, pp. 6–7). Despite the lack of temporal co-ordinates in the novel (one is given the day or the month but never the date or the year of occurrences), one can devise an historical narrative underlying the events depicted (though they are subject to irony). Chapters 1–5, in their references to the founding of Macondo, church-building, and the amnesia plague brought on by Rebeca the Indian girl, narrativise the discovery of the New World, the foundation of the Christian church there, and the concomitant destruction of the Amerindian cultures; seemingly random references to a fifteenth-century suit of armour, a Spanish galleon, Sir Francis Drake and an effeminate Italian piano tuner, help to fill out the European historical context. Chapters 6–9 possess their own backdrop, namely the struggle between Liberals and Conservatives in nineteenth-century Colombia following independence; the Buendía family are inveterate Liberals. Chapters 10–14 are set against the period of export-import growth characteristic of the late nineteenth and early twentieth centuries in Latin America, the emphasis here being on the banana fever which emerged during this period as a result of United States investment. Chapters 15–20 begin with the description of a

strike initiated by José Arcadio Segundo (that is itself based on the strike
which took place in Ciénaga, Colombia, in 1928), which is the first step of a
phase of gradual economic deterioration in Macondo leading to its destruction by a biblical hurricane at the conclusion of the novel. Despite the recog-
nisable historical phases implicit in the novel, and it is interesting that the
great figures of the independence, Simón Bolívar and José de San Martín, are
conspicuously absent even in displaced form, *Cien años de soledad* cannot be
seen as an historical novel in any empiric sense. It strives rather to blur the
dividing-line between reality and fantasy, but not simply in the manner of the
surrealists for whom the two terms were meant to be interchangeable, but
rather in a cultural-political sense. A leitmotif of the novel is the sense in
which occurrences seen as supernatural in the First World (such as ghostly
apparitions, human beings with the ability to fly, levitate, disappear or
increase their weight at will) are presented as natural from a Third-World
perspective, while occurrences seen as normal in the First World (magnets,
science, ice, railway trains, the movies, phonographs) are portrayed as supernatural from the point of view of an inhabitant of the Caribbean. García Márquez's playing with the distinction between fantasy and fact – his recourse to
what is commonly termed magical realism – does, indeed, have a political
edge since one of the episodes on which there is the least agreement is the
alleged murder and disposal of the three thousand banana plantation workers
described by José Arcadio Segundo in Chapter 15, but not credited by the
authorities (García Márquez 236–52). *Cien años de soledad* therefore con-
fronts the reader not only with the question of what the real is but also forces
him to reconsider the boundaries of that (unconsciously politicised) ideology
which informs the structure of his mental universe. A further twist is given to
the reality/fiction interface at the end of the novel. In Chapter 18 Aureliano,
the son of Meme and Mauricio Babilonia, discovers that the text which the
gypsy, Melquíades, left in the workshop and which the Buendía descendants
successively attempt to decipher, is written in Sanskrit and, two chapters
later, he also cracks the code in which it is written. (The code – a typically
magical-realist detail – is written in a combination of the private cipher of the
Emperor Augustus and a Lacedemonian military code; García Márquez 333.)
The last two pages of the novel describe Aureliano deciphering the history of
Macondo – the very story we have been reading for three hundred pages –
until the point at which he reads about himself reading the text (García
Márquez 334), when the text ends. The implication of this clever device is
that the text gives the impression – via reference to Melquíades's authorship
of the text we hold in our hands – of having written itself. The empiric author
of the novel, Gabriel García Márquez, as if to confirm this hypothesis, is
found in the text in two distinct projections, one as the Liberal military leader
who shares the destiny of Colonel Aureliano Buendía, namely, Colonel Ger-
ineldo Márquez, and the other as one of the four literary bohemians who
appear in Macondo in Chapters 19–20 and who divide their time between lit-

erary pursuits and whorehouses, namely, Gabriel. (The reference to the 'sabio catalán' in the same chapter, it should be added, is also highly autobiographical; García Márquez 320–23.) In this final image of the novel as it were disappearing into itself, we have a concrete linguistic embodiment of the incestual desire which had haunted every male member of the Buendía lineage. In its use of myth – and principally in Lévi-Strauss's theory of the prohibition of incest as the corner-stone of culture which figures strongly in García Márquez's novel – its disruption of linear temporality, and the use of individual history to signify the national narrative, *Cien años de soledad* was to become famous as the prototype of the Boom novel.[3]

## *The Short Story*[4]

One of the most significant short-story writers of this period is Julio Cortázar whose work has already been reviewed in the section on the novel (see pp. 128–29). Though his novels have received rave reviews, his short stories are probably better. Similar to his novels, Cortázar's short stories are centred on an unsolvable mystery. *Cartas de mamá* (1959), for example, tells the story of Luis and Laura who have run away from Argentina to Paris after a shotgun wedding. One day Laura's mother in a letter mentions that Nico has been asking after them, and this is taken by Luis to be a sign of senility since Nico was Luis's brother from whom Luis effectively stole Laura (they were engaged) and who subsequently died. The story gradually builds up the tension until, finally, Luis 'becomes' Nico, or so we are led to believe by the

---

3 There were a number of significant novels contemporary with the Boom which are not discussed here; they include *Los recuerdos del porvenir* (1963) by Elena Garro (1920–1998), *Juntacadáveres* (1964) by Juan Carlos Onetti (1909–1994), *Tres tristes tigres* (1964) by G. Cabrera Infante (b.1929), *El obsceno pájaro de la noche* (1970) by José Donoso (b.1924), *Oficio de difuntos* (1976) by Arturo Uslar Pietri (b.1906), and *Yo el Supremo* (1974) by Augusto Roa Bastos (b.1917). For a discussion of these works see a good overview in Randolph D. Pope, 'The Spanish American Novel from 1950 to 1975', *Cambridge History*, vol. 2, 365–424.

4 One genre which has not been discussed in this work is the novella. An argument could be made for there being a separate category reserved for the Spanish-American novella, seen as a shrunk novel rather than an extended short story, but in length somewhere in between. Examples of the Spanish-American novella would be María Luisa Bombal's *La última niebla* (1935), Juan Carlos Onetti's *El pozo* (1939), Adolfo Bioy Casares's *La invención de Morel* (1940), Ernesto Sábato's *El túnel* (1948), Gabriel García Márquez's *El coronel no tiene quien le escriba* (1958), discussed in this chapter as a short story, Carlos Fuentes's *Aura* (1962), Mario Vargas Llosa's *Los cachorros* (1967), finally leading to a rapid growth of the genre in the 1980s with works such as Mempo Giardinelli's *Luna caliente* (1983), discussed in Chapter 7, and Alvaro Mutis's *La última escala del Tramp Steamer* (1988). The kernel of this argument is found in a recent doctoral dissertation which uses the term 'nouvelle' rather than novella; see Cardona-López 63–67, *passim*.

concluding comments of the story. The realm of the strange and the terrifying has broken into the world of the quotidian. *Los buenos servicios* (1959) is likewise a bizarre story which centres on the perception which a widow, Madame Francinet, has of a rich household which she visits on two occasions to fulfil domestic tasks. She is later asked to attend the funeral of Monsieur Bébé and pretend that she is his mother; through naivety and greed (Monsieur Rosay offers her a considerable sum of money for the task) she agrees to do so, which she does and, in effect, we are none the wiser at the end of the story as to the manner of Monsieur Bébé's death (Susana Jakfalvi suggests there is a homosexual sub-plot; Cortázar, *Ediciones* 41). *Las babas del diablo* (1959), like the other stories, takes a mundane context – a young photographer, Michel, photographs a man and woman talking to each other by the Seine – and converts it into a mystery since something very untoward occurs when the photographs are developed (the narrator is turned into a still while the photographed couple seem to take on a life of their own [*Ediciones* 138]). The final paragraph of the story, with its references to passing clouds, the occasional falling of rain, and birds flying by, reinforces the eerie impression that the narrator has now been confined for eternity in the eye of the camera. *El perseguidor* (1959), a short story in which the narrator, Bruno, describes his relationship with a jazz musician, Johnny Carter, allows Cortázar once more to focus on the elusive interface between art and life, literature and reality, since Bruno is Johnny's biographer as well as his friend. Johnny Carter, like the real-life person on whom his character is based (the celebrated American saxophonist, Charlie Parker [1920–1955]), is a wild man, prone to outbursts of temper, bouts of insanity and suicidal clinical depression, but those around him recognise his musical gift to be something special which separates him from other men. This becomes evident particularly during the conversation in which Johnny explains to Bruno that he is able to experience time in a more inward way, as if he were entering a different time dimension, which, indeed, happens to him while he is on the Métro in Paris; '¿Cómo se puede pensar un cuarto de hora en un minuto y medio?' (*Ediciones* 153). The mystery underlying this experience is enhanced towards the end of the story in a conversation that Bruno has with Johnny shortly before the latter's death; Johnny angrily rejects Bruno's biography as a charade, in particular the latter's notion of God (*Ediciones* 196). This conversation between Johnny and Bruno, which leads to an intellectual impasse, builds on one of the main tropes of Cortázar's fiction: the intellectual comprehension of life destroys its beauty. It is not coincidental, thus, that, after Johnny's death, Bruno seems relatively unconcerned; he simply refers to how well his biography of Bruno is selling, and that there are plans for a new translation. The narrator is finally revealed to be part and parcel of the stultifying intellectualism which ruins the elusive and mysterious beauty of life. Finally *Las armas secretas* (1959) is centred on the mystery of bodily possession. Pierre and Michèle are two lovers in Paris; Michèle is hesitant to make love to

Pierre because of a previous experience (she was raped by a German during the occupation). But finally she invites Pierre to her home, only to stop him when the look in his eyes reminds her of the German; Pierre leaves, Michèle calls her friend, Babette, asking her to come and see her, and at this point the mystery begins. While driving through the woods where the German was killed in retaliation, Pierre suddenly swerves the car round and returns to the house, we presume, in order to re-enact the rape. Cortázar manages to create tension and mystery in this short story by leaving open the possibility that reincarnation occurs; thus Pierre had always imagined in the most vivid terms what Michèle's house would look like, he is obsessed with possessing her physically, and he has the odd habit of humming German songs. A change in Pierre's identity is suggested by the dog, Bobby, who seems to recognise him, accept him, but then barks at him later on. Perhaps the most intriguing detail of all is that Michèle's friends, Roland and Babette, who discovered and killed the German last time, have been alerted and are depicted as driving to the house when the narrative ends; it is likely, therefore, that not only will Michèle's rape be re-enacted, but also the murder of the rapist as well, who this time will be a Frenchman, Pierre. In this Cortázar is similar to other Spanish-American writers such as Borges and Fuentes; he is obsessed with the coincidence between the plot worked out between individuals in the past, and its re-enactment in the present. Cortázar's trump card is his use of suspense, at which he is an unrivalled master.

Equally important to mention here are the short stories by Gabriel García Márquez, whose novel, *Cien años de soledad*, has been discussed above (see pp. 130–33). *Los funerales de la Mamá Grande* (1962) epitomise some of the strengths of García Márquez's narrative skill. Each of the eight short stories in this collection focusses on a number of scenes taken from everyday life in order to address larger more problematic patterns of cultural life. 'La siesta del martes', for example, only allows the reader to know the purpose of the events being described (a woman and her daughter are taking a train ride to another village in order to visit the son's grave) halfway through the story. The reason why they wish to visit the cemetery where the thief is buried is presented laconically to the priest: 'Yo soy su madre' (*Funerales* 16). Often in these stories García Márquez will use an everyday scene in order to address a political issue. Thus, in 'Un día de éstos', a visit by the mayor to the dentist allegorises the struggle between the power of the state and the people's resistance. As the dentist remarks when he pulls out the mayor's tooth: 'Aquí nos paga veinte muertos, teniente' (*Funerales* 25). This story, like the others, works by innuendo and understatement; García Márquez leaves the reader to draw conclusions and authorial intervention is kept to a minimum. He uses the apparently trivial theft of three billiard balls in 'En este pueblo no hay ladrones' to portray the limited nature of people's lives (now the billiard balls have gone, the owner has to close down his establishment, and all social activity ceases). The short story which provides the title for this collection is different from the others in that it gives us an early indication of the style for which García Márquez would become famous, namely, the dead-pan description of fantastic events, or magical realism. The short stories in *Los funerales de la Mamá Grande* are visually-orientated, deliberately do not provide exact temporal or spatial parameters for the setting of the action, use dialogue at the expense of third-person description, and derive their power mainly through a clever balance of humour and suspense. Indeed, they are like snapshots whose significance is gradually unravelled before the reader's eyes.

García Márquez's best short story is *El coronel no tiene quien le escriba* (1957). Filmic and objectivist, this short story manages within a hundred pages or so to conjure up the political atmosphere of Colombia in the 1950s. The plot is so simple as to be almost non-existent. A man, called the Colonel, has been waiting for a letter for fifteen years which he believes to be imminent and in which he will receive news about his military pension. Much of the novel is taken up with the description of the various things he and his wife – simply called 'la mujer' – do in order to survive, while retaining their dignity. It takes place in a short period of time from October to December in an unspecified year in the 1950s (although it is probably 1956 since this was the year of the Suez crisis, which is mentioned twice in the narrative; *Coronel* 25, 41). No details are provided by an omniscient third-person narrator; instead the reader is seduced into constructing the outline of the characters' lives based on a number of asides which we, as readers, overhear. As we soon find out, the Colonel and his wife are severely affected by the loss of their son, Agustín, who, as it gradually emerges, was clearly involved in anti-government activities, for which he paid with his life. (He probably died in the period of political violence which occurred after the assassination of the leftist politician, Jorge Eliécer Gaitán, in 1948.) This, and a number of other clues, point to a sense of society as characterised by an overwhelming political oppression. The Colonel mentions that the person being buried at the time the novel opens is the first to have died a natural death in years (*Coronel* 11), the assumption being that everybody else in recent years has died a violent death caused by political conflict. The local priest rings the church bell a certain number of times to indicate whether the movie currently being shown in the local movie theatre is appropriate; for the last year no film has passed muster (*Coronel* 25). Another example of social control occurs during the scene when the funeral cortege is prohibited from passing in front of the police barracks (*Coronel* 16). There is frequent mention of press censorship, and in one scene the Colonel reads a sign which says: 'Prohibido hablar de política' (*Coronel* 64). Nothing is stated in an obvious manner; this elliptic quality of the novel is also evident in the dialogues which often consist of one or two words (*Coronel* 66). Typically, the narrative eye of the work stays locked onto the surface of things, refusing to penetrate into the mind of the characters; thus the characters' thoughts are often transcribed as if they were spoken sentences. The most elusive part of this short story concerns not the letter which appears in the title, but the cockerel which the Colonel refuses to sell, even though he and his wife are practically starving to death. It comes to have a symbolic value, being associated with leftist ideology, with the couple's dead son (it once belonged to Agustín), with the people's hope for a brighter future (the 'ilusión' mentioned towards the end of the novel; *Coronel* 70), as well as (rather ominously) with death (*Coronel* 71). Thus, the cock comes to stand for the people's determination to survive even in the face of the most abject political oppression. On a number of occasions, the Colonel's anguish is so great that he feels as if his body is excessive; political oppression is thus experienced in a physical, bodily sense by him. After the Colonel reads the sign that forbids political discussion, the immediately following sentence reads (with a Sartrian flavour): 'El coronel sintió que le sobraba el cuerpo' (*Coronel* 64). *El coronel no tiene quien le escriba* is a tour de force which manages to combine the allegorical portrayal of the destiny of a nation within the apparently over-small frame of the everyday life of an ageing couple.

In the short stories of the brilliant Argentine writer Luisa Valenzuela (b.1938) the notion of gender-specific writing is championed. In her well-known essay, 'Mis brujas favoritas', for example, Valenzuela forcefully rejects the apartheid suffered by women, their bodies and their writing, and proposes a 'lenguaje hémbrico' to counter the hegemony of patronymic discourse (*Brujas* 91). The question to be raised here is to what extent this 'lenguaje hémbrico' is in evidence in her creative writing. *Cambio de armas* (1982), a collection of stories and Valenzuela's most impressive work, addresses the notion of feminine writing in a complex manner. All of the five short stories follow the pattern of a birthing of feminine consciousness which typically is embodied by a linguistic metaphor. This motif is most clearly expressed in 'La palabra asesino' in which the act of pronouncing the word 'asesino' is a moment of liberation through knowledge for the female protagonist. Likewise, in 'Cambio de armas', it is not fortuitous that the point at which Laura reaches self-knowledge at the dénouement of the story is when she understands for herself the workings of the phenomenal universe indicated by the world of language; she points the revolver at the Colonel's back and (presumably) fires. The birthing of the feminine consciousness is predicated on a linguistic dynamic. Clearly the most important story in the context of 'lenguaje hémbrico' is 'Cuarta versión'. This particular story, the most metatextual of the collection, focusses on the *guerra sucia* in Argentina during the 1970s and early 1980s through three conflicting narrative points of view. On the one hand we have the perspective of Bella, the beautiful actress who is having an affair with Pedro the ambassador; secondly, we have the point of view provided by the 'narradora anónima' who relates Bella's story, and, thirdly, we have the perspective of the transcriber/narrator whose comments on the narrative proper are printed in italic script, and which are more in evidence at the beginning of the story. These three levels are, however, not distinct; in this Chinese-box-like configuration of narrative levels there is a good deal of overlapping. We are never sure, thus, when Bella is narrating or when her actions are being narrated by the 'narradora anónima'. The reader is, therefore, only half-prepared for the conclusion of the story in which Bella is the only target who is shot at and killed ('se oyó un único disparo'; Valenzuela, *Cambio* 63), and from which we must conclude that she was the most subversive of the group. This leads the reader to re-examine the previous events of the story. What is intriguing is that Bella's perspective seemed to emphasise the personal dimension of her love for Pedro the ambassador. Bella never once appeared to focus her action in political terms, which means that there is a disjunction between the way she is perceived from within the narrative – namely, according to the internal evidence of the narrative – and her actions as perceived by extradiegetical elements (who, in this case, are the Secret Police or the Ambassadorial Guards who kill her). The point of revelation, in 'Cuarta versión' as in the other stories, coincides with a linguistic birthing in that the text which we have just read, in a Borgesian sleight of hand which defies verisimilitude, is narrated by Pedro to Bella while she falls dying to the floor. It is between the official story of Bella's life given by the transcriber/narrator and the personal story of her life that the space of feminine consciousness lies. The linguistic mediation to which her story is subjugated, though, may make it ultimately indecipherable. But what finally emerges from 'Cuarta versión', as in Valenzuela's fiction taken as a whole, is that there is not only a difference between men's and women's writing but that the parameters of the latter must be actively explored.

One of the best short stories of this period by a female writer is *La muñeca menor* (1976) by the Puerto Rican short-story writer, Rosario Ferré (b.1942). It describes the strange Gothic horror tale of a young girl who is bitten by a *chágara* while in the water which then inserts itself in her leg and begins to live there. The local doctor is unable to do anything, or so it appears, until we discover later on in the story that he had deliberately not cured the young girl's illness in order to collect enough dues to put his son through college. The story ends with a gruesome twist. The aunt is an expert in making porcelain dolls which are exact replicas of her nieces. When the doctor's son falls in love with the youngest niece, the scene is set for the aunt's gruesome revenge. The doctor's son marries the youngest daughter and they go off to live in the provinces and, suddenly, the doll disappears. When the doctor checks on his wife, the following episode occurs: 'Una noche decidió entrar en su habitación para observarla durmiendo. Notó que su pecho no se movía. Colocó delicadamente el estetoscopio sobre su corazón y oyó un lejano rumor de agua. Entonces la muñeca levantó los párpados y por las cuencas vacías de los ojos comenzaron a salir las antenas furibundas de las chágaras' (Chang-Rodríguez, *Voces* 524). The story is not only a horror story in the style of Val Newton's *The Body Snatchers* (1945) with its symbolism of the body being destroyed from within by an alien force, it is an acerbic critique of a patriarchal ideology which turns women's bodies into objects designed for men's pleasure, and which is prepared to make a profit out of suffering. The story is, thus, not only feminist but also anti-capitalist. This is clear given the symbolism surrounding the fact that the son, like his father, becomes very rich as a result of his trade and, thus, does not have time to notice the gradual transformation of his wife into a porcelain doll. There are a few details which point to a distrust of male sexuality; the fact that the *chágara* is described as emitting sperm ('aquella inmensa vejiga abotagada que manaba una esperma perfumada'; Chang-Rodríguez, *Voces* 523), and that it is contained within a perpetually-open wound, suggests that the *chágara* is a symbol of the penis within the vagina. A powerful story, *La muñeca menor* is able to combine a radical feminist message with a magical-realist style in a unique, unforgettable way.

Another intriguing short story of this period by a female writer is *Encaranublado* (1983) by Ferré's compatriot, Ana Lydia Vega (b.1946). It is set on a small boat stranded in the Caribbean, whose owner, the Haitian Antenor, is attempting to reach Miami in the hope of making a fresh start in life. On the way, he picks up a Dominican, Diógenes, and then a Cuban, Carmelo, both of whom are intent on the same plan. They begin to squabble over the provisions, the water bottle, and then proceed to insult each others' countries, unaware of the storm which is brewing all around them. Luckily saved by a passing United States ship they are sent down to the hold; the moral of this humorous tale is that, despite their 'pursuit of happiness' in the United States, each of these representatives of a Caribbean country, the Haitian, the Dominican, and the Cuban, is about to have his dreams rudely shattered; the Puerto Rican already knows what to expect. The subaltern status of each of the representatives of a Caribbean nation is neatly expressed by their position below deck in the American ship, the latter being a symbol of their so-called economic salvation.[5]

## Theatre

One of the distinguishing features of Spanish-American theatre during this period is the Nuevo Teatro movement which arose at the end of the 1950s and spread, mainly in the 1960s and 1970s, thoroughout the Sub-Continent. It was galvanised by the creation of a number of independent theatrical groups such as El Teatro Libre in Argentina (1969), the Grupo Aleph in Chile (1969), the Teatro Escambray in Cuba (1971), the Cuatrotablas group in Peru (1971), and the Rajatabla group in Venezuela (1971). Nuevo Teatro is char-

---

[5]   One of the most interesting developments in contemporary short-story writing is the ascendancy of the female writer; for a good selection (in English), see *Scents of Wood and Silence*, edited by Kathleen Ross and Yvette E. Miller.

acterised by: (i) the desire to speak on behalf of the 'pueblo', (ii) the espousal of the notion of collective authorship in which there is no single author, (iii) an emphasis on everyday life and historical themes, and (iv) the Brechtian distancing effect ('Verfremdung') whereby actors – and audience – do not empathise with the characters portrayed. Latin American Nuevo Teatro also has similarities with United States and European 'hippie' theatre, and Living Theatre. Its most important characteristic, though, is its break with the notion of authorial ownership. As one Colombian dramatist put it memorably: 'El teatro ha cambiado de proprietario' (Carlos José Reyes 77). Often the practitioners of Nuevo Teatro will take an historical event in which the have-nots were pitted against the rich and use it for the political purpose of attacking a regime currently in power. Staging and acting is improvised; and the important part is the message rather than the style or artistry of the performance. Predictably, the Nuevo Teatro movement often found itself in conflict with the society it attempted to depict. In Argentina, a week after the Teatro Abierto '81 event in which more than two hundred authors, directors, and actors put on their work in the Teatro del Picadero in Buenos Aires, the theatre suffered an arson attack which completely destroyed its premises.

One of the most successful theatrical enterprises, and the prototype for the Nuevo Teatro, is the Teatro Experimental de Cali, Colombia, pioneered by Enrique Buenaventura (b.1925); its origins can be traced back to 1955 when Buenaventura took over the directorship of the Teatro Escuela in Cali. This company has put on over a hundred plays, has shown its work in thirty-seven European cities, seven United States cities, and twenty-three Latin-American cities. The first work put on was 'Misterio de adoración de los Reyes Magos', in which the Sacred Family was turned into an allegory of the Colombian people, with Herod as a dictator (Jaramillo 140–42). Fame arrived with the production of *A la diestra del Dios padre* (1958); this play is based on the Faustus theme and, more concretely, on a short story of the same title by Tomás Carrasquilla. It has five versions which were elaborated over the period 1958–1984 (Jaramillo 156). One of the aims of Buenaventura's theatre is not simply to entertain his audience but to construct culture: 'consideramos nuestros espectáculos aportes discutibles y discutidos a la construcción de una cultura de liberación y de divulgación' (qtd. in Jaramillo 144). Very much following in the Nuevo Teatro tradition founded by Buenaventura, there are at the present time a great number of contemporary theatrical groups in Colombia; Jaramillo lists twenty-five (289–335). An example of outdoor theatre is TECAL (Teatro Estudio Calará) of Bogotá. Its *Preludio para andantes o Fuga eterna* (1990) is a fast-moving piece based on the life of a musician which delights in quick, ironic repartee, and is reminiscent of Beckett's Theatre of the Absurd and, particularly, *En attendant Godot*.

If one were to identify one feature of Spanish-American theatre in the 1960s to the present which differentiates it from the work of the preceding generation, it would be its new awareness of, and expression of, the voice of the lower classes.[6] Buenaventura's *El menú* is typical in this respect. It describes the world of those preparing the meal for a VIP who is about to be initiated into membership of the 'Círculo Cerrado'. The language used by the characters, who range from the cook, to a man/woman figure, to various types of beggars, and hired assasins, is humorous, sparkling with slang, and, at times, vulgar. When the candidate finally arrives, they force him to eat so much that, when he is about to give his speech, he vomits and falls over. *El menú* provides great opportunity for slapstick, and is a satire against the rich who feed on fine French food, while the poor and destitute starve around them. *Los papeleros* (1964), by the Chilean dramatist Isidora Aguirre (b.1928), likewise focusses on the trials and tribulations of the lower classes. It describes the growing politicisation of garbage collectors, and the language of the characters, like that of *El menú*, is down-to-earth and vivid. There is some mention of the significant role that women play in civil rights movements (Solórzano, *El teatro actual* 272), and it is not by accident that the most authentic voice of the oppressed is a woman, Romelia, who is accused in the last scene of being 'mad'; her final words, before being led off, convey that the world has been turned upside-down: '¡este es el mundo al revés!' (Solórzano, *El teatro actual* 288). Following the Brechtian model, the audience is called upon in the closing scene of the play to reflect upon what they have seen, rather than drowning all critical analysis in an Aristotelian emotional involvement: 'El teatro cuenta los hechos/ tan absurdos como son/ a vosotros corresponde/ ¡pensar en la solución!' (Solórzano, *El teatro actual* 290).

One of the more artistically sophisticated plays written in this vein is *Los invasores* by Egon Wolff (b.1926), which was first staged in 1963 in the Teatro Antonio Vares by the Instituto de la Universidad de Chile, and directed by Víctor Jara. It expresses the polarisation in Chile at that time between the haves and the have-nots of Chilean society. More than anything it is a household drama since everything takes place within four walls. The husband and wife, Meyer and Pietá, and their children, Marcela and Bobby, are presented as a stable, upper-middle-class family whose world is suddenly invaded by the poor, spearheaded by their ringleaders, China and Alí Baba, who live on the other side of the river in a city which is almost certainly Santiago. The play begins realistically enough with a typical domestic setting,

6 It is important to recognise the Manichean split within contemporary Spanish-American drama. While it is undeniable that the works mentioned above project the voice of the lower classes, there are a number of works which have gained some notoriety but which do not do so. Examples are Carlos Fuentes's *Todos los gatos son pardos* (1970), a play recreating the drama of the conquest (for more discussion, see Hart, *Other* 29–35), and Vargas Llosa's *Kathie y el hipopótamo* (1983), the latter of which was staged very successfully in English translation in London in the mid-1980s (for more discussion see Gerdes 530). These works, and others like them, should be seen as 'overflow' works from another genre rather than works central to the contemporary dramatic canon.

although the wife, Pietá, is feeling apprehensive about something she cannot define. That night, however, an intruder breaks in and, from that point on, the play becomes gradually more unrealistic and even absurd. Meyer refuses to stop the invaders from taking over his home, and even turns a blind eye when one of them strikes his daughter (Act I, Scene ii; Wolff 162). The process described in the play, as Bobby lucidly points out, is '[e]l ocaso de la propiedad privada' (Act I, Scene ii; Wolff 176). Other elements underline the supernatural nature of the events described; thus, the individuals who torment Marcela at the beginning of Act II (Toletole, Alí Baba, and el Cojo) entered the bedroom by going through the wall, as Toletole explains (Act II; Wolff 186). Furthermore, these intruders know too much about Meyer's life to be accidental thieves. China, for example, knows enough about Meyer's life to wheedle the truth out of him about an unsavoury event committed by him in the past (Meyer murdered a business partner in order to get the insurance; Wolff 156, 205). Given this uncanny knowledge on the part of the intruders, it comes therefore as no surprise to the audience when we discover, after Meyer's screaming fit, that the play has been nothing more than a dream; the characters are therefore projections of Meyer's guilty imagination. But *Los invasores* has a final twist. Just when the audience is letting its defences down, Bobby mentions that one of the events described in the dream actually happened (the Gran Jefe Blanco who burned all the students' coats for warmth). At that moment a window shatters downstairs, conveying that Meyer's dream is about to be enacted for real. The conclusion of the play is convincing in that it confirms the previous actions as subconsciously valid (that is in Meyer's dream world), while introducing the possibility that it was also empirical. The inner and outer worlds are finally revealed to be identical.

## The Essay

A great deal of contemporary essay writing in Latin America addresses the problem of identity, ethnicity and origins. One of the more searching examples of this line of enquiry is *Calibán* (1971) by Roberto Fernández Retamar (b.1930), which Fredric Jameson calls 'the Latin American equivalent of Said's *Orientalism*' (Jameson viii). It begins with the question put to Fernández Retamar by a European journalist ('Does a Latin-American culture exist?'), and uses this as a spring-board to dismantle the premises underpinning such a question. The Cuban critic then takes the figure of Caliban as used by Shakespeare in *The Tempest*, and homes in on his rebuke to Prospero: 'You taught me language, and my profit on't/ Is. I know how to curse. The red plague rid you /For learning me your language' (Act I, Scene ii; lines 362–64). Fernández Retamar compares this situation to that of the Latin American who, unlike the inhabitants of other post-colonial nations, still speaks the language of his conqueror, Spanish. In particular, he sees Shakespeare's vision of Caliban as specifically Caribbean-centred since Caliban is Shakespeare's anagram for 'cannibal', by which term the Carib Indians were known. He argues that the notion of an 'anthrophagus' is a fiction produced by a vigorous emerging bourgeoisie, as likely, he says, as 'one-eyed men'. In effect, Fernández Retamar rejects Enrique Rodó's defence of Ariel (who symbolised the spiritual, Hispanic heritage of America) and instead proposes Caliban as a more apt symbol for the people of Latin America since they were enslaved and taught a foreign tongue by their conquerors. Using Martí as a yardstick, and specifically his notion that 'Nuestra Grecia es preferible a la Grecia que no es nuestra', Fernández Retamar then goes on to berate those writers and intellectuals who, in his view, have sold out to the forces of imperialism, among them Borges. Fernández Retamar concludes by rejecting the pro-Western and overtly racist stance underlying Sarmiento's *Facundo* and Martínez Estrada's *Radiografía de la pampa*. By untying the barbarism/civilisation binary opposition promoted by Sarmiento, *Calibán* in effect becomes a defiant re-writing of the First-World mythology which excludes the Third World from the arena of culture. The space inhabited by Caliban becomes the authentic ground in which popular, revolutionary culture can grow.

A specifically Marxist interpretation of Latin-American culture is found in *La ciudad letrada* (1984) by the Uruguayan essayist Angel Rama (1926–1983). Unlike Fernández Retamar, who pursues a synchronic reading, Rama's approach is diachronic. In the first three chapters of *La ciudad letrada* Rama focusses on the ordering principles animating the culture which was built in the New World, the first on the city as the site of civilisation, as opposed to the barbarism of Amerindia, the second and third on the lettered elites whose writings 'planned' the cities in which they lived, and, roughly speaking, concentrate on the early years of the conquest and the colonial period. The last three chapters turn their attention to the modern period from 1870 to the present day, the emphasis here being on the modernisation process, the growth of the economy, the formation of new social classes, the politicisation of the masses and the revolutions which shook the Sub-Continent after 1911. Rama's approach is vigorously eclectic, but it often takes the form of setting the historical scene (main historical events, ideologies, etc.), and discussing the literature as mediating those historical processes, and his insights are new and original. Rama's discussion of the literature of orality has opened up new avenues of research (Rama, *Ciudad* 86–88). Fundamental to his approach, and in this his work echoes Foucault's, is that different types of writing, ranging from legal documents to poetry, are social discourse. His historicist re-readings of literary works are undoubtedly some of the most challenging written.

Chapter 7

# SOME POST-MODERN DEVELOPMENTS

These final remarks on some post-modern developments are intended as a postscript to the previous chapters. They concentrate on a number of new developments in contemporary Spanish-American literature and analyse a representative sample of works from those new genres. As we saw in Chapter 6, the decade of the 1960s witnessed a boom of Spanish-American literature such as never before had been seen; as a result of a number of developments – among which should be mentioned political events such as the Cuban Revolution, economic events such as the commodification of literature, and cultural events such as the growth of the New Latin American Cinema – there emerged a new sense of a common cultural voice in Spanish America. Paradoxically enough, following close on the heels of the creation of a new Spanish-American literary canon in the 1960s, new dissident voices became audible. The canon became gradually more diversified, the old hegemony of white, male, middle-class literature came more and more to be questioned, until, certainly by the 1980s, it became difficult to talk of a single canon. New canons, such as women's writing, Afro/a/-Hispanic writing, Latino/a literature, gay literature, and *testimonio*, to give a few examples, began to emerge and claim space exclusively for themselves.

## *The Post-Boom Novel*

While there is much debate about the difference between the Boom and the post-Boom novel (some critics have even gone as far as to deny that there is any difference), it is clear that the progression from Boom to post-Boom constitutes a change of paradigm. As Philip Swanson has suggested: '[F]rom, roughly, the late sixties/early seventies, the Latin American novel began to experience a shift away from complex, even tortuous narrative forms towards more popular forms, often (though not always) relatively straightforward and sometimes, too, more directly political: a shift from the Boom to the post-Boom. The new novel had acquired an official air, lapsing into stereotype and a kind of heavy neo-classicism. The re-evaluation of popular culture (meaning, again, broadly speaking, mass culture rather than a form of indigenism) . . . brought a wind of change' (Swanson 161). It is also important to note that the post-Boom novel differs from the Boom novel in terms of the gender of the author; the Spanish-American new novel, as has been suggested, 'was a male-dominated affair' (Payne & Fitz 15), while there are a significant number of female authors of post-Boom novels, including, *inter alia*, Isabel Allende, Marta Traba, Carmen Peri Rossi, and Laura Esquivel.[1]

## The Men of the Post-Boom

*La guaracha del Macho Camacho* (1976), by the Puerto Rican Luis Rafael Sánchez (b.1936), is typical of the post-Boom novel in its playful eroticism and its allusiveness to popular culture, since it, effectively, novelises the 'popular culture of Caribbean music and American television' (Raymond Leslie Williams 102). The title of the novel is based on a pop song and is the refrain which laces together a number of otherwise disconnected *tranches de vie* of various stereotypical individuals from Puerto Rico, including a senator and his antics with a clandestine lover, a playboy who is addicted to his Ferrari and masturbation, and a high-class woman interested in art and the psychoanalyst's couch. The narrative switches easily and unexpectedly between scenes in the lives of these and other people, often in mid-sentence. Likewise a demeaning view is taken of human activity; social culture is reduced to copulation (a recurrent metaphor of the novel), eructation, vomit-

---

1   It is worthy of note that, during the period in which a new genre, the post-Boom novel, began to assert its dominance in the literary landscape of the 1980s and 1990s, the Boom novelists continued to write, and, in some cases, went on to write some of their best works. What is striking, however, is that the narrative of the Boom novelists typically alternated between two poles, that of the traditional Boom format, and a new style of writing in which some post-modern trends were assimilated. García Márquez, for example, continued to write novels in the traditional 'mythical' style of the Boom novel, such as his complex Dictator novel, *El otoño del patriarca* (1975), arguably his most sophisticated work, while at the same time writing works with a more post-modern feel, such as *Crónica de una muerte anunciada* (1981), which incorporates typical post-Boom features such as the detective-novel style and the 'reportaje' format (Hart, *Crónica* 17). The focus of Vargas Llosa's novels has shifted noticeably. His best work, *La guerra del fin del mundo* (1981), dealing with the transcendence of events which occurred during a massacre of thousands of religious fanatics near Canudos in Brazil at the turn of the century, follows the established format of the Boom novel. But some of his later works, such as *Historia de Mayta* (1984) and *¿Quién mató a Palomino Molero?* (1986), show him experimenting with post-modern techniques such as rapportage and the detective-novel formula. Cortázar's work in the 1970s continued exploring the Boom blueprint he created with *Rayuela* (*Libro de Manuel* [1973] being a good example of this) but in some works, particularly *Fantomas contra los vampiros multinacionales* (1975), Cortázar attempted to integrate popular culture into his work. Even Carlos Fuentes, of all the novelists the most impervious to the popularising techniques of the post-Boom (his masterpiece, *Terra Nostra* [1975], is a grandiose novel reminiscent of the epic and totalising scale of the Boom formula) approaches the neo-Realism of the post-Boom novel in his more recent novel, *Gringo viejo* (1985), which has been made into a successful movie.

ing and spitting. In this post-modern world, all is levelled and a pop song is neither more nor less significant than the foundation of the United States. Culture is not only inter-changeable, it is also repeatable; thus, scenes from the novel are repeated verbatim (Rafael Sánchez 103, and 149–50). As the narrator suggests at one point: 'el misterio del mundo es un mundo de misterio: cita citable' (Rafael Sánchez 77). The notion of a quotable quote itself repeated throughout the novel emphasises an epistemological strategy in which culture is experienced by the individual as a repeatable, interchangeable and empty reality, in which 'el aquí es esta desamparada isla de cemento nombrada Puerto Rico' (Rafael Sánchez 34). In contradistinction to the lyrics of the pop song, according to which 'la vida es una cosa femonemal', life is shown to be trite, nasty and pointless.

*Luna caliente* (1983), by the Argentine novelist Mempo Giardinelli (b.1947), epitomises the demythifying ethos of pastiche. It tells the story of a young man, Ramiro Bermúdez, recently returned to Buenos Aires from Paris, who has a distinguished career before him, and whose life swiftly disintegrates once he becomes fascinated with Araceli, the thirteen-year-old daughter of a doctor friend, Braulio Tennembaum. He rapes and kills Araceli, or at least so he thinks, and, as a result, decides to kill Braulio when they are out driving. Ramiro returns to Buenos Aires only to find that Araceli did not die after all. At this point, the narrative becomes gradually more fantastic; Ramiro is apprehended by the police but they are unable to press charges against him when Araceli provides him with an alibi. Later on, Ramiro, in a fit of rage inspired by Araceli's sexuality, kills her, and then flees to Paraguay. The novel ends with a twist. Waiting in a run-down hotel in Asunción, Ramiro is awakened by the porter's phone call informing him: 'Que lo busca una señorita, señor, casi una niña' (Giardinelli 158). At this point, it becomes clear that Araceli is a supernatural being who is able to return from the dead. *Luna caliente* basically derives from three sources. The most important of these is the 'novela negra' (or hard-boiled crime novel) which centres on the discovery of the identity of the murderer, although here the narrative is written in the first person. The second main source for Giardinelli's novel is the Gothic novel, above all in its combination of mystery and horror. The third basic ingredient is the political thriller, expressed mainly in the murky business in chapter xvi when Ramiro is informed by the Chief of Police that he will be looked after if he admits to having committed the murder and agrees to collaborate on the Police side against the subversives (the novel is set during the *guerra sucia*). The confluence of these three sources contrives to produce a text which has a rapidly-moving plot, and a clear sense of time and place as in the Realist novel, combined with a Cortazarian sense of the uncanny which unexpectedly explodes that world from within. Intriguingly, the appearance of the Chief of Police is as uncanny and unexplained as is Araceli's presence in the novel, which suggests the extent to which the political plot is a micro-narrative contained within the overarching paradigm of the mystery thriller. Though almost devoid of literary references in the first part of the book, literary allusions abound in the final chapter of the novel. Ramiro compares his love of Araceli to the ill-starred love of Paolo and Francesca in Dante's *Inferno*, as well as to that of Vergil's Dido and Homer's Helen (Giardinelli 156–57). His final thought, just before Araceli returns to him, is to compare himself to a prisoner of Dante's seventh circle of Hell (Giardinelli 157). *Luna caliente*, in its use of devices such as melodrama, coincidence, suspense and the supernatural derived from narratives of popular culture, is a good example of the more immediate appeal of the post-Boom novel as distinct from its rather erudite forebear, the Boom novel.

*Ardiente paciencia* (1983) by the Chilean Antonio Skármeta (b.1940), like *Luna caliente*, has a number of post-Boom features, in particular, its subversive allusiveness to the 'petite histoire' of popular culture. The plot centres around the love affair and eventual marriage of Mario Jiménez and Beatriz González. In order to win Beatriz's heart, Mario seeks the help of Pablo Neruda, for whom he works as the postman; given his fame and the quantity of letters he receives, Neruda has to have a postman all to himself to deliver his mail to his residence in Isla Negra in southern Chile. While the novel does focus to some extent on the turbulent political landscape of the late 1960s and early 1970s in Chile (references are made to Neruda's political involvement and to Salvador Allende's election in 1970 and the coup d'état which unseated him in 1973 and ushered in Pinochet's dictatorship), the emphasis is much more on the texture of everyday life; this is the Neruda of *Odas elementales* rather than *Canto general*. Thus, in one of the most successful scenes of the novel, we see Neruda explaining to his postman what a metaphor is, only to find himself put in his place afterwards: '– ¿Y por qué si es una cosa tan fácil, se llama tan complicado?' (Skármeta 11). As this passage makes quite clear, one of the most important techniques of the novel is humour. Nothing is spared, including romantic love (after one graphic sexual scene when Beatriz has an orgasm, she says: 'Me hiciste acabar, tonto'; Skármeta 63), the mother-in-law (Antonio is described as coming a cropper against 'una institución temible en Chile: las suegras'; Skármeta 36). The novel is also very amusing in its use of repartee; the following exchange between Mario and Neruda just before his death is typical: '– ¿Cómo se siente, don Pablo?/ – Moribundo. Aparte de eso nada grave' (Skármeta 112). Another feature of the novel which suggests its post-Boom pedigree is the way in which it blends different cultural codes. Like *Luna caliente*, *Ardiente paciencia* contains allusions to literary masterpieces, such as Shakespeare's play, *Hamlet* (Skármeta 112), and to Dante (Beatriz's name is an overt reference to Dante's beloved), but it also has many references to popular culture, such as the Peruvian soap-opera, *Simplemente María* (it is referred to in the novel as Mexican, but this is a slip of the pen; Skármeta 71), popular songs (such as 'no me digas que Merluza no, Maripusa, que yo sí como merluza'; Skármeta 85), classic movies (such as *West Side Story*, Skármeta 5), and the

Beatles' song 'The Postman' (Skármeta 51). The allusions to popular culture are not surprising given that, strictly speaking, *Ardiente paciencia* is not a novel but, rather, a film-script; it won prizes at the Biarritz and the Huelva film festivals and has recently led to a very successful Italian film version. Nevertheless, it is typical of the post-Boom novel's fondness for the language of film. A good example of this occurs when Mario uses a filmic metaphor to express the plenitude of sexual love: 'Las escenas vividas en el rústico lecho de Beatriz durante los meses siguientes hicieron sentir a Mario que todo lo gozado hasta entonces eran una pálida sinopsis del film que ahora se ofrecía en la pantalla oficial en Cinerama y technicolor' (Skármeta 67). Literature is explored in this novel not as a high-brow intellectual activity but as a cultural reservoir which, especially in its refinement of the language of love, plays a direct formative role in the everyday lives of ordinary people.

*Gazapo* (1985) by the Mexican Gustavo Sainz (b.1940), as Raymond Williams suggests, 'was a notable innovation for the Mexican postmodern: it brought the young language of adolescents into the Mexican novel, as well as the new technologies of communicating by means of tape recorders and other media' (Raymond Leslie Williams 26). It did have some roots in the past, however; like the Boom novel, Sainz's novel strove to undermine the structured nature of chronological time. The novel starts *in medias res* and seems to end there as well; it tells the story of group of a adolescent boys living in Mexico City who share their tales of sexual and criminal exploits with each other, retelling them to each other, and even going to the extreme of recording each others' stories with a tape recorder – to such an extent that it becomes difficult to separate the fact from the fiction. *Gazapo* is decidedly post-modern in that it focusses on the play-acting involved in their stories, namely, how the telling of the stories is more important than the events which they supposedly relate, and how the stories live each time they are related, with no version having more validity than any other. Apart from the main narrative of the boys' exploits, there are no real other subtexts, apart from the medieval texts which interrupt the narrative towards the end of the novel, and the snatches of the Catechism. Both are meant to throw an ironic light on the gang's deeds. But, perhaps more important, the text is interrupted by snatches of the narrator's diary and his tape-recorded narratives, all of which give the novel a play-back feel.

## The Women of the Post-Boom

*Conversación al sur* (1981) by Marta Traba (1930–1983) centres on the memories of two women, Dolores and Irene, who were involved in the revolutionary movement in the Southern Cone during the 1970s; as a result, both suffer mental and physical torture and lose their loved ones. Traba's presentation of the political conflict is gendered in that it projects femaleness and political insurgency as indivisible notions. Thus the political reality of oppression is experienced by one sex in particular (women); men are depicted in *Conversación al sur* as associated with the Right (if they are Leftist they are ineffectual, such as Andrés and Enrique). The women, however, as typified by Dolores and Irene, direct and sustain political insurgency. One of the most important rhetorical strategies of this novel is synecdoche; thus, the visible reality drawn in Traba's text alludes to the invisible reality which the reader is forced to reconstruct (the latter being the systematic abduction and torture of political subversives by the Argentine Armed Forces of which no empiric details are given in the text). The objective facts are reduced to tantalising allusions, the metaphor shorn from its concrete referent. As Dolores says to Victoria at one stage: 'Peor es imaginarse las cosas' (Traba 123). Not surprisingly, fear pervades Dolores's whole existence; she becomes paranoid, at one point suspecting the bus-driver of informing on her (Traba 155). Despite the pain which is inflicted on the subversives' minds and particularly their bodies, they are able, through political solidarity, to achieve a new identity. This is most evident during the description of the women who congregate every Thursday in the Plaza de Mayo to protest at the disappearance of their loved ones, a voice that one day would be heard. Thus, although *Conversación al sur* has a pessimistic level, since it seems to accept defeat as inevitable and ends with a scene in which Irene and Dolores are about to meet their doom, it also has a positive message in that the sense of solidarity shared by the women points the way forward to the path of social justice (Hart, *White* 99–107).

*La casa de los espíritus* (1982) by Isabel Allende (b.1942), published a year after *Conversación al sur*, is typical of a certain type of women's writing of the 1980s which flies in the face of the notion of the woman writer as interested only in the space of the home and the emotions (and especially love), since it addresses political issues directly. The novel traces, through the vicissitudes of three generations of women – Clara, Blanca, and Alba – the political struggle in twentieth-century Chile between the Left (symbolised by Pedro García and his son Pedro Segundo and grandson Pedro Tercero) and the Right (personified by Esteban Trueba). The women of the family are consistently portrayed as the mediators in this political struggle; thus Blanca, though Esteban Trueba's daughter, falls in love with Pedro Segundo, and Alba falls for a revolutionary by the name of Miguel. Whereas the Left is presented in terms of continuity through family lineage, the Right is shown finally to be issueless since Esteban Trueba's male progeny either become Marxists (Jaime) or dropouts (Nicolás) and his female progeny fall in love with revolutionaries. The exception to this rule is Esteban García, the second-generation illegitimate offspring of Esteban Trueba and Pancha García (Pedro García's sister); he ends up being a colonel in the police force and takes terrible revenge on Alba for the wrong he sees his unacknowledged grandfather as having committed to him. By this token Allende presents the military who took over power in Chile in the 1973 coup as a bastard breed issued from the landed classes (Esteban Trueba) and the unlanded (Pedro García); the insult could not be more carefully chosen. This sardonic depiction of the military class in the person of Esteban García is made all the more striking since, as the last chapter informs us, the text we have before us is the result of the collaborative effort of the Conservative Right (Esteban Trueba) and the Left (Alba). Indeed, it is only in the last chapter that we discover why Esteban Trueba's mini-memoirs are recorded in the text. As the collaboration between Esteban Trueba and Alba in the epilogue demonstrates, *La casa de los espíritus* traverses class as well as gender boundaries (landed/unlanded, male/female), this despite the often stereotyped portrayal of identity in gendered terms (Hart, *White* 91–99). Even though the reader is not spared some of the more gruesome details of tyranny, political oppression and sadism in the prison camps of Pinochet's Chile, Allende's novel is ultimately a positive affirmation of the value of solidarity in the face of evil and political oppression.

   *Como agua para chocolate* (1989) by the Mexican novelist Laura Esquivel (b.1950) is best seen in terms of the quotidianisation of the value of love; it merges high and low culture (ranging from motifs from Mexican soap opera to cookery book recipes), gives high priority to the mass-media notion of love as an all-consuming passion, and, most importantly, lends itself well to the language of film; a very successful film version was released in 1985, and broke box-office records. The book is set up like a 'folletín' (its subtitle is 'Novela de entregas mensuales'), and it is redolent of the 'telenovela' (a great favourite in Mexico, where there are two television channels which exclusively play soaps back to back all day long) in its reference to the next episode once one has finished ('Continuará'). *Como agua para chocolate* is, in essence, a feminine counter-version of the Mexican Revolution, offering a kitchen-eye's view of those turbulent years, which is at odds with the masculinist rhetoric of the history books with their emphasis on battles and the struggle for civic power. The most striking characteristic of the novel, as its title suggests, is the use of food as a metaphor for the human emotions. There are various examples of this; Tita's tears which drop into the cake being prepared for Rosaura and Pedro's wedding meal produce a fit of vomiting in the guests (Esquivel 44–45), and Tita's blood mixed up with rose petals, when added to the quails, produces an aphrodisiac reaction in those who consume it (Esquivel 54–61), an idea which is repeated in the last chapter of the novel when Tita makes *chile en nogada* and unleashes an orgy of the senses (Esquivel 240–42). While the link between food and sex is a traditional one, *Como agua para chocolate* manages to extend this association in unexpected ways. Perhaps the best illustration of this occurs when Tita has to sing to the 'frijoles' to make them cook; in a house where there have been arguments, so popular knowledge suggests, the food is 'annoyed' and therefore will not cook (Esquivel 218). Most intriguing of all is the way in which the emotions

are depicted as emanating from the body like a cloud, influencing everything in their path. Exemplary in this regard is the cloud of rose perfume
which emanates from Gertrudis's body and attracts Juan, the *villista*, to her,
at which point, following a Romantic stereotype, they sail off into the sunset
on a horse, copulating as they go (Esquivel 56–60); another example is the
anger which invades Tita when she has a tiff with Pedro (Esquivel 154).
Alongside its sensitivity to the ways of the flesh, the novel is also alert to the
realm of the spirit; Tita sees John Brown's Indian grandmother, 'la kikapú',
when recovering from an illness, and she is haunted by the spirit of her
mother, Mamá Elena (Esquivel 115–18, 177, 200–201). These events, and
here Esquivel shows her roots in the magical-realist tradition, are presented
as if they were part of everyday life, as are other fantastic occurrences, which
include those already mentioned, such as tears in food producing botulism, or
food producing sexual frenzy, or others such as Tita suddenly lactating and
therefore being able to feed her nephew (Esquivel 82), and people dying of
love (this is essentially what happened to Nacha [Esquivel 45], as well as Tita
and Pedro [Esquivel 243–44]). With its roots so firmly in popular culture, it is
not surprising that *Como agua para chocolate* should have only one reference to high culture, namely, the comparison between Tita and Ceres, the
Roman god of fertility (Esquivel 82), or that it deals in stereotypes, a good
example being the difference between the Anglo-Saxon male, John Brown,
and the Hispanic male, Pedro. Written from a feminine perspective – its
thesis is essentially that women are closer to food, love and life – *Como agua
para chocolate* is one of the best of the novels to emerge in the post-Boom
era. Its humour (a good example being when Tita explains, in the presence of
John Brown's deaf aunt, that she does not love him; Esquivel 220–22), and
metaphoric flair are carried over successfully into the movie version.

## Testimonio

*Testimonio*, or testimony (the word in Spanish suggests the act of testify-
ing or giving witness in a legal or religious sense), refers to a new type of
autobiography in Spanish America which denounces political injustice. On
the one hand, there are those works which are pure autobiographies, that is,
narratives in which the teller is/was also the actor. Some of the more gripping
examples are autobiographies by *guerrilleros*, such as the Argentine Ernesto
Che Guevara's *Paisajes de la guerra revolucionaria* (1969).

Beside these autobiographical narratives are those *testimonios* in which
the teller is not also the actor. These are potentially more intriguing since
they combine the artistry of a good novelist with the freshness of the account
of an action-packed life (novelists are, after all, not always the people who
lead exciting lives). A good early example of this was the series of articles

written for *El Espectador* by García Márquez, about the experiences of a shipwreck, and which was put together in book-form subsequently; it has an extraordinarily long title: *Relato de un náufrago que estuvo diez días a la deriva en una balsa sin comer ni beber, que fue proclamado héroe de la patria, besado por las reinas de la belleza y hecho rico por la publicidad, y luego aborrecido por el gobierno y olvidado para siempre* (1970). The beauty of the account, the irony of its title, are due to García Márquez's story-telling ability; it is easy to imagine that the shipwreck's story would have been distinctly unmemorable were it not for García Márquez's role in the process. The best example of the *testimonio* occurs when at least two factors are present; firstly, as in García Márquez's narrative, there is a split between the actor and the teller, and, secondly, when the story speaks on behalf not of one individual, but of a social group, or a nation. This occurred in the case of *Biografía de un cimarrón* (1966), the matrix text of the *testimonio* genre.

*Biografía de un cimarrón* is based on the life of Esteban Montejo, and particularly his experiences in Cuba as a runaway slave in late nineteenth-century Cuba, and it is recounted by the university ethnologist, Miguel Barnet. This text is the classic of the genre since it combines the two levels of quotidian personal narrative and ethnographic epic (González Echeverría 117–18). It allows a vision of the life of a slave 'from the inside', as it were, and gains authenticity as a result of there being two hands in the work, compiler and author. The narrative begins with Montejo's early life; he was born on 26 December 1860 and became a maroon living in the 'monte' soon afterwards (and therefore did not know his parents). It describes how he managed to survive while there (what he ate, where he hid), then portrays his life as a wage-earner in the sugar plantations immediately after the abolition of slavery (the main freedom he appreciated in the post-slavery world seems to have been that of pursuing women), as well as his role in the militias during the War of Independence. The description of his life – the vicissitudes of everyday life, the subversion of official culture as expressed by the work ethic, the institution of the family, and adherence to Christianity – is a useful corrective to the versions of slaves' lives which appear in other nineteenth-century texts, such as Gómez de Avellaneda's *Sab*. *Biografía de un cimarrón* has an air of authenticity even when the account of Montejo's everyday life is bizarre. The predominance of the African religion in Cuba ('los dioses más fuertes son los de Africa'; Barnet 15), the horrors of war and guerrilla warfare, especially the use of the machete by the Cubans (Barnet 169), the use of hand-picked slaves for breeding purposes, which effectively doomed many of the men to a life of male-male sex (Barnet 38, 40–41), and (most bizarre of all) the description of two sisters from a wealthy familiy who used to sleep with monkeys (Barnet 153), all contrive to produce a gruesomely believable *tranche de vie* of life in pre- and post-Independence Cuba. Though based on Montejo's personal life, *Biografía de un cimarrón* speaks on behalf of a people denied access to the fruits of this earth, and therefore stands as a testimony to the injustice of colonialist political systems.

One other extremely important *testimonio* of this period is Rigoberta Menchú's autobiography, which, like *Biografía de un cimarrón*, is at once personal testimony and ethnobiography. A book of thirty-four carefully-organised chapters, *Me llamo Rigoberta Menchú y así me nació la conciencia* (1983) tells the story of Rigoberta's life, beginning with her childhood in Chimel, a small village in the *altiplano* in Guatemala near San Miguel de Uspantán, which is the capital of the north-western province of Quiché. We learn of how as a young girl she was forced, like the rest of her family, to work at the *finca* in the lowlands in subhuman conditions at the hands of the *mestizo ladinos*, of how landowners referred to as the Garcías, the Brols and the Martínez, and soldiers gradually destroyed the Indian community, and of how the Indians decided to resist – with force if necessary – the unlawful expropriation of their lands. Rigoberta describes the role played by her father, Vicente Menchú, in this consciousness-raising process in which he networked with unions and other Indian communities and then joined the Comité de Unidad Campesina, an organisation defending peasants' rights, for which he suffered imprisonment and torture, as did Rigoberta's brother and mother. (A Revolutionary Christian Group was formed bearing Vicente Menchú's name, after his death by burning in the Spanish Embassy in Guatemala on 31 January 1980.) Rigoberta also describes her own role as a catalyst in enabling surrounding Indian communities to defend themselves, for which she used her previous experience as a catechist. The narrative shows how this conflict between the peasants and the military gradually took on political connotations, suggested by the later use of the word 'compañero/compañera' to indicate 'comrade'. *Me llamo Rigoberta Menchú* concludes with a description of the forced exile from Guatemala of its author. What is remarkable about this autobiography is that it is, like no other text published to date, an authentic example of the vision of life for a Quiché community, harassed by an enemy that, literally and linguistically, it does not understand. Rigoberta Menchú herself, though clearly one of the most adept communicators in her community (in this she followed in her father's footsteps), only learned Spanish some three years before she began telling her story, sitting in Paris with an interviewer and a tape-recorder, at the age of twenty-three. It is not a text for the faint-hearted as the 'horror movie' description in chapter XXIV of the torture and public burning of the so-called subversives, including Rigoberta's brother, in Chajul on 24 September 1979, makes quite clear. An important statement on the injustice suffered by the Amerindian population of Central America, *Me llamo Rigoberta Menchú* was awarded the Nobel Peace Prize in 1992; the medal is being kept on display in the Museum of the Templo Mayor in Mexico City until democracy returns to Guatemala.

## *Latino/a Literature*

In this period a completely new genre, or sub-genre, emerged within the Spanish-American literary canon, namely Latino/a literature, which may be defined as literature written in Spanish, English, or Spanglish, by authors of Hispanic descent who presently reside in the United States on a permanent basis, and/or which has a Hispanic focus. Certainly some important examples of Latino literature were published in the 1940s, and according to some critics a long time before that, but the crescendo of its popularity may be located in the period stretching from the 1970s until the present day.[2] During the 1970s Latino/a writers were mainly published in Latino presses such as Bilingual Review and Arte Público Press, but since the 1980s they have branched out into the major presses: Julia Alvarez (Alonquin Books), Ana Castillo (Norton), Sandra Cisneros (Random House), Dagoberto Glib (Grove Press), Cristina García (Knopf), and Helena Viramontes (Dutton) (Torres, 'U.S. Latino/a Literature' 1). Latino/a literature has some way to go before it is officially 'canonised' in the university curriculum. In the words of one critic, '[a]s a stepchild of both English and Spanish departments it participates in the literary canons of neither' (Torres, 'U.S. Latino/a Literature' 2).

One of the classics of Latino literature is *Mi querido Rafa* (1981) by Rolando Hinojosa (b.1929). Set in Klail City, it tells the story of Jehú, a Chicano loan officer, who works in a local bank, and uses his position there to back the political campaign of Ira Escobar, who won the democratic primary while running against the incumbent candidate, Roger Terry; Ira is outwitted by Terry, however, when the latter decides to run as an independent and gets the coveted seat in Washington. As the complicated plot unfolds, it becomes clear that Jehú has been set up by Noddy, his boss, and the story ends with a scene in which he is asked to resign. The striking features of the novel are its structure and its language. The first half of the novel consists of twenty-two letters from Jehú to his cousin, Rafa, which show how Jehú gets caught up in the muddy waters of politics, unbeknownst to him, while the second half incorporates a series of testimonies of people who knew Jehú during the period in which he supported Ira Escobar's election campaign. The language is a delicious blend of Spanglish; it interjects Spanish words in

---

2   A critic such as Luis Leal, for example, traces Latino literature back to the seventeenth century, his definition of the genre being literature written in Spanish which focusses on the land now known as the United States. Thus, the chronicle *Historia de la Nueva México, 1610*, by Gaspar Pérez de Villagrá (1555–1620), is included as an early example of Chicano literature (Arias & Gonzales-Berry 654), but it is preferable to retain the term for late twentieth-century literature, when it achieved canonic status. The desire to rewrite the canon of Spanish-American literature from the vantage-point of Latino literature is not uncommon, as the recent *Masterpieces of Latino Literature*, ed. Frank Magill, suggests; this anthology contains sections on writers such as Cortázar and Manuel Puig whose connections with what is normally known as Latino literature are sketchy, to say the least.

English sentences, and vice-versa, and thereby sustains a credible code-switching linguistic environment. A very subtle novel, *Mi querido Rafa* has established Hinojosa as one of the most important Chicano writers of his time; this was confirmed when he was awarded the Casa de las Américas Prize.

Latino literature is also commonly interpreted to mean literature written in English by writers of Hispanic descent; one of the most well-known Latino writers within this vein is Oscar Hijuelos (b.1951) whose novel, *The Mambo Kings Sing of Love* (1989), won the Pulitzer Prize in 1990. In some senses like a *Bildungsroman*, the novel describes the adventures of a group of Cuban musicians, with a particular focus on the Castillo brothers, Cesar and Nestor, who arrived in New York in 1949, hoping to make their fame as musicians. A raunchy and raw novel, *The Mambo Kings Sing of Love* is not for the puritanical reader. Unlike the classic formation-novel, however, *The Mambo Kings Sing of Love* does not describe a learning curve in the mind of the main protagonist, Cesar; his life is described as a seemingly endless procession from one woman's body to another and bears more traces of a maroon biography than that of a classic *Bildungsroman*. When Cesar lies dying at the end of the novel, for example (he is suffering from kidney failure because of his excessive drinking), his life is not provided with a perspective produced by hindsight; rather he simply longingly recalls the many women he has slept with. Perhaps most skilful about the novel, it underlines the interplay between the life of the lover described in their songs, and the life the singers lead (during the short period of happiness before his demise as a result of kidney failure, Cesar becomes '[l]ike a character in a happy habanera'; Hijuelos 368).

One genre in which there has been an effective presence of Latino/a writers has been the short story. The *Cuentos Chicanos* anthology, edited by Rudolfo Anaya and Antonio Márquez, gives a good indication of the dominant themes within short Chicano fiction. In general, the stories in this collection are witness to a people in transition, struggling to cling on and assert its identity, caught in a no-man's land between two cultural identities. Thus, some of the stories have an epic quality about them. 'The Migrant', by Mario Suarez, for example, tells the story of a young man, Teofilo, who attempts to keep mind and soul together as a migrant worker; his struggle to bring up a family despite a hostile economic environment, though personalised, is meant as an ethno-history of a displaced people. Not surprisingly, given their ethnographic bent, a number of the stories use allegory to convey their message. Ana Castillo's 'Ghost Talk', for example, which tells the story of a young girl whose Mexican mother was seduced by her Anglo work supervisor and made pregnant, describes the means whereby the young girl enacts her revenge and is meant to be understood as an allegory of the clash of Hispanic and Anglo cultures, since it essentially re-writes the trauma of the conquest in a new geographical context. Denise Chávez's 'Willow Game' re-enacts, through the allegory of an uprooted willow tree, the pain felt by women at male violence. Not all the stories are ethnographic – Rudolfo Anaya's 'B. Traven is Alive and Well in Cuernavaca' and Juan Bruce-Novoa's 'The Manuscript' defiantly focus on the process of their own telling – but the majority of them use the narrative of an individual's biography as a vehicle with which to express a community's experience of political disempowerment.

Also important within this genre are those literary works written by Latinas. As Lourdes Torres has pointed out, Latina writers such as Cherríe Moraga (b. 1942), Aurora Levins-Morales (b.1954), Rosario Morales (b.1930), and Gloria Anzaldúa (b.1942), 'subvert both Anglo and Latino patriarchal definitions of culture', thereby appropriating a new space which 'seeks to integrate ethnicity, class, gender, sexuality, and language' (Torres, 'Construction' 272). Indeed, Cherríe Moraga's work expresses a triple disenfranchisement, that of being Latino/a in an Anglo society, that of being female in a macho society, and that of being gay in a heterosexual society. A poet, playwright and essayist, Moraga uses each of these genres to express this disenfranchisement, sometimes in a vituperative manner. What is fascinating about Moraga's work is the way she works through cultural symbols, feminising them as well as lesbianising them; in the primal scene of the birth of the New World, she identifies not with Cortés or la Malinche, or with Christ or Moctezuma, but with Coyolxauhqui, the daughter of Coatlicue, the principal female Aztec goddess, who is murdered by her brother, Huizilopotchli, the God of War ('El mito azteca', *The Last* 73–76). Her utopia is a place she calls Queer Aztlán, a nation in which Latino/a culture is respected, gays are free, and the environment is respected (*The Last* 145–74); in a sense, one could argue that her work is an attempt to body that land into existence.

One of the most significant of the Latina writers is Helena Maria Viramontes (b.1954) who has published a number of short stories, including *The Moths and Other Stories* (1985) and *Under the Feet of Jesus* (1995). Two main themes emerge within her work: family relationships and the female body, evident in stories such as 'Growing', 'Birthday', and 'The Cariboo Cafe'. The experience of womanhood is positivised, and that of masculinity negativised. The universe of the male is typified by the Church which is presented in Viramontes's short stories as a social institution which alienates women. It is, perhaps, not surprising to discover that murder by women of their male tormentors is presented as a comprehensible outcome in stories such as 'The Broken Web' and 'Neighbors'. Viramontes's most anthologised short story, 'Moths', focusses on the bonding between a miscreant, fourteen-year-old girl and her grandmother. When the narrator works in the garden she feels a oneness with the universe, which is noticeably absent from her experience of the chapel in Jay's Market (Viramontes 25). Perhaps most distinctive about this story, though not a common technique in her work, is the note of magical realism which occurs in the final paragraphs of the story. The protagonist and her *abuelita*, now deceased, are in a bath: 'Then the moths came. Small, gray ones that came from her soul and out through her mouth fluttering to light, circling the single dull light bulb of the bathroom' (Viramontes 28). Viramontes's fiction, as 'The Moths' suggests, is complex and sophisticated, and evokes with great poignancy the 'feminine' within the universe.

The other main chord within the symphony of contemporary Latino/a writing, although some would dispute the validity of its presence in this section, includes those Spanish-American writers who were born in Latin America but who now reside in the United States, and who write in Spanish. Unlike Latino/a authors who write in English and whose audience is located within the United States, these writers are writing for an audience which is Spanish-speaking. Typically, this genre is created by writers who also teach at the university level in the United States. Examples are Eduardo Espina, born in Uruguay, Carlota Caulfield and Jesús Barquet, born in Cuba, José Antonio Mazzotti and Miguel Angel Zapata, born in Peru, and Armando Romero, born in Colombia. Their work might be characterised in terms of a letter sent home to their compatriots. Like the writing more traditionally associated with Latino/a literature, it focusses on the experience of life in the United States. Since, unlike other Latino/a writers, they tend to write in Spanish even though they inhabit an Anglophone linguistic environment, it could be argued that they are self-consciously using their literature in order to create a 'magic capsule' of Spanish which separates them from the language-world they inhabit on a day-to-day basis (Hart, 'La cápsula mágica').

## The Gay/Lesbian Novel

Gay and lesbian writing has only recently been co-opted into the Spanish-American literary canon, and that largely as a result of the 1991 study by David William Foster, *Gay and Lesbian Themes in Latin American Writing*. Most of the works he studies come from Argentina and Mexico, countries with historically active gay communities; the main authors he studies are Reinaldo Arenas, Isaac Chocrón, Sylvia Molloy, and Luis Zapata.[3] In this section I have decided to focus on four novels, two by men (Puig and Arenas) and two by women (Peri Rossi and Molloy), and concentrate on their literary qualities rather than their gayness. This is an appropriate approach, since in none of these works is there an explicit campness, or, indeed, a revelation-

---

3   An important and theoretically sophisticated analysis of gay culture appears in Paul Julian Smith's work, *Laws of Desire*. A good gay reading of modern narrative by Hispanic women, including discussion of Peri Rossi and Sylvia Molloy, appears in Inmaculada Pertusa's dissertation, 'Escribiendo entre corrientes: Carmen Riera, Esther Tusquets, Cristina Peri Rossi y Sylvia Molloy'.

scene in which the protagonist suddenly realises who (s)he is. The insights in these writers' novels echo those in the work of critical theorists such as Paul Julian Smith, Eve Kosofsky Sedgwick and Jonathan Dollimore, who problematise the notion that homosexuality is a discrete or essentialist identity, and instead see it as a discursive construct.[4] In the case of Manuel Puig, as we shall see, the discursive construct of homosexuality is seen to be predicated upon the performativity of art.

The most significant Hispanic gay writer, and indeed, post-Boom writer, is the Argentine Manuel Puig (1932–1989), whose best work, arguably, is *El beso de la mujer araña* (1973). The sixteen chapters of this novel focus on the relationship in a prison cell between Valentín, a revolutionary subversive convicted of terrorist activites, and Luis Alberto Molina, a gay man convicted of corrupting a minor. Puig's novel is multi-discursive in the sense that it includes a number of different discourses which include: (i) the colloquial conversations between Valentín and Molina about their everyday life in the prison cell (eating, going to the toilet, etc.), (ii) the Hollywood films Molina lovingly recounts to Valentín, (iii) discussions between Molina and the Prison Inspector, and (iv) the footnotes which give scientific psychoanalytic information about the 'perverse' nature of homosexuality. An important aspect of *El beso de la mujer araña* is its willingness to address the issue of gender difference; in Puig's novel this takes the form of reference to Molina's homosexuality and paedophilia (since the latter crime is the cause of his imprisonment). The relationship between Valentín and Molina eventually becomes homoerotic and, in telescoped form, the novel alludes to male-male sex (Puig 265–66). Again it is difficult to extract the precise nature of the relationship and, indeed, know if Molina actually did betray Valentín to the authorities; chapter 14 ends with Molina asking for the sensitive information Valentín wants to relay to the outside world, and chapter 15 is based on a police report describing Molina's movements once released from jail and his eventual murder, by parties presumably close to Valentín in retaliation for (actual or presumed) betrayal (Puig 279). In an about-turn of roles, Molina dies as a martyr for a cause in which he is not immediately involved. The final message of Puig's novel is fundamentally ambiguous in that it relates the dissidence of perverse sexual behaviour to political dissidence in such a way that the parallels sought between the sex and politics, the personal and the public, are ambivalent. And yet, finally, despite the seriousness of the themes treated (political versus sexual deviance, the law and the penal system, the normal and the dysfunctional), Puig's novel ultimately reduces the various functions of the novel's characters to the performance of roles: since Molina performs as a martyr for the cause, does that make him a communist? Since Valentín performs sexually with a homosexual, does that

---

4   See Smith, *Laws of Desire*; Kosofsky Sedgwick, *Epistemology of the Closet*; and Dollimore, *Sexual Dissidence*.

make him gay? The fact that both Molina and Valentín do something out of character questions the notion of the character as a self-coherent identity understood in an Aristotelian sense. *El beso de la mujer araña*, thus, emphasises the ontological falseness but unavoidability of roles; in Oscar Wildesque fashion Puig suggests that human beings simply play different roles (bourgeois, woman, man, etc.) and are in essence nothing more than masks. In this resides the most subversive point of Puig's text. Since the various footnotes which periodically puncture the text lead to no conclusion about homosexuality that is not subversive, and, since they simply expose the lack of validity of societal, cultural and, indeed psychoanalytic systems used to interpret homosexuality, we must see them as acting – not as a true subconscious, which we might expect, given the Freudian references – but as an inappropriate hermeneutic taxonomy having no power to judge the relationship between Molina and Valentín. Indeed, the footnotes simply constitute a misreading of a sexuality which remains undefined and indefinable throughout the novel; the nearest approximation we have to the riddle of sexuality are the suspension points which punctuate the description of the sexual relationship between Molina and Valentín (Puig 266–67). Sexuality becomes an ambiguous trace in the novel's structure; once more Puig's text underlines the notion of the performance of roles rather than the discovery of an authentic, self-identical self.

An important writer of the post-Boom novel is the gay Cuban novelist, Reinaldo Arenas (1943–1992). One of his best novels, *Otra vez el mar* (1982), treats themes which are common in his work: desire, love, and the individual pitted against society. Part I of the novel is written from the perspective of a young Cuban woman married to Héctor, a dreamy young man who finds it difficult to keep down a job, while they are spending a holiday at the beach in September 1969, with their small child. There is a type of plot; a woman moves in with her son into the cabin next door to Héctor and his wife, and, later that evening, the son is found dead on the beach, although the cause of his death remains a mystery. More important than the plot, however, is the novel's Joycean rejection of the limitations of Euclidean space and time. At various points the narrative is punctuated, without any warning, by scenes from the past (as when Héctor goes off to become a revolutionary in the mountains before the 1959 Revolution, and they witness a death by murder squad in Havana soon afterwards), as well as dream scenes (such as the episode early on in which the Trojan war over Helen is enacted on a beach with the soldiers using their penises for swords, or when the Virgin Mary and God appear, accompanied by angels who walk across the ocean and then fly off in an airplane, or when a food line in Havana is merged with a Nazi concentration camp in which individuals are burnt alive on the slightest pretext). The main aim of Part I of the novel is to assert a new type of language in contradistinction to the language of state power, one which rejects the dictates of time (as encapsulated by the government slogan of 'ten million tons of sugar by next year, 1970!'; Arenas 52) and, indeed, space (since the time of the Trojan war is shown to be porous with that of present-day Cuba), in order to pursue a vision of life which privileges desire over all else. This defiance of the official version of Castro's Cuba (Arenas was persecuted and imprisoned for being a homosexual by Castro), submerged in Part I, emerges openly in Part II, in a series of angry, free-verse poems, prose passages, timid first encounter conversations between gays on the beach, gay love scenes, and exposure of the hypocrisy of the Castro regime. The criticism of the regime meant, of course, that *Otra vez el mar* could not be published in Cuba; Part IV has a section which ironically describes the business of officially-sponsored literary publication as a monster whose anus exhales the perfume of odes and whose mouth disgorges vomit 'in its moments of greatest orgy' (Arenas 294). Arenas's work is significant not only in terms of its expression of the gay's right to free speech in Spanish America but also because of its lyric search for a world as yet untouched by human hypocrisy.

*La nave de los locos* (1984) by Cristina Peri Rossi (b.1941) is a playfully post-modern gay text which re-writes the alphabet of Christian culture. It describes the misadventures of a character whose name is simply a letter of the alphabet, Equis (that is, 'X'), in a variety of urban settings; the novel includes episodes describing sordid sexual encounters, far-fetched dream-sequences, and Equis's philosophizing about life and the universe with his companions, Vercingetorix and Graciela. The novel has little narrative structure and is, furthermore, punctuated by a backdrop-discourse which describes in meticulous, and indeed factual, details the celebrated eleventh-century tapestry depicting the creation of the world which is held in Gerona Cathedral, Spain. Peri Rossi's text declares its own epigonic status with regard to a variety of other texts such as Sebastian Brandt's *Narrenschift* (1494), Pío Baroja's *La nave de los locos* (1925), and Katherine Anne Porter's *Ship of Fools* (1959). All of these works ultimately derive inspiration from the historical custom common in Europe, and especially Germany, in the first half of the fifteenth century, when ships were loaded with mad people and sent downstream in order to drop their human cargo off at another unsuspecting town; though rooted in a particular historical event, the *navis stultiferum* soon became a literary *topos* emblematising the uncertainties of man's life. This notion is used in Peri Rossi's text to undercut ironically the masculinocentric narrative of the Creation, as symbolised by the *Tapestry of the Creation* alluded to in the novel; in effect her novel strives to deconstruct the patriarchal notion of Godhead, which itself is the madness of the world. Thus, the bathetic vicissitudes of the life the protagonist, Equis, and his friends, Vercingetorix and Graciela, are interspersed with grandiose, eloquent descriptions of the cathedral tapestry (see Hart, *White* 124–31). *La nave de los locos* is a sardonic, feminocentric text which contrasts the macro-narrative of the Creation story with the micro-narrative of the sordid antics of three individuals caught in the trap of modern urban life.

A significant gay novel of the post-Boom is Sylvia Molloy's *En breve cárcel* (1981) which, as the title of its translation into English suggests (*Certificate of Absence*, published in 1989), is a textual memory which focusses on absence, in this case, that of the narrator's previous lovers, Vera and Renata. Described by one critic as 'a self-conscious feminist text that defends its marginality and refuses to comply with many of the expectations traditional readers may have of masculine texts' (Raymond Leslie Williams 88), this novel possesses a strikingly intra-feminine quality. No men are present in the narrative, and the focus of the plot is on the triangular (and troublesome) relationship between the three female protagonists. Indeed, the second chapter of the novel focusses on the narrator's memory of her sister, how they were bathed together and used each other as mirrors of being, and Part II, chap. 7, concludes with a jubilant sense of the unity between the women in her life: 'yo quería – madre, hermana, amante – que estuvieran conmigo, yo no vivo sino por ustedes' (*Breve* 147). *En breve cárcel* is at the furthest remove from the action-packed, magical-realist novel format; it concentrates on the details of everyday life, social etiquette, meeting people, eating meals, and so forth, at times in a disorientatingly perceptive way. Molloy's novel is being written in the room in which the narrator had an affair with Vera, and is an attempt to remember that relationship and salvage it from the ravages of time. Each detail, even the most trivial, is lovingly and painfully recorded, and becomes obsessive in a way which is redolent of Proust. One striking metaphor, which occurs twice, is the connection between bones and text (which are negativised) and skin and voice (which are valorised); the important thing is to record the past before it fades, the voice before it turns into text, and the skin before it turns into bones (*Breve* 122; see also 38). Despite this loving attention to detail, there is a sense throughout the novel that the true meaning of the events lies in an elsewhere which is unrecorded, but which nevertheless gives rise to the events narrated, as when the narrator speaks of 'Conversaciones . . . alrededor de algo que no se nombra' (*Breve* 54). The effect of distance with regard to 'something unnamed' is re-textualised in the novel through the distance created by the reported speech mode of the novel; speech in Molloy's novel is reported rather than transcribed. *En breve cárcel* alludes to its own genesis, particularly in the detailed description of the room in which the narrator is sitting. The novel is also intertextual in that it defiantly alludes to other literary texts; Proust in its anguished, recording mode, and Shakespeare, specifically in the figure of Desdemona from *Othello*, whose cruel death at the hand of her husband is used as a metaphor to describe the relationship between the narrator and Vera in Part II, chap. 5. And yet, just as the text is gradually consumed by its literariness – this story is also the story of growing into literature – so a sense of otherness creeps into the text. And since the body and writing are seen as mutually dependent – '[p]ero hoy escribe, y quería escribirse y leerese en un cuerpo: está ahora sola con el suyo, también con la imagen de la que escribe,

162 STEPHEN M. HART

de la que lee' (*Breve* 107) – the alienation produced by writing also leads to an alienation of the body: 'El cuerpo – su cuerpo – es de otro. Desconocimiento del cuerpo, contacto con el cuerpo, placer a violencia, no importa: el cuerpo es de otro' (*Breve* 31). In this sense, the act of writing is built on an attempt to find a space in which to reside, and specifically within the house of language, to use Heidegger's favourite metaphor. Words and the phenomenal world fuse, for example, in a remarkable descriptive passage in Part I, chap. 5: 'Ve que las palabras se levantan una vez más, como se levanta ella, agradece la letra ondulante que la enlaza, reconoce las cicatrices de un cuerpo que acaricia' (*Breve* 67). While *En breve cárcel* ends on a pessimistic note – a nihilism predicated on the title, taken from one of Quevedo's gloomy, death-inspired poems to Lisi – there is also a sense, hinted at in the above passage, that language offers a home.

## Afro/a/-Hispanic Literature

Like Latino/a literature and Spanish-American women's writing, Afro/a/-Hispanic literature, that is, literature written by Spanish-American writers of African descent, has created space for itself in the new Spanish-American canon, especially since the 1970s, as Richard Jackson has pointed out ('Emergence' 4). The term Afro/a/-Hispanic literature covers work produced by a multitude of writers ranging from Nicolás Guillén, the national poet of Cuba, to Leoncio Evita (b.1929), a novelist of Spanish Guinea. The main aim of many of the writers included for discussion here is that of formulating an authentic vision of the life and identity of blacks living in Hispanic America, as expressed from the inside by writers of African descent, rather than by *criollo* writers (the classic case being Gómez de Avellaneda's nineteenth-century novel, *Sab*, which spilt 'crocodile tears' for the Negro). Often the Afro/a/-Hispanic is portrayed as an individual who has suffered political, economic, and emotional oppression by the culture in which (s)he has lived. The work of the Afro-Hispanic writers discussed here constitutes a means whereby the political powerlessness of their race is given voice. What Jean-Paul Sartre said in his now famous essay, *Orphée Noir*, which served as an introduction to an anthology of African and West Indian poets published in 1948, is emblematic of these writers: 'These black men are addressing themselves to black men about black men; their poetry is neither satiric nor imprecatory: it is an awakening to consciousness' (Sartre 16).

An important poet whose work emblematises what the French philosopher calls an 'awakening to consciousness' is the Dominican Blas Jiménez (b.1949). His poem 'Diálogo negro', from *Exigencias de un cimarrón (en sueños)* (1987), for example, dramatises the poet's discovery of blackness: 'Vino un negro y me dijo/ que el viejo del tío Tom/ era un negrito creado/ por la discriminación' (Watson Miller 73). As the poem concludes, the 'negro' who brings knowledge of cultural oppression is actually the poet himself. Based on the idea of self-discovery in the mirror, this poem is also meant to be understood as a rallying-cry for all blacks imprisoned by what Jiménez calls the 'white imagination'. A similar type of consciousness-raising occurs in the work of the Ecuadorian poet Adalberto Ortiz (b.1914). Like Nicolás Guillén, Ortiz evokes the nuances of black-Hispanic speech in his poetry. His poem 'Yo no sé', for example, though based on apparent unknowing, evokes the injustice of social oppression. As the poem opens: '¿Po qué será,/ me pregunto yo,/ que casi todo lo negro/ tan pobre son/ como yo soy?/ Yo no lo sé./ Ni yo ni Uté' (Watson Miller 99). Likewise his poem 'Contribución' speaks of the need for the sounds of African music to 'shake up' the whites; as the poem concludes, the Hispanic African symbolises not only the sweetness of sugar cane, but also the 'fire' of revenge: 'porque el alma, la del Africa/ que encadenada llegó/ a esta tierra de América/ canela y candela dio' (Watson Miller 100).

One of the best contemporary Afro-Hispanic short-story writers is Carlos Guillermo Wilson, aka 'Cubena', who was born in Panama City in 1941. His short stories are intentionally shocking, and, given their political message, it is perhaps not surprising that they have been censored in Panama. 'El niño de harina', for example, from *Cuentos del negro Cubena* (1971), describes the strange behaviour of a young boy living in the San Miguel district of Panama who persists in pouring flour on himself at night. At first interpreted as a childhood aberration similar to bed-wetting, the last sentence of the story, however, shows the motive for this behaviour to be a profoundly cultural one: 'El niño de harina era negro' (Watson Miller 83). Other works offer a vision of the dispossessed of this earth. The moving tale, 'Una carta', from *Una canción en la madrugada* (1970) by Quince Duncan (b.1940), for example, presents the world-view of an older woman whose son has left her with eight children to look after (each by a different woman); the son follows the *cimarrón* prototype so common in Duncan's fiction (Smart 156). While the mother refuses to hear any wrong said about her son, the anger associated with this injustice is expressed – poetically – by the image of boiling water which opens the tale and concludes it: 'Afuera, todavía hervía el agua en las venas de la tierra' (Watson Miller 91).

Aida Cartagena Portalatín (1918–1994) is one of the few Afra-Hispanic writers known outside her country of origin; she was born in Moca, Dominican Republic. Her work, which spans the genres of poetry, novel and short story, focusses on the dilemma of black identity in Hispanic culture. Her short story, 'La llamaban Aurora (Pasión por Donna Summer)', is written from the 'innocent' perspective of a young black girl who is unable to work out the contradiction between white people's love of Donna Summer's music, and the violent political discrimination that blacks suffer around the globe (Watson Miller 70). The reader is asked to focus on this cultural inconsistency, and invited to conclude that white culture's love of Donna Summer's music is merely another form of cultural oppression.[5]

The work of two Hispanic writers of African descent deserves special mention, and they are the Peruvian Nicomedes Santa Cruz (1925–1982) and the Colombian Manuel Zapata Olivella (b.1920). Nicomedes Santa Cruz is best known for his *décimas*, a traditional poetic form dating from the seventeenth century which he has Africanised. Perhaps the single most famous poem by an Afro-Hispanic writer is Santa Cruz's 'Ritmos negros del Perú', which is to be understood as a cultural memorial of the history of his race: 'De Africa llegó mi abuela/ vestida con caracoles,/ la trajeron lo' españoles/ en un barco carabela' (Watson Miller 103). His poem 'De ser como soy, me alegro' speaks in a straightforward manner on behalf of a non-racialist society: 'Muy claramente se explica/ que, viviendo con honor,/ nacer de cualquier color/ eso a nadie perjudica' (Watson Miller 106). His work has its roots in the oral tradition of poetic repartee; his poem 'Si tú eres cantor completo', for example, in which he manages to use every letter of the alphabet in four rhymed *décimas*, clearly grows out of this tradition.

Zapata Olivella's masterpiece is *Changó, el gran putas* (1983), which takes as its theme 'the psychical and physical liberation of an entire ethnic group in its confrontation, as African prisoners, with Western culture' (Lewis, *Treading* 112). The novel has five parts, each of which focusses on a defining moment of history for the peoples of African descent; the first on the slave trade in the early sixteenth century, the second on the early colonial days in the New World, the third on the slave rebellions in the last decade of the eighteenth century in the Caribbean which led to a black republic in Haiti, the fourth on the fight for independence in the Sub-Continent, and the fifth on the struggle against racism in the United States as seen particularly through the perspective of Malcolm-X's life. Given its broad panoramic focus, *Changó, el gran putas* can legitimately be seen as the epic of the Afro/a/-Hispanic peoples. The most striking feature about the form of the novel is the narrative voice which is transferred from person to person without warning. This technique – which is now part of the narratological repertoire of the modern novel since Faulkner first introduced it in *The Sound and the Fury* in 1929 – is utilised in *Changó, el gran putas* for a specific reason, namely, that of stressing the symmetry between the different lives described, a pattern which is woven round the 'Fall' of the African peoples, their banishment from Africa by Shango, the Yoruba God of thunder and lightning, and their subsequent experience of the diaspora. Olivella's novel is Afrocentric in one other important way, and that is its skill in presenting the historical events of

---

[5] It is important to note that a new canon has begun to emerge within Afro-Hispanic literature: Afra-Hispanic literature, that is, literature written by Spanish-American women of African descent. Portalatín is part of this new canon; see Miriam DeCosta and Rosemary G. Feal for some discussion of the themes and theorisation of this canon.

this world from the perspective of the realm of the spirit as inhabited by the African gods. In the stomach-churning description of life on the slavers in the first part of the novel, for example, Zapata Olivella shows how the African gods accompanied their people on their transatlantic journey to be sure that they were present if they died during the voyage. Similarly, the slave rebellion led by Toussaint L'Ouverture in the French colony of Haiti in 1791 is portrayed through the lens provided by voodoo. These various themes are brought triumphantly together in the very last paragraph of the novel when the dead are addressed by their ancestors and their actions are placed in the larger, teleological context of Last Things (Zapata Olivella 511). This makes it quite clear that Olivella's novel is meant to be understood as transcending the three-dimensional limitations of literature in order to enter the fourth dimension of politics; the last sentence of this 'selfconsciously-liberationist' novel, as one critic puts it (Smart 115), functions as a wake-up call for all Americans of African descent to take up the fight for the right to own their own culture.

# POSTLUDE

Cada estado social trae su expresión a la literatura, de tal
modo, que por las diversas fases de ella pudiera contarse la
historia de los pueblos con más verdad que por sus croni-
cones y sus décadas.
(Martí, *Prosas* 98)

A number of ideas raised in this study deserve mentioning. As a direct
result of emphasising the continuity of the genres from the conquest until the
present day, rather than, say, following the literary trends within each of the
separate republics of Spanish America, a number of ideas have emerged:
firstly, that poetry in Spanish America can be divided into two mutually
exclusive camps of civic verse and personal/contestatory verse, a distinction
which holds remarkably well over the evolution of the genre; secondly, the
novel form in Spanish America grew out of the chronicles which described
the early post-conquest world, and specifically those with a personal autobiographical focus; and, thirdly, the genre of theatre has been dogged from the
very beginning in the New World with a split between the more popular
manifestation of the genre and its socially elevated mirror image which was
often European in inspiration and catered to the social elite.

As we have seen, Spanish-American literature went through a variety of
phases from its humble beginnings in the sixteenth century until the present
day when it competes on its own terms with any produced in the world. The
notion of literature and the role of the writer in society changed substantially
during that period. While in the sixteenth century literature was still at the
mercy of its aristocratic benefactors, nowadays the writer is more often than
not an outspoken critic of state policies and practices. Yet, despite the difference in perspectives, the press, and its production of the printed word, can be
seen as the common denominator binding together, in different ways over
time, the complex and variable relationship between the writer, the reader
and the state.

Three clear defining moments are evident in that evolution. From the conquest until the independence movements which occurred at the beginning of
the nineteenth century, literature was subject to the Maecenal law of literary
production, and its source of support was often the Spanish King, the Viceroy's palace, or the Church. The most famous writer of the colonial period,
Sor Juana Inés de la Cruz, epitomised the social network in which literature

played out these power struggles; she was alternately lionised and rejected by the Church and the viceregal court. The advent of serialised printing during the era of independence, however, dealt the final death blow to the Maecenal mode of literary production. The new printing presses, owned by individuals who supported Republicanism at the expense of Monarchism, determined in quite specific ways what was published. Print technology continued to improve through the remainder of the nineteenth century and, by the end of that century, many writers, such as the *modernistas* in particular, were living off their pens as journalists. The growth of print-runs and sales of literary works continued apace in the first half of the twentieth century, but it was only in the 1960s that Spanish-American literature suddenly burst onto the world stage. The period now associated with the Boom novel witnessed a sudden leap forward which was so drastic that no student of Spanish-American literature, unless blessed with unusually effective prophetic powers, could have predicted it. Spanish-American literature had finally arrived.

# SUGGESTIONS FOR FURTHER READING

These suggestions for further reading are arranged by the chapter sequence in the text, which necessarily leads to overlap in coverage; some suggestions listed in the general section are also relevant for the other chapters. The titles were chosen to provide an indication of further profitable reading in Spanish-American literature. In most cases these texts have been tried and tested in the classroom environment. Readers who want greater detail will find a wealth of leads in the books suggested.

The best detailed introduction to Spanish-American literature is provided by the first two volumes of *The Cambridge History of Latin American Literature*, edited by Enrique Pupo-Walker and Roberto González Echeverría, and published in 1995. Though the volume is not uniform in approach to the different areas and there is a degree of unevenness in the contributions, it is, nevertheless, the necessary first stepping-stone in any analysis of Spanish-American literature. For a broader approach, the *Encyclopedia of Latin American Literature*, edited by Verity Smith and published in 1997, is invaluable; not only does it cover canonical literary authors as well as providing helpful separate short commentaries on their main works, but it also introduces new topics, such as 'Resistance Literature in Spanish America' and 'Popular Culture', into the canon.

Jean Franco's *An Introduction to Spanish American Literature*, and José Miguel Oviedo's two-volume *Historia de la literatura hispanoamericana* offer the best in balanced appraisals and continuous narratives, and are highly recommended. Also worth mentioning are Jacques Joset's *La literatura hispanoamericana* which, not surprisingly, given its length, is unable to give even the major works more than a cursory glance; and José Juan Arrom's *Esquema generacional de las letras hispanoamericanas: ensayo de un método*. The drawback of this latter work, despite the wisdom of the judgements on individual works, is that Arrom splits the literature from the conquest to 1983 into seventeen thirty-year periods, which is too tidy to be believable. For a traditional approach to the authors of the canon which has the advantage of a uniform format, see *Latin American Writers*, edited by Carlos A. Solé and Maria Isabel Abreu, in three volumes; the quality of the contributions, though, is variable. Though the present study reads against the grain of a nationalist approach, for an introduction to the literature of the Sub-Continent which is country-based, see David William Foster's edition of a *Handbook of Latin American Literature*. This handbook has the advantage of offering separate sections on Latino literature and paraliterature.

A representative sample of the best of the criticism on the main authors of the canon is to be found in *Spanish American Literature: A Collection of Essays*, edited by David William Foster and Daniel Altamiranda, and published in five volumes. Volume 1 treats theoretical debates such as post-colonialism, post-modernism, and ethnicity; volume 2 colonial literature; volume 3 nineteenth-century literature; volume 4 literature from 1900 to 1960, while volume 5 concludes with a selection of essays on authors published after the 1960s. A collection of the main canonic texts, ranging from Bartolomé de las Casas to Rigoberta Menchú, is provided in Foster's *Literatura hispanoamericana: una antología*. Also helpful is Chang-Rodríguez and Filer's annotated anthology *Voces de Hispanoamérica*. The best way to research recent criticism on Spanish-American authors is to use a combination of the following three methods: (i) conduct a PMLA on-line search giving the author as subject, (ii) consult the appropriate years of the *Year's Work in Modern Language Studies*, and (iii) consult the online HAPI data base, which gives an up-to-date list of journal articles published on the Latin-American canon.

## Chapter 1

For an excellent introduction to Amerindian culture, see Gordon Brotherston's *Book of the Fourth World*, and for more on the *Chilam Balam*, consult Munro S. Edmonson's *Heaven Born*. Regina Harrison's *Signs, Songs and Memory in the Andes* is an authoritative introduction to Quechua culture. Aybar's *Literatura quechua* provides an excellent selection of Quechua literature. León-Portilla is the best critic on Aztec literature and culture of Mexico; his *The Broken Spears* and *Fifteen Poets of the Aztec World* are highly recommended. There are also excellent introductory surveys of Aztec, Maya and Quechua literature in Verity Smith's *Encyclopedia of Latin-American Literature*. Particularly good on the issue of transculturation is Boone & Mignolo's *Writing Without Words*. On the conquest, see Tzvetan Todorov's *La conquista de América*, George Baudot's *Utopía e historia en México*, and Antonello Gerbi's *La naturaleza de las Indias Nuevas*. A good overview of Cortés's work is provided in Marcel Bataillon's *Hernán Cortés*; see also Inga Clendinnen's 'Cortés, Signs and the Conquest of Mexico'. For an insightful introduction to the literature of conquest and discovery, see Beatriz Pastor, *Discuros narrativos*; Rolena Adorno, 'Cultures in Contact: Mesoamerica, the Andes, and the European Written Tradition', *Cambridge History*, vol. 1, 33–57; Stephanie Merrim, 'The First Fifty Years of Hispanic New World Historiography: The Caribbean, Mexico and Central America', *Cambridge History*, vol. 1, 58–100; Kathleen Ross, 'Historians of the Conquest and Colonization of the New World: 1550–1620', *Cambridge History*, vol. 1, 101–90; and Stephen Greenblatt's *Marvelous Possessions*. James Murray's *Spanish Chronicles of the Indies* is a clear, no-nonsense introduction to the 'crónicas'. A competent overview of the main writers of this period is provided by Mario Hernández Sánchez-Barba in his *Historia y literatura en Hispanoamérica (1492–1820)*. David William Foster, *Spanish American Literature: A Collection of Essays*, vol. 2, has accurate, introductory essays on authors of this period, such as Bartolomé de las Casas, Alvar Núñez Cabeza de la Vega, Bernal Díaz del Castillo, El Inca Garcilaso de la Vega, Alonso de Ercilla y Zúñiga, and others such as Sor Juana Inés de la Casa, Juan del Valle y Caviedes, and Alonso Carrió de la Vandera. For an authoritative introduction to El Inca Garcilaso's work, see Margarita Zamora's *Language, Authority and Indigenous History*.

*Chapter 2*

Students wishing to flesh out the historical background of the viceroyalty of Peru should consult Kenneth Andrien's excellent *Crisis and Decline: The Viceroyalty of Peru in the Seventeenth Century*. For a detailed overview of the culture of this period, see Asunción Lavrín, 'Viceregal Culture', *Cambridge History*, vol. 1, 286–335; and Karen Stolley, 'The Eighteenth Century: Narrative Forms, Scholarship and Learning', *Cambridge History*, vol. 1, 336–74. For a well-written overview of colonial literature full of original insight, see René Prieto, *The Identity of Hispanoamerica*. Essential background reading are Lanning's *Academic Culture in the Spanish Colonies* and Irving Leonard's *Books of the Brave*. For a balanced appraisal of the poets in particular, see Roberto González Echeverría, 'Colonial Lyric', *Cambridge History*, vol. 1, 191–259. A good selection of colonial poets is provided in Campa and Chang-Rodríguez's edition of *Poesía hispanoamericana colonial*. For an introduction to the theatre, see Frederick Luciani, 'Spanish American Theatre of the Colonial Period', *Cambridge History*, vol. 1, 260–85. A selection of theatrical works is found in Luzuriaga and Reeve's *Los clásicos del teatro hispanoamericano*, which should be complemented with José Rojas Garcidueñas's *Tres piezas del virreinato*. A good sampling of essays by established scholars on the main authors of the colonial period may be found in *Historia de la literatura hispanoamericana. Tomo 1. Epoca colonial*, edited by Luis Íñigo Madrigal; it contains separate essays on, *inter alia*, Sor Juana Inés de la Cruz, Juan del Valle y Caviedes, and colonial theatre; highly recommended. An anthology which is still worth consulting is Flores and Anderson's *Masterpieces of Spanish American Literature: The Colonial Period to the Beginnings of Modernism*. David Brading provides a wonderful overview of the main thinkers of New Spain in his study, *The First America*. Mark Burkholder's *Politics of a Colonial Career* fleshes out the backdrop on the role of the writer/politician in the Spanish colonies. Julie Greer Johnson's *Satire in Colonial Spanish America* also functions as an authoritative overview of the main writers of this period. The best overall introduction to the history of the press during this period is Steinberg's fascinating *Five Hundred Years of Printing*. Clive Griffin's study of *The Crombergers of Seville* is the definitive study of print culture of the time. Also helpful are Vicente Quesada's *The History of Printing and Early Publications in the Spanish American Colonies* and Lawrence Thompson's *Printing in Colonial Spanish America*. Cruickshank's article, 'Literature and the Book Trade in Golden-Age Spain', is excellent. Essential readings on Sor Juana Inés de la Cruz are Stephanie Merrim, *Feminist Perspectives on Sor Juana Inés de la Cruz*; Ludwig Pfandl, *Sor Juana Inés de la Cruz*; Octavio Paz, *Sor Juana Inés de la Cruz o las trampas de la fe*; and Georgina Sabat de Rivers, *El sueño de Sor Juana Inés de la Cruz*.

## *Chapter 3*

For a selection of criticism on the main authors of the nineteenth century, see David William Foster, *Spanish American Literature: A Collection of Essays*, vol. 3. A helpful overview of the novel is found in Antonio Benítez-Rojo, 'The Nineteenth-Century Spanish American Novel', *Cambridge History*, vol. 1, 417–89. The classic study of Realism is Auerbach's *Mimesis*, which should be complemented with Ian Watt's study of *The Rise of the Novel*. The best study of the nineteenth-century Spanish-American novel is Doris Sommer's *Foundational Fictions*. For the background on drama of this period, see Frank Dauster, 'The Spanish American Theatre of the Nineteenth Century', *Cambridge History*, vol. 1, 536–55; and for an overview of the essay during this period, consult Nicholas Schumway, 'The Essay in Spanish America: 1800 to Modernismo', *Cambridge History*, vol. 1, 556–89; and Martin S. Stubb, 'The Essay of Nineteenth-Century Mexico, Central America, and the Caribbean', *Cambridge History*, vol. 1, 590–607. Benedict Anderson's *Imagined Communities* is essential reading on the interface between print and nationalism in the nineteenth century. An excellent overview of the press in Spanish America is provided by Antonio Checa Godoy in his *Historia de la prensa en Iberoamérica*. The best introduction to Spanish-American Romanticism is Emilio Carilla's *El romanticismo en la América Hispánica*. For an overview of the main themes and motifs of the Romantic movement Praz's *The Romantic Agony* should be consulted. For more on Bello, see Rafael Caldera, *Andrés Bello*. Antonio Cussen, *Poetry and Politics in the Spanish American Revolution*, is excellent on Bello and Bolívar. For a good overview study which places Echeverría's work in a cultural context, see H. Katra, *The Argentine Generation of 1837*. A review of Fernández de Lizardi's work which has stood the test of time is Jefferson Rea Spell's *The

*Life and Works of José Joaquín Fernández de Lizardi.* For excellent, probing discussions of Sarmiento's work, see Noé Jitrik's *Muerte y resurreción de Facundo* and Enrique Anderson Imbert's *Genio y figura de Sarmiento.* For a good overview of Isaacs's work see Susana Zanetti's *Jorge Isaacs.* Vera Kutzinski's *Sugar's Secrets* has thought-provoking chapters on Plácido and Villaverde. For a competent overview of Avellaneda's work, see Hugh H. Harter, *Gertrudis Gómez de Avellaneda.* Susan Kirkpatrick, *Las Románticas,* has a good chapter on Avellaneda.

*Chapter 4*

For a good introduction to *modernismo,* Cathy L. Jrade, 'Modernist Poetry', *Cambridge History,* vol. 2, 7–68; and Aníbal González, 'Modernist Prose', *Cambridge History,* vol. 2, 69–113, should be consulted. A judicious selection of *modernista* poetry is found in Schulman and Picón Garfield's *Poesía modernista hispanoamericana y española.* Given that the notions of imitation and originality became crucial for the *modernistas,* Harold Bloom's study, *The Anxiety of Influence,* provides a good context with which to analyse the movement. Since the *modernistas* experimented so much with rhyme schemes, Tomás Navarro Tomás's *Métrica española* should be consulted; also helpful is Antonio Quilis's *Métrica española.* For an excellent discussion of Darío's work, see Angel Rama, *Rubén Darío y el modernismo.* Gwen Kirkpatrick's *The Dissonant Legacy of 'Modernismo'* is cogent on Herrera y Reissig and Lugones. There is some excellent discussion of the post-modernist poets, including Agustini, in Emir Rodríguez Monegal, *Sexo y poesía en el 900 uruguayo.* A good overview of Mistral's work is Fernando Alegría, *Genio y figura de Gabriela Mistral,* and a good general study of Storni's work is provided by Rachel Phillips in her *Alfonsina Storni: From Poetess to Poet.* For a good introduction to Ibarbourou's work, see Jorge Arbeleche, *Juana de Ibarbourou.* Excellent background information on the prose of this era is available in Aníbal González's *Journalism and the Development of Spanish American Narrative;* this study also has a good chapter on Palma's *Tradiciones.* For information on *costumbrismo,* see Enrique Pupo-Walker, 'The Brief Narrative in Spanish America: 1835–1915', *Cambridge History,* vol. 1, 490–535. A good clear introduction to José Hernández's work is provided by Aragón and Calcetti in their *Genio y figura de José Hernández.* For more on the backdrop to the literature inspired by the *gaucho,* see Josefina Ludmer, 'The Gaucho Genre', *Cambridge History,* vol. 1, 608–31. Rowe and Schelling's *Memory and Modernity* also has some good discussion of the *gaucho.* Lafleur's study of literary magazines of this period, *Las revistas literarias argentinas 1893–1967,* is indispensable. For an introduction to Villaverde's work, see Imeldo Alvarez García, *La obra narrativa de Cirilo Villaverde.* There are good chapters on *Aves sin nido* in John

Brushwood, *Genteel Barbarism*; Efraín Kristal, *The Andes Viewed from the City*; and Francine Masiello, *Between Civilization and Barbarism*. An absorbing selection of women writers' essays of this period appears in Doris Meyer's *Rereading the Spanish American Essay*. For the theatre, Judith Weiss's *Latin American Popular Theatre* is the definitive study. For a challenging reading of Martí's work, see Blanca Rivera-Meléndez, *Poetry and the Machinery of Illusions*.

*Chapter 5*

For an excellent overview of the poetry of this period, see Gordon Brotherston, *Latin American Poetry*. For the main outlines of the avant-garde, see Hugo J. Verani, 'The Vanguardia and its Implications', *Cambridge History*, vol. 2, 114–37. For a good discussion of Huidobro's work, see René de Costa, *Vicente Huidobro: The Careers of a Poet*. On Vallejo, see Jean Franco, *Poetry and Silence*. On Paz, see Jason Wilson, *Octavio Paz*, and John M. Fein, *Octavio Paz*; and on Nicolás Guillén, see Lorna Williams, *Self and Society in the Poetry of Nicolás Guillén*. René Prieto's 'The Literature of Indigenismo', *Cambridge History*, vol. 2, 69–113, provides a competent overview of *indigenismo*, which should be complemented with Manuel Aquézolo Castro's edition, *La polémica del indigenismo*, which is a judicious selection. Also worth consulting are Luis Alberto Sánchez, *Indianismo e indigenismo en la literatura peruana*, and Julio Rodríguez-Luis, *Hermenéutica y praxis del indigenismo*. On Arguedas, see William Rowe, *Mito e ideología en la obra de José María Arguedas* and Antonio Cornejo Polar, *Los universos narrativos de José María Arguedas*. For the background to the *novela de la tierra*, see Carlos J. Alonso, 'The *criollista* Novel', *Cambridge History*, vol. 2, 95–212, as well as the same author's *The Spanish American Regional Novel*. For more on *Los de abajo*, see John Rutherford, 'The Novel of the Mexican Revolution', *Cambridge History*, vol. 2, 213–25; and Verity Smith, *Encyclopedia*, 91–92. For good preliminary discussions of Ricardo Güiraldes's *Don Segundo Sombra* and Teresa de la Parra's *Las memorias de la Mamá Blanca*, not discussed in this study, see Verity Smith, *Encyclopedia*, 403–404, 631–32. *Spanish American Literature: A Collection of Essays*, edited by David William Foster, vol. 4, provides excellent overview essays on Quiroga, Mistral, Vallejo, Huidobro, Asturias, Borges, Guillén, Neruda, and Carpentier. For a discussion of two of Carpentier's novels not treated here (*El reino de este mundo* and *El siglo de las luces*), see Verity Smith, *Encyclopedia*, 171–74. For a succinct analysis of Asturias's *El Señor Presidente*, see Verity Smith, *Encyclopedia*, 79–81. Frank Dauster, *Historia del teatro hispanoamericano*, is a magisterial introduction to the theatre of this period; also worth consulting is Diana Taylor's *Theatre of Crisis*. For a good selection of plays consult Carlos Solórzano's edition of *El teatro actual lati-*

*noamericano*, as well as his edition of *Teatro breve hispanoamericano*. For some probing analyses of women writers of this period, see Francine Masiello's *Between Civilization and Barbarism*. A good overview of Rulfo's work is found in Luis Leal, *Juan Rulfo*. On Quiroga, see Peter R. Beardsell, *Quiroga*. *Cuentos de amor, de locura y de muerte*, and Emir Rodríguez Monegal, *Genio y figura de Horacio Quiroga*. On Borges, see Harold Bloom's collection of essays, *Jorge Luis Borges*; Donald Shaw, *Borges' Narrative Strategy*; Sylvia Molloy, *Signs of Borges*; Ronald Christ, *The Narrow Act*; and John Sturrock, *Paper Tigers*. The best introduction to Usigli is Peter Beardsell, *A Theatre for Cannibals*; for more on René Marqués, see Bonnie Hildebrand Reynold, *Space, Time and Crisis*. For an imaginative discussion of Mariátegui's work, see Roland Forgues, *Mariátegui: la utopía realizable*. There are excellent chapters on Castellanos in Debra Castillo, *Talking Back*, and Naomi Lindstrom, *Women's Voices in Latin American Literature*.


*Chapter 6*

José Quiroga, 'Spanish American Poetry from 1922 to 1975', *Cambridge History*, vol. 2, 303–64, offers background information on the poetry of this period. For a good poetic anthology, see José Olivio Jiménez's *Antología de la poesía contemporánea*. The best study of Parra's work is Edith Grossman, *The Antipoetry of Nicanor Parra*, and the best study of Cardenal's work is Paul W. Borgeson, Jr., *Hacia el hombre nuevo*. The definitive overview of Pizarnik's work is Cristina Piña, *Alejandra Pizarnik*; for a good selection of essays on Claribel Alegría, see Boschetto-Sandoval and Phillips McGowan's *Claribel Alegría and Central American Literature*. The first port of call for the Boom novel is Randolph D. Pope, 'The Spanish American Novel from 1950 to 1975', *Cambridge History*, vol. 2, 226–78; also indispensable are José Donoso's *Historia personal del Boom*, Carlos Fuentes's *La nueva novela hispanoamericana*, Luis Harss's *Into the Mainstream*, Gerald Martin's *Journeys Through the Labyrinth*, and Angel Rama's *Ciudad letrada*. There are some good authoritative essays on the Boom writers in John King's *Modern Latin American Fiction: A Survey*. For discussion of Fuentes's novellas, see Verity Smith, *Encyclopedia*, 330–33. For excellent studies on Cortázar's novels, see Steven Boldy, *The Novels of Julio Cortázar*, and Carmen Ortiz, *Julio Cortázar*. For a brief analysis of Donoso's *Casa de campo*, Onetti's *El astillero*, and Vargas Llosa's *Histora de Mayta*, none of which are treated in this study, see Verity Smith, *Encyclopedia*, 269–70, 598–99, 833–34. For Sábato's *Abaddón el exterminador*, and *El túnel*, see Verity Smith, *Encyclopedia*, 739–42. Succinct and insightful discussions of two important novels by García Márquez not discussed in this study (*El amor en los tiempos del cólera* and *El general en su laberinto*) are to be found in Verity Smith, *Encyclopedia*, 350–51, and 353–54. Daniel Balderston, 'The

Twentieth-Century Short Story in Spanish America', *Cambridge History*, vol. 2, 465–96, is a thematic analysis. For an overview of Cortázar's short stories, see Ilan Stavans, *Julio Cortázar*. José Miguel Oviedo, 'The Modern Essay in Spanish America', *Cambridge History*, vol. 2, 365–424, is a well thought-out piece on the essay. For a competent overview of the theatre, Sandra M. Cypess, 'Spanish American Theatre in the Twentieth Century', *Cambridge History*, vol. 2, 497–525, should be consulted. Beatriz Rizk's *El nuevo teatro latinoamericano* is authoritative. Angel Flores, *Spanish American Authors: The Twentieth Century*, is an excellent reference manual; it has hard facts, critical judgements and impressive bibliographies. Also useful is *Masterpieces of Latino Literature*, edited by Frank N. Magill, which contains biographies of the main writers of the Latin-American as well as the Latino literary canon, along with separate sections on their key works. The intriguing feature of this volume is that it allows Latin-American writers and Latino writers to rub shoulders indiscriminately. Two recent excellent encyclopedias edited by Peter Standish, *Hispanic Culture of South America*, and *Hispanic Culture of Mexico, Central America, and the Caribbean*, place contemporary literature within the context of other cultural expressions such as music, dance, and film. A canon-creating anthology of women poets of this era is provided by Mary Crow in her excellent *Woman Who Has Sprouted Wings*. Julio Ortega's *Reapropiaciones* has two excellent essays on Ferré's fiction; Margarite Fernández Olmos judiciously compares the short stories of Ferré and Ana Lydia Vega in her *Contemporary Women Authors of Latin America*.

*Chapter 7*

For an insightful discussion of the post-Boom, see Gustavo Pellón, 'The Spanish American Novel: Recent Developments, 1975 to 1990', *Cambridge History*, vol. 2, 274–302; also indispensable are Philip Swanson's *The New Novel in Latin America*, Payne & Fitz's *Ambiguity and Gender in the New Novel of Brazil and Spanish America*, and Donald Shaw's *The Post-Boom in Spanish American Fiction*. The best introduction to Luis Rafael Sánchez's work is Efraín Barrandas, *Para leer en puertorriqueño*. Karl Kohut is the editor of a good selection of essays on Giardinelli, *Un universo cargado de violencia*. The best study of Skármeta's work is Donald Shaw, *Antonio Skármeta and the Post Boom*. There is some good discussion of Traba's work in Elia G. Kantaris, *The Subversive Psyche*. The best introduction to Isabel Allende's work is Patricia Hart's *Narrative Magic in the Fiction of Isabel Allende*. Roberto González Echeverría's *The Voice of the Masters* has a good chapter on Miguel Barnet's *Biografía de un cimarrón*. For the backdrop to Afro-Hispanic literature the reader is advised to consult Vera M. Kutzinski, 'Afro-Hispanic American Literature', *Cambridge History*, vol. 2, 164–94, as well as Richard Jackson's *The Black Image in Latin American Literature*.

Also important is the same author's more recent *Black Writers and the Hispanic Canon* which has discussion of the work of Blas Jiménez, Carlos Guillermo Wilson, Nicomedes Santa Cruz, and Manuel Zapata Olivella. An excellent anthology is provided by Ingrid Watson Miller in her *Afro-Hispanic Literature*; a canon-defining essay on Afra-Hispanic literature appears in the guise of Miriam DeCosta's 'Afra-Hispanic Writers and Feminist Discourse'. For a good introduction to Chicano literature, consult Charles Tatum, *Chicano Literature*, as well as Luis Leal and Manuel M. Martín-Rodríguez, 'Chicano Literature', *Cambridge History*, vol. 2, 357–86. For competent discussions of Latino literature, see William Luis, 'Latin American (Hispanic Caribbean) Literature Written in the United States', *Cambridge History*, vol. 2, 526–56. For a good selection of Chicano short stories, see Rodolfo Anaya's edition of *Cuentos chicanos*. For some indication of the debate currently raging on the *testimonio*, see *Spanish American Literature: A Collection of Essays*, vol. 1, 99–153. John Beverley's *Against Literature* also has some important essays on this topic. For individual essays on Puig, Luis Rafael Sánchez, Luisa Valenzuela, Isabel Allende, Reinaldo Arenas, and Rigoberta Menchú, see David William Foster, *Spanish American Literature: A Collection of Essays*, vol. 5. For an authoritative introduction to postmodernism, see Lyotard's *The Postmodern Condition*; also worth consulting are Jameson's *Postmodernism, or the Cultural Logic of Late Capitalism*, Best's *Postmodern Theory*, and Connor's *Postmodernist Culture*. For some canonical essays on the Latin-American post-modern, see *Spanish American Literature: A Collection of Essays*, vol. 1, 205–98. Raymond Williams, *The Postmodern Novel in Latin America*, offers a detailed account of postmodernism in the novel. The best introduction to Latin-American gay literature is David William Foster's *Gay and Lesbian Themes in Latin American Writing*. Indispensable studies on Puig's work are Pamela Bacarisse, *The Necessary Dream*, and Lucille Kerr, *Suspended Fictions*. Hernández-Miyares and Rozencvaig have edited a collection of essays on Reinaldo Arenas entitled *Reinaldo Arenas: alucinaciones, fantasías y realidad*. Amy Kandinsky has an excellent discussion on Peri Rossi's work in her *Reading the Body Politic*.

# WORKS CITED

Acosta, José de, *Obras del P. José de Acosta*, ed. P. Francisco Mateos. Madrid: Atlas, 1954.

Adorno, Rolena, 'Cultures in Contact: Mesoamerica, the Andes, and the European Written Tradition', *The Cambridge History of Latin American Literature*, vol. 1, 33–57.

*Delmira Agustini: Poesías completas*, ed. Alberto Zum Felde. 4th ed. Buenos Aires: Losada, 1971.

Ahern, Maureen, 'The Cross and the Gourd: The Appropriation of Ritual Signs in the *Relaciones* of Alvar Núñez Cabeza de Vaca and Fray Marcos de Niza', *Early Images of the Americas: Transfer and Invention*, ed. Jerry M. Williams & Robert E. Lewis. Tucson & London: University of Arizona Press, 1993. 215–44.

Alegría, Ciro, *El mundo es ancho y ajeno*. Madrid: Alianza, 1993.

Alegría, Claribel, *Flowers from the Volcano*, trans. Carolyn Forché. Pittsburgh: University of Pittsburgh Press, 1982.

Alegría, Fernando, *Genio y figura de Gabriela Mistral*. Buenos Aires: Editorial Universitaria, 1966.

Alonso, Carlos J., *The Spanish American Regional Novel*. Cambridge: Cambridge University Press, 1990.

———, 'The *criollista* Novel', *The Cambridge History of Latin American Literature*, vol. 2, 95–212.

Alvarez García, Imeldo, *La obra narrativa de Cirilo Villaverde*. Havana: Letras Cubanas, 1984.

Anaya, Rodolfo A., & Antonio Márquez (eds.), *Cuentos Chicanos: A Short Story Anthology*. Albuquerque: University of New Mexico Press, 1984.

Anderson, Benedict, *Imagined Communities: Reflections on the Origin and Spread of Nationalism*. London: Verso, 1987. 4th impression. [1983]

Anderson-Imbert, Enrique, *Spanish-American Literature. A History*, trans. John V. Falconieri. Detroit: Wayne State University Press, 1969. 2 vols.

———, *Genio y figura de Sarmiento*. Buenos Aires: Editorial Universitaria, 1967.

Andrien, Kenneth J., *Crisis and Decline: The Viceroyalty of Peru in the Seventeenth Century*. Albuquerque: University of New Mexico Press, 1985.

Aquézolo Castro, Manuel (ed.), *La polémica del indigenismo*. Prólogo y notas de Luis Alberto Sánchez. Lima: Mosca Azul, 1976.

Aragón, Roque Raúl, & J. Calcetti. *Genio y figura de José Hernández*. Buenos Aires: Editorial Universitaria, 1972.

Arbeleche, Jorge, *Juana de Ibarbourou*. Montevideo: Editorial Técnica, 1978.

Arenas, Reinaldo, *Farewell to the Sea: A Novel of Cuba*, trans. Andrew Hurley. New York: Viking, 1986.

Arguedas, José María, *Los ríos profundos*. Lima: Editorial Horizonte, 1993.

Arias, Santa, & Erlinda Gonzales-Berry, 'Latino Writing in the United States', *Handbook of Latin American Literature*, ed. David William Foster. New York & London: Garland, 1992. 649–85.

Arrom, Juan José, *Esquema generacional de las letras hispanoamericanas: ensayo de un método*. 2nd ed. Bogotá: Caro y Cuervo, 1977.

Arzáns de Orsúa y Vela, Bartolomé, *Tales of Potosí*, ed. R. C. Padden, trans. Frances M. López-Morillas. Providence, RI: Brown University Press, 1975.

Asturias, Miguel Angel, *Hombres de maíz*. Madrid: Alianza, 1979. 3rd ed.

*Audiencia de Lima. Correspondencia de Presidentes y Oidores. Documentos del Archivo de Indias. 1549–1564*, ed. Roberto Levillier. Madrid: Juan Pueyo, 1922. vol. 1.

Auerbach, Erich, *Mimesis. Dargestelle Wirklichkeit in der Abländischen Literatur*. Bern, 1946.

Aybar, Edmundo Bendezú, 'Introducción', *Literatura quechua*. Caracas: Ayacucho, 1980. xv–xxxii.

Azuela, Mariano, *Los de abajo*, ed. W. A. R. Richardson. London: Harrap, 1980.

Bacarisse, Pamela, *The Necessary Dream: A Study of the Novels of Manuel Puig*. Cardiff: University of Wales Press, 1988.

Balderston, Daniel, 'The Twentieth-Century Short Story in Spanish America', *The Cambridge History of Latin American Literature*, vol. 2, 465–496.

Barnet, Miguel, *Biografía de un cimarrón*. Havana: Editorial Letras Cubanas, 1980.

Barradas, Efraín, *Para leer en puertorriqueño: acercamiento a la obra de Luis Rafael Sánchez*. Río Piedras, PR: Cultural, 1981.

Bataillon, Marcel, *Hernán Cortés: autor prohibido*. Mexico: Universidad Nacional Autónoma Metropolitana, 1956.

Batres Montúfar, José, *Poesías*. Guatemala, CA: Tipografía nacional, 1944.

Baudot, Georges, *Utopía e historia en Mexico: las primeras cronistas de la civilización mexicana (1520–1569)*. Madrid: Espasa Calpe, 1983.

Bautista Avalle-Arce, Juan, 'El poeta en sus poemas: el caso Ercilla', *Historia y crítica de la literatura hispanoamericana*, ed. Cedomil Goic. Barcelona: Editorial Crítica, 1988. vol. 1. 220–26.

Beardsell, Peter R., Quiroga. *Cuentos de amor, de locura y de muerte*. London: Grant and Cutler, 1986.

———, *A Theatre for Cannibals. Rodoflo Usigli and the Mexican Stage*. London: Associated University Presses, 1992.

Belli, Carlos Germán, *Boda de la pluma y la letra*. Madrid: Ediciones Cultura Hispánica, 1985.

Bello, Andrés, *Obra literaria*. Selección y prólogo, Pedro Grases & Cronología Oscar Samrano Urdaneta. Caracas: Biblioteca Ayacucho. 1985. [1979]. 2nd ed.

Benítez-Rojo, Antonio, 'The Nineteenth-Century Spanish American Novel', *The Cambridge History of Latin American Literature*, vol. 1, 417–89.

Best, Steven, & Douglas Kellner, *Postmodern Theory: Critical Interrogations*. New York: The Guilford Press, 1991.

Beverley, John, *Against Literature*. Minneapolis: University of Minneapolis Press, 1993.

Bloom, Harold, *The Anxiety of Influence. A Theory of Poetry*. New York: Oxford University Press, 1973.

—— (ed.), *Jorge Luis Borges*. New York: Chelsea House, 1986.

Boldy, Steven, *The Novels of Julio Cortázar*. Cambridge: Cambridge University Press, 1980.

Bolívar, Simón, *Documentos*, ed. Manuel Galich. Cuba: Casa de las Américas, 1964.

——. *Obras completas*, ed. Vicente Lecuna. La Habana: Lexis, 1950. 3 vols.

Boone, Elizabeth, & Walter D. Mignolo (eds.), *Writing Without Words: Alternative Literacies in Mesoamerica and the Andes*. Durham, NC: Duke University Press, 1994.

Borgeson, Jr., Paul W., *Hacia el hombre nuevo: poesía y pensamiento de Ernesto Cardenal*. London: Tamesis, 1984.

Boschetto-Sandoval, Sandra M., & Marcia Phillips McGowan, *Claribel Alegría and Central American Literature: Critical Essays*. Athens, OH: Ohio University Center for European Studies, 1994.

Brading, D. A., *The First America: The Spanish Monarchy, Creole Patriots, and the Liberal State 1492–1867*. Cambridge: Cambridge University Press, 1991.

Brotherston, Gordon, *Latin American Poetry: Origins and Presence*. Cambridge: Cambridge University Press, 1976.

——, *Mexican Painted Books: Originals in the United Kingdom and the World They Represent*. Colchester: University of Essex Press, 1992.

——, *Book of the Fourth World: Reading the Native American Through their Literature*. Cambridge: Cambridge University Press, 1992.

Brushwood, John, *Genteel Barbarism: Experiments in the Analysis of Nineteenth-Century Spanish American Novels*. Lincoln, NE: University of Nebraska Press, 1981.

Burkholder, Mark A., *Politics of a Colonial Career: José Baquíjano and the Audiencia of Lima*. Albuquerque: University of New Mexico Press, 1980.

Caldera, Rafael, *Andrés Bello: Philosopher, Poet, Philologist, Educator, Legislator, Statesman*, trans. John Street. London: Allen and Unwin, 1977.

*Cambridge History of Latin American Literature, The*, ed. Roberto González Echeverría & Enrique Pupo-Walker. Cambridge: Cambridge University Press, 1996. 3 vols.

Campbell, Joe R., & Frances Kartunnen, *Foundation Course in Nahuatl Grammar*. Austin: Institute of Latin American Studies, University of Texas at Austin, 1989. 2 vols.

Campa, Antonio R. de la, & Raquel Chang-Rodríguez (eds.), *Poesía hispanoamericana colonial: antología*. Madrid: Alhambra, 1985.

Cardenal, Ernesto, *Poesía escogida*. Barcelona: Barral, 1975.

Cardona-López, José, 'La *nouvelle* hispanoamericana reciente', Dissertation, University of Kentucky, 1996.

Carilla, Emilio, *El romanticismo en la América Hispánica*. 2nd ed. Madrid: Gredos, 1967. 2 vols.

Carlyle, Thomas, *On Heroes, Hero-Worship and the Heroic in History*. Philadelphia: Henry Altemus, 1894.

Carpentier, Alejo, *Los pasos perdidos*. Barcelona: Barral, 1974.

Carrió de la Vandera, Alonso, *El lazarillo de ciegos caminantes*. Caracas: Biblioteca Ayacucho, 1985.

Casas, Bartolomé de las Casas, *Breuissima relacion de la destruycion de las Indias colegida por el Obispo don fray Bartolome de las Casas* (1552). Cambridge University Library, Microfiche 163.

Caso, Fernando, *Explicación del reverso del Codex Vindobonensis*. Mexico: Colegio Nacional, 1950.

Castellanos, Rosario, *Album de familia*. Mexico: Joaquín Mortiz, 1985.

———, *Meditation on the Threshold*. New York: Bilingual Press, 1988.

———, *Oficio de tinieblas*. Mexico: Joaquín Mortiz, 1966. 2nd ed. [1962]

———, *Balún-Canán*. Mexico: Fondo de Cultura Económica, 1987. 14th printing. [1957]

———, *El eterno femenino*. Mexico: Fondo de Cultura Económica, 1990. 7th printing. [1975]

Castillo, Debra, *Talking Back: Toward a Latin American Feminist Criticism*. Ithaca, NY: Cornell University Press, 1992.

Castillo, sor Francisca Josefa de la Concepción de, *Análisis crítico de los 'Afectos espirituales' de Sor Francisca Josefa de la Concepción de Castillo*. Texto restablecido, introducción y comentarios de Darío Acury Valenzuela. Bogotá: Imprenta Nacional, 1962.

Cervantes, Miguel de, *El Ingenioso Hidalgo Don Quijote de la Mancha*, ed. John Jay Allen. Madrid: Cátedra, 1977. 2 vols.

Chang-Rodríguez, Raquel, & Malva E. Filer, *Voces de Hispanoamérica: antología literaria*. Boston: Heinle & Heinle, 1988.

Charno, Steven M., *Latin American Newspapers in United States Libraries: A Union List*. Austin & London: University of Texas Press, 1968.

Checa Godoy, Antonio, *Historia de la prensa en Iberoamérica*. Seville: Alfar, 1993.

Christ, Ronald J., *The Narrow Act: Borges's Art of Allusion*. New York: New York University Press, 1969.

*Christopher Columbus: Journal of the First Voyage (Diario del primer viaje)*, ed. & trans. B. W. Ife, together with an essay on Columbus's language by R. J. Penny. Warminster: Aris & Phillips Ltd., 1990.

Cieza de León, Pedro, *La Chronica del Perv, nvevamente escrita, por Cieça de Leon, vezino de Sevilla*. Antwerp: Martin Nucio, 1554. Sala de Investigaciones, Biblioteca Nacional, Lima. X985.0092.

Cisneros, Antonio, *Propios como ajenos: antología personal (Poesía 1962–1969)*. Lima: Peisa, 1991. 2nd ed.

Clendinnen, Inga, 'Cortés, Signs, and the Conquest of Mexico', *The Transmission of Culture in Early Modern Europe*, ed. Anthony Grafton & Ann Blair. Philadelphia: University of Pennsylvania Press, 1990. 87–130.

Cobo Borda, Juan Gustavo, *Usos de la imaginación*. Buenos Aires: El Imaginario, 1984.

*Códice de 1576 (Códice Aubin). Historia de la nación mexicana. Reproducción a todo color,* ed. Charles E. Dibble. Madrid: Ediciones José Porrúa Turanzas, 1963. [Original in the British Museum.]

*Codex Dresden. Commentary on the Maya Manuscript in the Royal Public*

*Library of Dresden*. By Ernst Förstemann, trans. Selma Wesselhoeft & A. M. Parker. Cambridge, Mass.: Peabody Museum of American Archeology and Ethnology, 1906.

*Codex Kingsborough. Códice Kingsborough. Memorial de los indios de Tepetlaoztoc al monarca español contra los encomenderos del pueblo*, ed. Francisco del Paso y Troncoso. Madrid: Hauser y Memet, 1912.

*Codex Mendoza. Códice Mendocino. Documento mexicano del siglo XVI que se conserva en la biblioteca bodleiana de Oxford, Inglaterra*. Facsímile fototípico dispuesto por don Francisco del Paso y Troncoso. Mexico: Museo Nacional de Arqueología, Historia y Etnografía, 1925.

*Codex Mendoza*. Berdan, Frances F., & Patricia Rieff Anawalt, ed. Berkeley-Los Angeles-Oxford: University of California Press, 1992. 4 vols.

*Códice Osuna: reproducción facsimilar de la obra del mismo título, editada en Madrid, 1878. Acompañada de 158 páginas inéditas encontradas en el Archivo General de la Nación (México) por el Prof. Luis Chávez Orozco*. Mexico: Ediciones del Instituto Indigenista Interamericano, 1947.

*Codex Perez, The, and the Book of Chilam Balam of Maní*, trans. Eugene R. Craine & Reginald C. Reindorp. Norman: University of Oklahoma Press, 1979.

*Codex Tro-Cortesianus (Codex Madrid). Museo de América, Madrid*. Introduction and summary F. Anders. Graz, Austria: Akademische Druck. -u. Verlagsanstalt, 1967.

Connor, Steven, *Postmodernist Culture: An Introduction to Theories of the Contemporary*. Oxford: Basil Blackwell, 1989.

Cornejo Polar, Antonio, *Los universos narrativos de José María Arguedas*. Buenos Aires: Losada, 1973.

Corominas, Joan, & J. A. Pascual, *Diccionario crítico etimológico hispánico*. 5 vols. Madrid: Gredos, 1980.

Cortázar, Julio, *Rayuela*. Buenos Aires: Editorial Sudamericana, 1977. 21st ed. [1963]

——, *Las ediciones secretas*, ed. Susana Jakfalvi. Madrid: Cátedra, 1979.

Cortés, Hernán, *Cartas de relación*. Mexico: Editorial Porrúa, 1960.

Costa, René de, *Vicente Huidobro: The Careers of a Poet*. Oxford: Clarendon, 1984.

Craine, Eugene R., & Reginald C. Reindorp, 'Preface', *The Codex Pérez and the Book of Chilam Balam of Maní*, trans. Craine & Reindorp. Norman: University of Oklahoma Press, 1979. xiii–xviii.

Crow, Mary (ed.), *Woman who has Sprouted Wings: Poems by Contemporary Latin American Poets*. 2nd ed. Pittsburgh: Latin American Literary Review Press, 1987.

Cruickshank, D. W., 'Literature and the Book Trade in Golden-Age Spain', *Modern Language Review* 73 (1978): 799–824.

Cruz, Sor Juana Inés de la, *Obras completas. Lírica personal*, ed. Alfonso Méndez Plancarte. Mexico: Fondo de Cultural Económica, 1951. vol. 1.

Cussen, Antonio, *Poetry and Politics in the Spanish American Revolution: Bello, Bolívar and the Classical Tradition*. Cambridge: Cambridge University Press, 1991.

Cypess, Sandra M., 'Spanish American Theatre in the Twentieth Century', *The Cambridge History of Latin American Literature*, vol. 2, 497–525.

Darío, Rubén, *Poesías completas*, ed. Alfonso Méndez Plancarte. Madrid: Aguilar, 1968.

Dauster, Frank N., *Historia del teatro hispanoamericano. Siglos XIX y XX.* Mexico: De Andrea, 1973.

———, 'The Spanish American Theatre of the Nineteenth Century', *The Cambridge History of Latin American Literature*, vol. 1, 536–55.

DeCosta, Miriam, 'Afra-Hispanic Writers and Feminist Discourse', *NWSA Journal* 5 (1993): 204–17.

Díaz del Castillo, Bernal, *Historia verdadera de la conquista de la Nueva España*, ed. Miguel León-Portilla. Madrid: Historia 16, 1984. 2 vols.

*Diccionario de la lengua española*, Madrid: Espasa-Calpe, 1992.

Diego de Landa, Fray, *Relación de las cosas de Yucatán*. Mérida: Editorial San Fernando, 1992.

Dollimore, Jonathan, *Sexual Dissidence: Augustine to Wilde, Freud to Foucault*. Oxford: Oxford University Press, 1991.

Donoso, José, *Historia personal del 'Boom'*. 2nd ed. Barcelona: Seix Barral, 1983.

Eagleton, Terry, *Literary Theory: An Introduction*. Minneapolis: University of Minnesota Press, 1985.

Echeverría, Esteban, *Obras completas*, ed. Juan María Gutiérrez. Buenos Aires: Ediciones Antonio Zamora, 1951.

Edmonson, Munro S. (ed.), *Heaven Born. Mérida and its Destiny: The Book of Chilam Balam of Chumayal*. Austin: University of Texas Press, 1986.

*Enciclopedia Universal Ilustrada Europea-Americana*. Barcelona. Hijos de J. Espasa, Editora. n.d. vol. XXX.

*Encyclopedia Britannica*, Chicago: Encyclopedia Britannica Inc., 1995. 15th ed.

Espinosa Pólit, Aurelio, '*La victoria de Junín* de José Joaquín de Olmedo', *Historia y crítica de la literatura hispanoamericana*, ed. Cedomil Goic. Barcelona: Editorial Crítica, 1988. vol. 1, 536–41.

Esquivel, Laura, *Como agua para chocolate*. Mexico: Editorial Planeta Mexicana, 1992. 17th reprint. [1989]

Feal, Rosemary G., 'Reflections in the Obsidian Mirror: The Poetics of Afro-Hispanic Identity and the Gendered Body', *Afro-Hispanic Review* 14 (1995): 26–32.

Fein, John M., *Octavio Paz: A Reading of his Major Poems, 1957–1976*. Lexington: Kentucky University Press, 1986.

Fernández Olmos, Margarite, *Contemporary Women Authors of Latin America*. Brooklyn, NY: Brooklyn College Press, 1983.

Fernández de Lizardi, José Joaquín, *El Periquillo Sarniento*. Mexico: Porrúa, 1984.

Fernández de Oviedo, Gonzalo, *De la natural historia de las Indias (Sumario de historia natural de las Indias)*, ed. Enrique Alvarez López. Madrid: Summa, 1942.

Fernández Retamar, Roberto, *Caliban and Other Essays*, trans. Edward Baker. Minneapolis: Minnesota University Press, 1989.

————, 'Prologue to Ernesto Cardenal', *Caliban and Other Essays*, trans. Edward Baker. Minneapolis: Minnesota University Press, 1989. 100–10.

Flores, Angel, & Helene M. Anderson (eds.), *Masterpieces of Spanish American Literature. The Colonial Period to the Beginnings of Modernism*. New York: Macmillan, 1974. vol. 1.

*Juan del Valle Caviedes. Obra completa*, ed. Daniel R. Reedy. Caracas: Biblioteca Ayacucho, 1984.

Foreno Benavides, Abelardo, *Impresión y represión de los derechos del hombre*. Bogotá: Universidad de los Andes, 1967.

Forgues, Roland, *Mariátegui: la utopía realizable*. Lima: Amauta, 1995.

Foster, David William, *Gay and Lesbian Themes in Latin American Writing*. Austin: University of Texas Press, 1991.

———— (ed.), *Handbook of Latin American Literature*. New York & London: Garland, 1992. 2nd ed.

———— (ed.), *Literatura hispanoamericana: una antología*. New York & London: Garland, 1994.

————, & Daniel Altamiranda (eds.), *Spanish American Literature: A Collection of Essays*. New York & London: Garland, 1997. 5 vols.

Foucault, Michel, *The Order of Things: An Archeology of the Human Sciences*. New York: Pantheon, 1970.

Franco, Jean, *An Introduction to Spanish-American Literature*. Cambridge: Cambridge University Press, 1969.

Fuentes, Carlos, *La muerte de Artemio Cruz*. Mexico: Fondo de Cultura Económica, 1962.

————, *Cambio de piel*. Barcelona: Seix Barral, 1980. 2nd ed. [1967].

————, *La nueva novela hispanoamericana*. Mexico: Joaquín Mortiz, 1972.

García Goyena, Rafael, *Fábulas*, ed. Carlos Samayoa Chinchilla. Guatemala, C.A.: Ediciones del Gobierno de Guatemala, 1950.

García Márquez, Gabriel, *Cien años de soledad*. Barcelona: Argos Vergara, 1980.

————, *El coronel no tiene quien le escriba*. Barcelona: Plaza & Janés, 1979. 6th ed.

————, *Los funerales de la mamá grande*. Buenos Aires: Editorial Sudamericana, 1977.

Garro, Elena, *Los recuerdos del porvenir*. Mexico: Joaquín Mortiz, 1963.

Gerbi, Antonello, *La naturaleza de las Indias Nuevas: De Cristóbal Colón a Gonzalo Fernández de Oviedo*. Mexico: Fondo de Cultura Económica, 1978.

Gerdes, Dick, 'Peru', *Handbook of Latin American Literature*, ed. David William Foster. New York & London: Garland, 1992. 2nd ed. 493–553.

Giardinelli, Mempo, *Luna caliente*. Buenos Aires: Planeta Argentina, 1995.

Goic, Cedomil (ed.), *Historia y crítica de la literatura hispanoamericana*. Barcelona: Editorial Crítica, 1988. vol. 1.

Gómez de Avellaneda, Gertrudis, *Antología poética*. La Habana: Editorial Letras Cubanas, 1983.

González, Aníbal, *Journalism and the Development of Spanish American Narrative*. Cambridge: Cambridge University Press, 1993.

————, 'Crónica y cuento en el modernismo', *El cuento hispanoamericano*, ed. Enrique Pupo-Walker. Madrid: Castalia, 1995. 155–70.

————, 'Modernist Prose', *The Cambridge History of Latin American Literature*, vol. 2, 69–113.

González Echeverría, Roberto, *The Voice of the Masters: Writing and Authority in Modern Latin American Literature*. Austin: University of Texas Press, 1985.

————, 'Colonial Lyric', *The Cambridge History of Latin American Literature*, vol. 1, 191–259.

————, & Enrique Pupo-Walker (eds.), *The Cambridge History of Latin American Literature*. Cambridge: Cambridge University Press, 1996. 3 vols.

Greenblatt, Stephen, *Marvelous Possessions: The Wonder of the New World*. Chicago: University of Chicago Press, 1991.

Greer Johnson, Julie, *Satire in Colonial Spanish America: Turning the New World Upside Down*. Foreword by Daniel R. Reedy. Austin: University of Texas Press, 1993.

Griffin, Clive, *The Crombergers of Seville. The History of a Printing and Merchant Dynasty*. Oxford: Clarendon, 1988.

Grossman, Edith, *The Antipoetry of Nicanor Parra*. New York: New York University Press, 1975.

Guaman Poma de Ayala, *Nueva corónica y buen gobierno*, ed. Franklin Pease. Caracas: Biblioteca Ayacucho, 1980. 2 vol.

Güiraldes, Ricardo, *Don Segundo Sombra*. Buenos Aires: Losada, 1971. 30th ed.

Gutiérrez, Eduardo, *Juan Moreira*. Buenos Aires: La Patria Argentina, 1879.

Harss, Luis, *Into the Mainstream. Conversations with Latin-American Writers*. New York: Harper & Row, 1969.

Harrison, Regina, *Signs, Songs and Memory in the Andes: Translating Quechua Language and Culture*. Austin: University of Texas Press, 1989.

Hart, Patricia, *Narrative Magic in the Fiction of Isabel Allende*. Rutherford, NJ: Fairleigh Dickinson University Press, 1989.

Hart, Stephen M., *The Other Scene: Psychoanalytic Readings in Modern Spanish and Latin-American Literature*. Boulder, Colorado: Society of Spanish and Spanish-American Studies, 1992.

————, *White Ink: Essays on Twentieth-century Feminine Fiction in Spain and Latin America*. London: Tamesis, 1993.

————, 'Some Reflections on the Spanish American Literary Canon', *Siglo XX/20th Century* 1 (1994): 145–55.

————, *García Márquez: 'Crónica de una muerte anunciada'*. London: Grant & Cutler, 1994.

————, 'Is Women's Writing in Spanish America Gender-Specific?' *Modern Language Notes* 110 (1995): 335–52.

————, 'La cápsula mágica: los poetas latinoamericanos que viven en los Estados Unidos y su Público', *The Seventeenth Louisiana Conference on Hispanic Languages and Literatures. Louisiana State University, Baton Rouge, 1996*, ed. by Jesús Torrecilla *et al*. Baton Rouge, LA: Department of Foreign Language and Literatures, 1996. 3–10.

Harter, Hugh A., *Gertrudis Gómez de Avellaneda*. Boston: Twayne, 1981.

Hellenbeck, Cleve, *Alvar Núñez Cabeza de Vaca. The Journey and Route of the First European to Cross the Continent of North America 1534–1536*. Port Washington, NY: Kennikat Press, 1971.

Hernández-Miyares, Julio, & Perla Rozencvaig (eds.), *Reinaldo Arenas: alucinaciones, fantasías y realidad*. Glenview, IL: Scott Foresman Montesinos, 1990.

Hernández Sánchez-Barba, Mario, *Historia y literatura en hispano-américa (1492–1820)*. Madrid: Castalia, 1978.

Hijuelos, Oscar, *The Mambo Kings Sing of Love*. London: Hamish Hamilton, 1990. [1989]

Hinojosa, Rolando, *Mi querido Rafa*. Houston, TX: Arte Público Press, 1981.

Huidobro, Vicente, *Poesía y prosa de Vicente Huidobro*, ed. Antonio de Undurranga. Madrid: Aguilar, 1957.

Jackson, Richard, *The Black Image in Latin American Literature*. Albuquerque: University of New Mexico Press, 1976.

———, 'The Emergence of Afro-Hispanic Literature', *Afro-Hispanic Review* 10 (1991): 4–10.

———, *Black Writers and the Hispanic Canon*. Boston: Twayne, 1997.

Jameson, Fredric, *Postmodernism, or the Cultural Logic of Late Capitalism*. Durham, NC: Duke University Press, 1991.

Jaramillo, María Mercedes, *El nuevo teatro colombiano: arte y política*. Medellín: Editorial Universidad de Antioquia, 1992.

Jiménez, José Olivio (ed.), *Antología de la poesía hispanoamericana contemporánea: 1914–1987*. Madrid: Alianza, 1988. 3rd ed.

Jitrik, Noé, *Muerte y resurrección de Facundo*. Buenos Aires: Centro Editor de América Latina, 1968.

Joset, Jacques, *La literatura hispanoamericana*. Barcelona: Ockros-Tau Ediciones, 1974.

Jrade, Cathy L., 'Modernist Poetry', *The Cambridge History of Latin American Literature*, vol. 2, 7–68.

Judson, C. Fred, 'Continuity and Evolution of Revolutionary Symbolism in *Verde Olivo*', *Cuba: Twenty-Five Years of Revolution, 1959–1984*, ed. Sandor Halesbsky & John M. Kirk. New York: Praeger, 1985. 233–50.

Kaminsky, Amy, *Reading the Body Politic: Feminist Criticism and Latin American Women Writers*. Minneapolis: University of Minnesota Press, 1993.

Kantaris, Elia G., *The Subversive Psyche. Contemporary Women's Narrative from Argentina and Uruguay*. Oxford: Oxford University Press, 1996.

Katra, William H., *The Argentine Generation of 1837: Echeverría, Sarmiento, Alberdi, Mitre*. Rutherford, NJ: Fairleigh Dickinson University Press, 1996.

Kerr, Lucille, *Suspended Fictions: Reading Novels by Manuel Puig*. Urbana: University of Illinois Press, 1987.

King, John (ed.), *Modern Latin American Literature: A Survey*. London: Faber and Faber, 1987.

Kirkpatrick, Gwen, *The Dissonant Legacy of 'Modernismo': Lugones, Herrera y Reissig, and the Voices of Modern Spanish-American Poetry*. Berkeley: University of California Press, 1989.

Kirkpatrick, Susan, *Las Románticas: Women Writers and Subjectivity in Spain, 1835–1850*. Berkeley: University of California Press, 1989.

Kohut, Karl (ed.), *Un universo cargado de violencia: presentación, aproximación y documentación de la obra de Mempo Giardinelli*. Frankfurt: Vervuert Verlag, 1990.

Kristal, Efraín, *The Andes Viewed from the City: Literary and Political Discourse on the Indian in Peru 1848–1930*. New York: Peter Lang, 1987.

Kutzinski, Vera M., *Sugar's Secrets. Race and the Erotics of Cuban Nationalism*. Charlottesville: University of Virginia Press, 1993.

———, 'Afro-Hispanic American Literature', *The Cambridge History of Latin American Literature*, vol. 2, 164–94.

Lafleur, Héctor René, Sergio D. Provenzano, & Fernando P. Alonso, *Las revistas literarias argentinas 1893–1967*. Buenos Aires: Centro Editor de América Latina, 1962.

Lagmanovich, David, 'Para una caracterización de *Infortunios de Alonso Ramírez*', *Historia y crítica de la literatura hispanoamericana*, ed. Cedomil Goic. Barcelona: Editorial Crítica, 1988. vol. 1. 411–16.

Lanning, John Tate, *Academic Culture in the Spanish Colonies*. Oxford: Oxford University Press, 1940.

Lavrín, Asunción, 'Viceregal Culture', *The Cambridge History of Latin American Literature*, vol. 1, 286–335.

Leal, Luis, *Juan Rulfo*. Boston: Twayne, 1983.

———, & Manuel M. Martín-Rodríguez, 'Chicano Literature', *The Cambridge History of Latin American Literature*, vol. 2, 357–86.

Leonard, Irving A., *Books of the Brave Being an Account of Books and of Men in the Spanish Conquest and Settlement of the Sixteenth-Century New World*. Cambridge, Massachusetts: Harvard University Press, 1949.

———, *Baroque Times in Old Mexico: Seventeenth-Century Persons, Places and Practices*. Ann Arbor: The University of Michigan Press, 1959.

——— (ed.), *Colonial Travelers in Latin America*. New York: Alfred A. Knopf, 1972.

León-Portilla, Miguel, 'Teatro náhuatl prehispánico', *La Palabra y el Hombre* (Mexico City) 9 (1959): 13–35.

——— (ed.), *The Broken Spears: The Aztec Account of the Conquest of Mexico*. Boston: Beacon Press, 1992.

———, *Fifteen Poets of the Aztec World*. Norman and London: University of Oklahoma Press, 1992.

Lewis, Marvin, *Treading the Ebony Path: Ideology and Violence in Contemporary Afro-Colombian Prose Fiction*. Columbia: University of Missouri Press, 1987.

Lindstrom, Naomi, *Women's Voices in Latin American Literature*. Washington, DC: Three Continents Press, 1989.

Lloyd, David, *Anomalous States: Irish Writing and the Post-Colonial Moment*. Durham, NC: Duke University Press, 1993.

López de Gómara, Francisco, *Historia general de las Indias y Vida de Hernán Cortés*, ed. Jorge Gurria Lacroix. Caracas: Ayacucho, 1979.

Lorente Medina, Antonio, 'Introducción', Carrió de la Vandera, Alonso. *El lazarillo de ciegos caminantes*. Caracas: Biblioteca Ayacucho, 1985. ix–xxxv.

Luciani, Frederick, 'Spanish American Theatre of the Colonial Period', *The Cambridge History of Latin American Literature*, vol. 1, 260–85.

Ludmer, Josefina, 'The Gaucho Genre', *The Cambridge History of Latin American Literature*, vol. 1, 608–31.

Luis, William, 'Latin American (Hispanic Caribbean) Literature Written in the United States', *The Cambridge History of Latin American Literature*, vol. 2, 526–56.

Luzuriaga, Gerardo, & Richard Reeve (eds.), *Los clásicos del teatro hispanoamericano*. Mexico: Fondo de Cultura Económica, 1975.

Lyotard, Jean François, *The Postmodern Condition: A Report on Knowledge*, trans. Geoff Bennington & Brian Massumi. Minneapolis: University of Minnesota, 1984.

Madrigal, Luis Iñigo (ed.), *Historia de la literatura hispanoamericana*. Madrid: Cátedra, 1982, 1987. 2 vol.

Magill, Frank N. (ed.), *Masterpieces of Latino Literature*. New York: Harper Collins, 1995.

Mariátegui, José Carlos, *Siete ensayos de interpretación de la realidad peruana*, ed. Aníbal Quijano & Elizabeth Garrels. Caracas: Ayacucho, 1979.

Martí, José, *Prosa escogida*, ed. José Olivio Jiménez. Madrid: Editorial Magisterio Español, 1975.

——, *Prosas*, ed. Andrés Iduarte. Mexico: Unión Panamericana, 1950.

——, *Versos libres*, ed. Ivan A. Schulman. Barcelona: Editorial Labor, 1970.

Martin, Gerald, *Journeys Through the Labyrinth: Latin American Fiction in the Twentieth Century*. London: Routledge, 1989.

Martinengo, Alessandro, 'La cultura literaria de Juan Rodríguez Freyle', *Historia y crítica de la literatura hispanoamericana*, ed. Cedomil Goic. Barcelona: Editorial Crítica, 1988. vol. 1. 147–52.

Masiello, Francine, *Between Civilization and Barbarism: Women, Nation, and Literary Culture in Modern Argentina*. Lincoln & London: University of Nebraska Press, 1992.

Melgar, Mariano, *Antología*, ed. Edmundo Cornejo. Lima: Ediciones Populares, 1972. 2nd ed.

Mendieta, Fray Jerónimo de, *Historia eclesiástica indiana*, ed. Francisco Solano y Pérez-Lila. Madrid: Atlas, 1973. 2 vols. 'Biblioteca de Autores Españoles' Series, nos. 260 and 261.

Menéndez Pidal, Ramón, *Colección de incunables americanos*. Madrid: Ediciones Cultura Hispánica, 1944.

Merrim, Stephanie, 'The First Fifty Years of Hispanic New World Historiography: The Caribbean, Mexico and Central America', *The Cambridge History of Latin American Literature*, vol. 1, 58–100.

—— (ed.), *Feminist Perspectives on Sor Juana Inés de la Cruz*. Detroit: Wayne State University Press, 1991.

Meyer, Doris (ed.), *Rereading the Spanish American Essay: Translation of 19th and 20th Century Women's Essays*. Austin: University of Texas Press, 1995.

Mignolo, Walter, 'Cartas, crónicas y relaciones del descubrimiento y la conquista', *Historia de la literatura hispanoamericana: época colonial*. Madrid: Cátedra, 1982. vol. 1. 57–116.

Miller, Ingrid Watson (ed.), *Afro-Hispanic Literature: An Anthology of Hispanic Writers of African Ancestry*. Miami, FL: Ediciones Universal, 1991.

Molloy, Sylvia, *En breve cárcel*. Barcelona: Seix Barral, 1981.

——, *Signs of Borges*. Durham, NC: Duke University Press, 1994.

Moraga, Cherríe, *Loving in the War Years: lo que nunca pasó por sus labios.* Boston, MA: South End Press, 1983.

———, *The Last Generation: Prose and Poetry by Cherríe Moraga.* Boston, MA: South End Press, 1993.

Motolonía, aka R. P. Fr. Toribio de Benavente, *Historia de los indios de la Nueva España.* Barcelona: Herederos de Juan Gili, Editores, 1914.

Murray, James C., *Spanish Chronicles of the Indies: The Sixteenth Century.* Boston: Twayne, 1994.

Mutis, Alvaro, *Summa de Maqroll Gaviero (Poesía 1948–1988).* Mexico: Fondo de Cultura Económica, 1990.

Navarro Tomás, T., *Métrica española: reseña histórica y descriptiva.* Madrid: Guadarrama, 1972. 3rd ed.

Nebrija, Antonio, *Gramática castellana*, ed. Pascual Galindo Romeo. Madrid: Junta del Centenario, 1965.

Neruda, Pablo, *Twenty Love Poems and a Song of Despair*, trans. W. S. Merwin. London: Jonathan Cape, 1975.

Núñez, Estuardo, 'Notas a la obra y vida de Don Pedro de Peralta', *Homenaje a Peralta.* Lima: Universidad Nacional Mayor de San Marcos, n.d. 21–33.

Olavide, Pablo de, *Obras dramáticas desconocidas*, ed. Estuardo Núñez. Lima: Biblioteca Nacional del Perú, 1971.

———, *El desertor (Teatro)*, ed. Trinidad Barrera & Piedad Bolaños. Sevilla: Imprenta Escandón, 1987.

Olivio Jiménez, José (ed.), *Antología de la poesía hispanoamericana contemporánea: 1914–1987.* Madrid: Alianza, 1988.

Ollé, Carmen, *Noches de adrenalina.* Lima: Lluvia Editores, 1992. [1981]

Olmedo, José Joaquín de, *Poesías completas*, ed. Aurelio Espinosa Pólit. Mexico: Fondo de Cultura Económica, 1947.

Ortega, Julio, *Reapropiaciones: culturas y nueva escritura en Puerto Rico.* Río Piedras, PR: Universidad de Puerto Rico, 1991.

Ortiz, Carmen, *Julio Cortázar: una estética de la búsqueda.* Buenos Aires: Almageste, 1994.

Oviedo, José Miguel, *Historia de la literatura hispanoamericana. 1. De los orígenes a la Emancipación.* Madrid: Alianza, 1995.

———, 'The Modern Essay in Spanish America', *The Cambridge History of Latin American Literature*, vol. 2, 365–424.

*Oxford English Dictionary*, 20 vols. Oxford: Clarendon, 1989, 2nd ed.

Palma, Ricardo, *Tradiciones peruanas.* Lima: Editorial Universo. 1980. 2 vols.

Pardo y Aliaga, Felipe, *Teatro: (selección). 'Frutos de la educación' & 'Una huérfana en chorrillos'.* Lima: Editorial Universo, 1977.

Parker, Alexander A., 'The Calderonian Sources of *El Divino Narciso* de Sor Juana Inés de la Cruz', *Romantisches Jarbuch* 19 (1968): 257–74; Spanish translation in Cedomil Goic, *Historia y crítica de la literatura hispanoamericana: 1: Epoca colonial.* Barcelona: Editorial Crítica, 1988. 360–65.

Parra, Nicanor, *Antipoems: New and Selected*, ed. David Unger. New York: New Directions, 1985.

*Obras completas de Teresa de la Parra.* Caracas: Editorial Arte, 1965.

Pastor, Beatriz, *Discursos narrativos de la conquista: mitificación y emergencia.* Hanover, NH: Ediciones del Norte, 1983.

Payne, Judith A., & Earl E. Fitz, *Ambiguity and Gender in the New Novel of Brazil and Spanish America: A Comparative Assessment*. Iowa City: University of Iowa Press, 1993.

Paz, Octavio, *Puerta al campo*. Barcelona: Biblioteca Breve de Bolsillo, 1981. [1966]

——, *Corriente alterna*. Mexico: Siglo Veintiuno Editores, 1967.

——, *Poesía en movimiento: México 1915–1966*. Mexico: Siglo XXI, 1979. 13th ed.

——, *Sor Juana Inés de la Cruz o las trampas de la fe*. Barcelona: Seix Barral, 1982.

——, *Conjunciones y disyunciones*. Mexico: Joaquín Mortiz, 1969.

——, *In/mediaciones*. Barcelona: Seix Barral, 1979.

——, *El laberinto de la soledad*. Mexico: Fondo de Cultura Económica, 1984. [1959]

——, ed. with Alí Chumacero, José Emilio Pacheco, & Homero Aridjis. *Poesía en movimiento: México 1915–1966*. Mexico: Siglo XXI Editores, 1979. 13th ed.

Pellón, Gustavo, 'The Spanish American Novel: Recent Developments, 1975 to 1990', *The Cambridge History of Latin American Literature*, vol. 2, 274–302.

Peri Rossi, Cristina, *La nave de los locos*. Barcelona: Seix Barral, 1989.

Pertusa, Inmaculada, 'Escribiendo entre corrientes: Carmen Riera, Esther Tusquets, Cristina Peri Rossi y Sylvia Molloy', Ph.D. dissertation. University of Colorado, 1995.

Pfandl, Ludwig, *Sor Juana Inés de la Cruz: la décima musa de México*. Mexico: Universdad Nacional Autónoma Metropolitana, 1963.

Phillips, Rachel, *Alfonsina Storni: From Poetess to Poet*. London: Tamesis, 1975.

Piedra, José, 'Literary Whiteness and Afro-Hispanic Difference', *The Bounds of Race: Perspectives on Hegemony and Resistance*, ed. Dominick LaCapra. Ithaca: Cornell University Press, 1991. 278–310.

Pierce, Frank (ed.), *The Heroic Poem of the Spanish Golden Age: Selections*. Oxford: Dolphin, 1947.

Pierce, Robert N. & Kurt Kent, 'Newspapers', *Handbook of Latin American Popular Culture*, ed. Harold E. Hinds, Jr., & Charles M. Tatum. Westport, CT: Greenwood Press, 1985. 230–50.

Piña, Cristina, *Alejandra Pizarnik*. Buenos Aires: Planeta, 1991.

'Plácido'. *Gabriel de la Concepción Valdés. Los poemas más representativos de Plácido*, ed. Frederick S. Stimpson & Humberto E. Robles. Chapel Hill, NC: University of North Carolina and Castalia, 1976.

Pope, Randolph D., 'The Spanish American Novel from 1950 to 1975', *The Cambridge History of Latin American Literature*, vol. 2, 226–78.

*Popol Vuh. The Sacred Book of the Ancient Quiché Maya*. English version by Delia Goetz & Sylvanus G. Morley from the translation of Adrián Recinos. Norman: University of Oklahoma Press, 1950.

Praz, Mario, *The Romantic Agony*. London: Oxford University Press, 1970.

Prieto, René, 'The Literature of *Indigenismo*', *The Cambridge History of Latin American Literature*, vol. 2, 69–113.

Promis, José, *The Identity of Hispanoamerica: An Interpretation of Colonial Literature*, trans. Alita Kelley & Alec E. Kelley. Tucson: University of Arizona Press, 1991.

Puig, Manuel, *El beso de la mujer araña*. Barcelona: Seix Barral, 1988. 8th ed.

Pupo-Walker, Enrique, 'El relato virreinal', *El cuento hispanoamericano*, ed. Enrique Pupo-Walker. Madrid: Castalia, 1995. 55–78.

———, 'El relato costumbrista', *El cuento hispanoamericano*, ed. Enrique Pupo-Walker. Madrid: Castalia, 1995. 79–110.

———, 'The Brief Narrative in Spanish America: 1835–1915', *The Cambridge History of Latin American Literature*, vol. 1, 490–535.

Quesada, Vicente G., *The History of Printing and Early Publications in the Spanish American Colonies*, trans. Gustavo E. Archilla. New York: Columbia University Press, 1938. (Translated as a report on Project 465-97-3-81 under the auspices of the Works Progress Administration and the Department of Social Science, Columbia University).

Quilis, Antonio, *Métrica española*. Barcelona: Ariel, 1989. 3rd ed.

Quiroga, Horacio, *Cuentos escogidos*, ed. Jean Franco. Oxford: Pergamon, 1968.

Quiroga, José, 'Spanish American Poetry from 1922 to 1975', *The Cambridge History of Latin American Literature*, vol. 2, 303–64.

Rama, Angel, *Rubén Darío y el modernismo*. Caracas: Biblioteca de la Universidad Central de Venezuela, 1970.

———, *La ciudad letrada*. Hanover: Ediciones del Norte, 1984.

———, *La crítica de la cultura en América Latina*, ed. Saúl Sosnowski & Tomás Eloy Martínez. Caracas: Ayacucho, 1985.

Reyes, Carlos José, 'La creación colectiva: una nueva organización interna del trabajo teatral', *El teatro latinoamericano de creación colectiva*, ed. Marina García. Havana: Casa de las Américas, 1978. 75–107.

Reynolds, Bonnie Hildebrand, *Space, Time, and Crisis: The Theatre of René Marqués*. York, SC: Spanish Literature, 1988.

Rivera, José Eustasio, *La vorágine*. Barcelona: Planeta, 1975.

Rivera-Meléndez, Blanca, *Poetry and the Machinery of Illusion: José Martí and the Poetics of Machinery*. Ithaca, NY: Cornell University Press, 1992.

Rizk, Beatriz J., *El nuevo teatro latinoamericano: una lectura histórica*. Minneapolis, MN: Institute of Ideologies and Literatures, 1987.

Roa Bastos, Augusto, *Yo el Supremo*. Mexico: Siglo Veintiuno Editores, 1976. 6th ed.

Rodó, José Enrique, *Ariel*. 3rd ed. Montevideo: Claudio García & compañía, n.d.

Rodríguez-Luis, Julio, *Hermenéutica y praxis del indigenismo: la novela indigenista de Clorinda Matto de Turner a José María Arguedas*. Mexico: Fondo de Cultura Económica, 1980.

Rodríguez Freyle, Juan, *El Carnero*, ed. Darío Achury Valenzuela. Caracas: Ayacucho, 1979.

Rodríguez Monegal, Emir, *Genio y figura de Horacio Quiroga*. Buenos Aires: Editorial Universitaria, 1967.

———, *Sexo y poesía en el 900 uruguayo*. Montevideo: Alfa, 1969.

Rodríguez Torres, Alvaro, 'Reseña histórica de la Biblioteca Nacional de Colombia', *Biblioteca Nacional de Colombia* (1994): 1–18.

Rosas y Oquendo, Mateo, *Sátira hecha por Mateo Rosas de Oquendo a las cosas que pasan en el Pirú, año de 1598*, ed. Pedro Lasarte. Madison: The Hispanic Seminary of Medieval Studies, 1990.

Ross, Kathleen, 'Historians of the Conquest and Colonization of the New World: 1550–1620', *The Cambridge History of Latin American Literature*, vol. 1, 101–90.

——, & Yvette E. Miller, *Scents of Wood and Silence: Short Stories by Latin American Women Writers*. Pittsburgh: Latin American Literary Review Press, 1991.

Rowe, William, *Mito e ideología en la obra de José María Arguedas*. Lima: Instituto Nacional de Cultura, 1979.

——, & Vivian Schelling, *Memory and Modernity: Popular Culture in Latin America*. London: Verso, 1991.

Rulfo, Juan, *Obra completa: 'El llano en llamas'/'Pedro Páramo'/Otros textos*, ed. Jorge Ruffinelli. Caracas: Ayacucho, 1985.

Rutherford, John, 'The Novel of the Mexican Revolution', *The Cambridge History of Latin American Literature*, vol. 2, 213–25.

Sabat de Rivers, Georgina, *El 'Sueño' de Sor Juana Inés de la Cruz: tradiciones literarias y originalidad*. London: Tamesis, 1976.

Sahagún, Bernardino de, *A History of Ancient Mexico*, trans. Fanny R. Bandelier. Nasheville: Fish University Press, 1932.

——, *Historia general de las cosas de Nueva España. Códice florentino*. Facsimile ed. Mexico: Secretaría de Gobernación, 1979.

Sainz, Gustavo, *Gazapo*. Mexico: Grijalbo, 1975.

Sánchez, Luis Alberto, *Indianismo e indigenismo en la literatura peruana*. Lima: Mosca Azul, 1981.

Sánchez, Luis Rafael, *La guaracha del Macho Camacho*. Barcelona: Argos Vergara, 1982.

Santa Cruz y Espejo, Eugenio de, *Obra educativa*, ed. Philip L. Astuto. Caracas: Ayacucho, 1981.

Sartre, Jean-Paul, 'Black Orpheus', *The Massachusetts Review* 6:1 (1964–65): 13–52.

Schulman, Ivan A., & Evelyn Picón Garfield (eds.), *Poesía modernista hispanoamericana y española (Antología)*. Madrid: Taurus, 1986.

Schumway, Nicholas, 'The Essay in Spanish America: 1800 to Modernismo', *The Cambridge History of Latin American Literature*, vol. 1, 556–89.

Sedgwick, Eve Kosofsky, *Epistemology of the Closet*. Berkeley: University of California Press, 1991.

Seed, Patricia, 'Taking Possession and Reading Texts: Establishing the Authority of Overseas Empires', *Early Images of the Americas: Transfer and Invention*, ed. Jerry M. Williams & Robert E. Lewis. Tucson & London: University of Arizona Press, 1993. 111–47.

Shaw, Donald L., *Gallegos: Doña Bárbara*. London: Grant & Cutler, 1972.

——, *Borges' Narrative Strategy*. Liverpool: Cairns, 1992.

——, *Antonio Skármeta and the Post Boom*. Hanover, NH: Ediciones del Norte, 1994.

——, *The Post-Boom in Spanish American Fiction*. Ithaca, NY: State University of New York Press, 1997.

*José Asunción Silva. Poesía y prosa*, ed. Eduardo Camacho Guizado. Bogotá: El Ancora Editores, 1993.

Sinfield, Alan, *Literature, Politics, and Culture in Postwar Britain*. Berkeley and Los Angeles: University of California Press, 1989.

Skidmore, Thomas E., & Peter H. Smith, *Modern Latin America*. New York: Oxford University Press, 1992. 3rd ed.

Smart, Ian Isidore, *Amazing Connections: Kemet to Hispanophone Africana Literature*. Washington DC, & Port-of-Spain: Original World Press, 1996.

Smith, Paul Julian, *Laws of Desire*. Oxford: Oxford University Press, 1994.

Smith, Verity (ed.), *Encyclopedia of Latin American Literature*. London: Fitzroy Dearborn, 1997.

Soley, Lawrence C., & John S. Nichols, *Clandestine Radio Broadcasting: A Study of Revolutionary and Counterrevolutionary Electronic Communication*. New York: Praeger, 1987.

Solís Alcalá, Emilio, trans. & intr., *Códice Pérez*. Mérida, Yucatán: Imprenta Oronte, 1944.

Solórzano, Carlos (ed.), *Teatro breve hispanoamericano contemporáneo*. Madrid: Aguilar, 1970.

—— (ed.), *El teatro actual latinoamericano*. Mexico: Ediciones de Andrea, 1972.

Sommer, Doris, *Foundational Fictions: The National Romances of Latin America*. Berkeley: University of California Press, 1991.

*Spanish American Literature: A Collection of Essays*, ed. David William Foster & Daniel Altamiranda. New York & London: Garland, 1997. 5 vols.

Spell, Jefferson Rea, *The Life and Works of José Joaquín Fernández de Lizardi*. Philadelphia: University of Pennsylvania Press, 1931.

Stavans, Ilan, *Julio Cortázar: A Study of the Short Fiction*. Boston: Twayne, 1996.

Steinberg, S. H., *Five Hundred Years of Printing*. Harmondsworth: Penguin, 1966. With a foreword by Beatrice Warde. 2nd ed.

Stolley, Karen, 'The Eighteenth Century: Narrative Forms, Scholarship and Learning', *The Cambridge History of Latin American Literature*, vol. 1, 336–74.

Stubb, Martin S., 'The Essay of Nineteenth-Century Mexico, Central America, and the Caribbean', *The Cambridge History of Latin American Literature*, vol. 1, 590–607.

Sturrock, John, *Paper Tigers: The Ideal Fictions of Borges*. Oxford: Clarendon, 1977.

Swanson, Philip, *The New Novel in Latin America: Politics and Popular Culture After the Boom*. Manchester: Manchester University Press, 1995.

Tamayo Vargas, Augusto, 'Obras menores en el teatro de Peralta', *Homenaje a Peralta*. Lima: Universidad Nacional Mayor de San Marcos, n.d. 5–20.

Tanner, Tony, *Adultery in the Novel: Contract and Transgression*. Baltimore: The John Hopkins Press, 1979.

Tatum, Charles, *Chicano Literature*. Boston: Twayne, 1982.

Taylor, Diana, *Theatre of Crisis: Drama and Politics in Latin America*. Lexington: The University Press of Kentucky, 1991.

Thomas, H., *Short-Title Catalogues of Portuguese Books and of Spanish-American Books Printed Before 1601 Now in the British Museum*. London: Bernard Quaritch Ltd., 1926.

Thompson, Lawrence S., *Printing in Colonial Spanish America*. Hamden, CT: The Shoe String Press, 1962.

Todorov, Tzvetan, *La conquista de América, la cuestión del otro*. Mexico: Siglo XXI, 1987.

Torres, Lourdes, 'The Construction of the Self in U.S. Latina Autobiographies', *Third World Women and the Politics of Feminism*, ed. Chandra Mohanty, Ann Russo & Lourdes Torres. Bloomington: Indiana University Press, 1991.

———, 'U.S. Latino/a Literature: Re-creating America', *Notes and Queries* (forthcoming).

Traba, Marta, *Conversación al sur*. Mexico: Siglo Veintiuno Editores, 1988. 3rd ed.

*Tres piezas teatrales del virreinato*, ed. José Rojas Garcidueñas & José Juan Arrom. Mexico: Universidad Nacional Autónoma de México, 1976.

Uslar Pietri, Arturo, *Oficio de difuntos*. Barcelona: Seix Barral, 1976.

Valenzuela, Luisa, 'Mis brujas favoritas', *Theory and Practice of Feminist Literary Criticism*, ed. Gabriela Mora & Karen S. Van Hooft. Ypsilanti, Michigan: Bilingual Press, 1982. 88–95.

———, *Cambio de armas*. Hanover: Ediciones del Norte, 1980.

Vallejo, César, *Obra poética completa*, ed. Américo Ferrari. Madrid: Alianza, 1983.

Vargas Llosa, Mario, *La orgía perpetua: Flaubert y 'Madame Bovary'*. Barcelona: Seix Barral, 1975.

———, *La ciudad y los perros*. Barcelona: Seix Barral, 1981. 19th ed.

———, *La historia secreta de una novela*. Barcelona: Tusquets Editor, 1981.

———, *La casa verde*. Barcelona: Seix Barral, 1978. 18th ed.

Vega, Ana Lydia, *Encaranublado y otros cuentos de naufragio*. Río Piedra, PR: Editorial Antillana, 1983.

Verani, Hugo J., 'The Vanguardia and its Implications', *The Cambridge History of Latin American Literature*, vol. 2, 114–37.

Viramontes, Helena Maria, *The Moths and Other Stories*. Houston: Arte Público Press, 1985.

Watson Miller, Ingrid (ed.), *Afro-Hispanic Literature: An Anthology of Hispanic Writers of African Ancestry*. Miami, FL: Ediciones Universal, 1991.

Watt, Ian, *The Rise of the Novel. Studies in Defoe, Richardson and Fielding*. Berkeley & Los Angeles: University of California Press, 1957.

Weiss, Judith A., *Latin American Popular Theatre: The First Five Centuries*. Albuquerque: University of New Mexico Press, 1993.

Wellek, René, 'The Concept of Realism in Literary Scholarship', *Concepts of Criticism*. New Haven: Yale University Press, 1963. 222–55.

Williams, Lorna, *Self and Society in the Poetry of Nicolás Guillén*. Baltimore: Johns Hopkins University Press, 1982.

Williams, Raymond Leslie, *The Postmodern Novel in Latin America: Politics, Culture, and the Crisis of Truth*. New York: St Martin's Press, 1995.

Wilson, Jason, *Octavio Paz: A Study of his Poetics*. Cambridge: Cambrige University Press, 1979.

Wold, Ruth, *El diario de México, primer cotidiano de Nueva España*. Madrid: Gredos, 1970.

Wolff, Egon, *Los invasores. Teatro chileno contemporáneo*, ed. J. Durán-Cerdá. Mexico: Aguilar, 1970. 131–209.

Woodyard, George (ed.), *The Modern Stage in Latin America: Six Plays*. New York: E. P. Dutton, 1971.

Zamora, Margarita, *Language, Authority, and Indigenous History in the 'Comentarios Reales de los Incas'*. Cambridge: Cambridge University Press, 1988.

Zanetti, Susana, *Jorge Isaacs*. Buenos Aires: Centro Editor de América Latina, 1967.

# INDEX